LIFE AT THE COURT OF

QUEEN VICTORIA

1861 - 1901

LIFE AT THE COURT OF QUEEN VICTORIA

1861 - 1901

ILLUSTRATED FROM THE COLLECTION OF LORD EDWARD PELHAM-CLINTON, MASTER OF THE HOUSEHOLD

WITH SELECTIONS FROM THE JOURNALS *OF QUEEN VICTORIA*

EDITED AND WITH ADDITIONAL MATERIAL BY BARRY ST-JOHN NEVILL

EXETER, ENGLAND

DEDICATION

To the memory of
my very dear Mother and Father
—who gave me so much

Endpapers: Queen Victoria with members of her family, 1881.

First published in Great Britain 1984 by
Webb & Bower (Publishers) Limited
9 Colleton Crescent, Exeter, Devon EX2 4BY

Picture research by Anne-Marie Ehrlich

Designed by Peter Wrigley

British Library Cataloguing in Publication Data

Victoria, *Queen of Great Britain*
Life at the Court of Queen Victoria
1861–1901.
1. Victoria, *Queen of Great Britain*
2. Great Britain—Kings and rulers—Biography
I. Title II. Nevill, Barry St-John
941.081′092′4 DA552

ISBN 0–86350–028–5

Typeset in Great Britain
by Keyspools Ltd, Golborne, Lancs

Colour and duotone origination by
Peninsular Repro, Exeter, England

Printed and bound in Italy by
New Interlitho SpA, Milan

CONTENTS

	PAGE
Introduction	7
The Children of Queen Victoria and Prince Albert	18
Queen Victoria's Prime Ministers and Their Terms of Office	24
The Pelham-Clintons	29
Principal Events 1861–70	31
Selections from the Journals of Queen Victoria	35
Principal Events 1871–80	68
Principal Events 1881–90	107
Principal Events 1891–1901	145
List of Precedence	174
Lord Edward's Diary	214
Acknowledgements	221
Index	222

Queen Victoria in her robes of State, painted by Winterhalter in 1859.

INTRODUCTION

Queen Victoria gave her name to arguably the greatest period in Britain's history and her reign of sixty-three years and seven months was the longest of any British monarch. Indeed, by the time she became Empress of India in 1876, she ruled the largest Empire the world had known, numbering her subjects in hundreds of millions.

In 1894 she appointed one of her friends Master of the Household. He was Colonel the Lord Edward Pelham-Clinton, who only accepted this great position with reluctance. Writing in her *Journal* on 28 September, 1894, she said: 'I forgot to mention that I have offered the post of Master of the Household to Lord Edward Clinton. At first he declined on account of his health and feeling himself unfit, as he said, for the office, but on being asked to reconsider it and try it for six months, he consented, though feeling very diffident. I saw him yesterday and was much pleased with all he said. He is so amiable and gentlemanly and good.'

Lord Edward's principal hobby was keeping scrap-books. First, from 1860 showing his early involvement with and interest in Court life and then, from 1881 as a Groom-in-Waiting, and finally from 1894 from the uniquely privileged position of Master of the Household. (He was also, for six months—until 22 July, 1901—Master of his old friend King Edward VII's Household, and then a Groom-in-Waiting to the King.) For about forty-seven years, from 1860 to 1907 when he died, Lord Edward amassed an extraordinary and large collection of royal memorabilia and ephemera. This collection is superbly bound and includes all kinds of royal invitations, letters from royalty (British and foreign) and other letters from distinguished men from all walks of life—from the young Pablo Casals to top army officers such as Field-Marshal Earl Roberts and Lord Kitchener. There are also letters from famous actors, musicians, painters and others in public life. The collection also includes a large number of programmes, silk-bound if intended for the royal hand; menus and detailed seating plans for state and private dinners; royal, and other visitors, and where they, their suites and servants stayed; details of journeys made at home and abroad by the Queen; protocol for the jubilees of 1887 and 1897 and service sheets of all the royal baptisms, weddings, funerals and memorial services, most of which were supervised by the Queen who had a reputation for enjoying the planning of a church service, particularly funerals and memorials. It is one of the paradoxes of the Queen's character that, although she much enjoyed services and hearing sermons and was very much a Christian monarch, she did not like bishops.

Among the many other things she disliked were loud voices; meeting people she knew when out for her afternoon drive; one of her Prime Ministers, Mr Gladstone; and smoking. Hot rooms, coal fires and death duties were also high on her list.

The Royal Household in the 1890s. Lord Edward Pelham-Clinton is seated on the right at the end of the front row.

Smoking had to be made as uncomfortable as possible for those who wished to indulge in the 'filthy habit'. The Queen made smokers go into the garden if they wished to smoke at Osborne House and when Prince Christian was courting her daughter, Princess Helena, she provided him with a damp, white-washed room near the servants' quarters. She had 'NO SMOKING' notices placed almost everywhere in her homes and when King Albert of Saxony visited her, he was warned about smoking. He was a heavy smoker and it was only with great difficulty that he managed to do without a cigar for two days. On the third day he remembered that he was a king and so walked up the grand staircase puffing a large cigar, which he said gave him great satisfaction. But it is reported that it deeply shocked those courtiers who witnessed it.

The 'discovery' of Lord Edward's collection has provided an excellent opportunity to publish more selected extracts from the Queen's *Journals* and to 'illustrate' them with items from his collection, from the death of the Prince Consort in 1861 to the death of the Queen herself in 1901.

Although after the Prince's death the Queen gave an impression to the world of secluded and inconsolable widowhood, seldom being seen in public and refusing to take her place in the social life of the country, as Lord Edward's collection and as her *Journals* show, she led an enormously active and varied life almost up to her death.

She began her journals in 1832 when she was thirteen and continued them until a few days before she died.

Queen Victoria with the Prince Consort.

Sir Philip Magnus in his superb biography of King Edward VII says of the *Journals*:

> Queen Victoria's diary passed in 1901 into the hands of her youngest child, Princess Beatrice. In fulfilment of a charge laid upon her by her mother, the Princess transcribed passages from that invaluable historical and personal record into a series of blue copybooks; and she destroyed Queen Victoria's manuscript by fire as she went along. That process of transcription and destruction which was spread over a great number of years distressed King George V and Queen Mary who were powerless to intervene; but no one could dispute Queen Victoria's absolute right to leave such directions as she thought proper about the disposal of her most intimate papers.... It can be stated that Princess Beatrice felt constrained not merely to destroy, without transcribing substantial portions of her mother's diary, but also to alter substantially a great many other portions which she did transcribe and it must be added that posterity has suffered in consequence an incalculable and irreparable loss.

The Queen herself published some of her *Journals*, and when she met the author, Charles Dickens, she gave him a copy of *More Leaves from a Journal of a Life in the Highlands* inscribed: 'From the humblest of authors to one of the greatest.'

Many historians feel that the death of the Prince Consort was the turning point in the Queen's life and there has been much speculation about the life she really led for the forty years she was the 'Widow of Windsor'.

In a letter to her uncle, the King of the Belgians, she described herself as

> an utterly heart-broken and crushed widow of 42. My life as a happy one is ended! The world is gone for me. Oh! to be cut off in the prime of life—to see our pure, happy, quiet domestic life, which alone enabled me to bear my much disliked position cut off at 42 when I had hoped with such instinctive certainty that God never would part us and he would let us grow old together (though he always talked of the shortness of life) is too awful. Too cruel.

For the next forty years, Queen Victoria kept her husband's room exactly as it had been. Hot water was brought in each morning, his chamber pot scoured with all the others in the household; fresh towels and bed linen laid out and a clean night shirt placed on his bed. For some years after his death, the Queen even slept with his nightclothes in her arms.

Although she cut herself off from the public, there were some things she simply had to do, and one of these was to receive Princess Alexandra of Denmark in November, 1862, after her betrothal to the Prince of Wales in the autumn. The princess spent a few weeks with her future mother-in-law and was determined to make a good impression. She did, and the Queen was later to write in her *Journal*: 'How beloved Albert would have loved her.'

Queen Victoria with the Prince and Princess of Wales. The Queen is gazing at a bust of the Prince Consort.

It was not until February, 1866, that she agreed to open Parliament. Hundreds of thousands of people were in London for the spectacle. The Queen wrote in her *Journal* that she could hardly touch her food before she left the palace and when the band played she had great difficulty in repressing her tears.

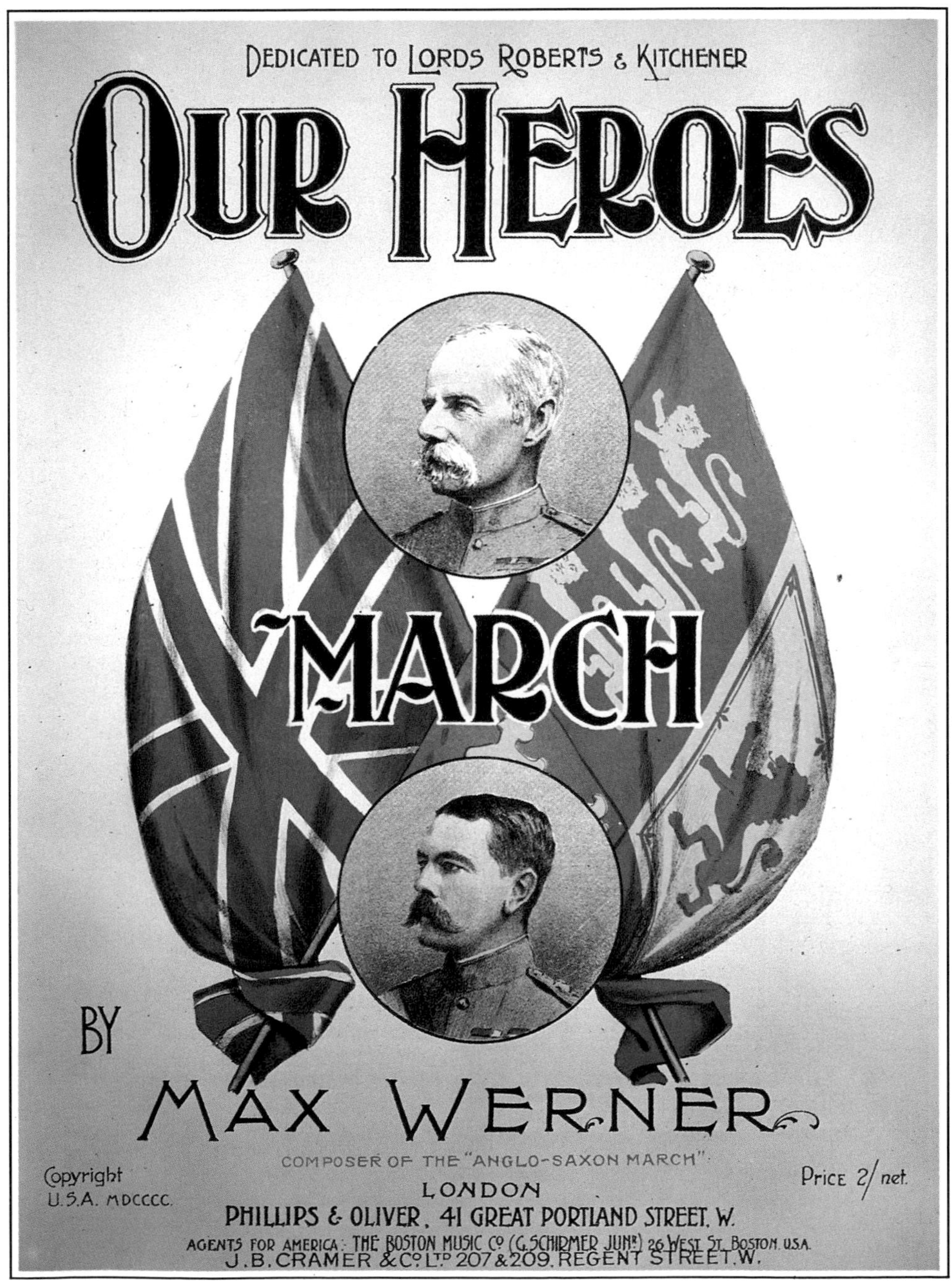

In the days before radio and television sheet music, like this march, had a ready market. It is dedicated to two of the heroes of the Victorian Empire, Lords Roberts and Kitchener.

The Lord Chancellor read her speech for her. It mentioned that her Empire was increasing in size with most of her people living in peace. But the Irish were troublesome—again! There were references to the covetous Bismarck; the drop in the slave trade and an increase in the overseas sale of our goods and the speech ended with just a hint of parliamentary reform. The Queen rose from the Throne, kissed the Princess of Wales (as Princess Alexandra had become) and began her right regal procession. Her behaviour was so impressive, so queenly, that *The Times*, which had not been on her side, referred to her grief: 'which everyone hoped would have been more speedily lessened . . . but hers was still the loftiest and most beloved head in the realm.'

Actually, the Queen had likened the opening of Parliament to an execution, but as Hector Bolitho wrote in his absorbing book, *The Reign of Queen Victoria*:

> During the months that followed, she tried to combat criticism by appearing in London more often. She held Courts at Buckingham Palace and went to Aldershot; she attended the marriage of her daughter, opened the Aberdeen Waterworks and while she was watching the Braemar Highland Gathering, was 'full of conversation' . . . these busy appearances seemed to help the battle against grief and the change was noticed by those who loved her.

The forty years of her widowhood were to be progressive and prosperous beyond anyone's wildest dreams. These years saw the perfection of earlier inventions such as railway travel and the telegraph. There was also the new morality. Victorians were proud of their decency and respectability after the brashness and crudeness of previous generations. They hoped that their moral standards would set the tone for subsequent generations. They did, for years. Indeed, those standards are still valued in certain circles over eighty years after the Queen's death.

Victorians positively gloated over the many British possessions scattered over the world and were particularly pleased when their beloved Queen was proclaimed Empress of India.

As she grew older, the working man had begun to have a say in the affairs of state and by 1882, all *men* over twenty-one could vote—and in secret. But the Queen did not really approve of the education and emancipation of the working classes, saying that education made them unfit for work as good servants and labourers, nor of women, and she was heard to say of the daughter of Earl Russell (a former Prime Minister), who had spoken in the cause of female suffrage: 'She ought to get a good whipping.'

The Queen's fears were groundless. Throughout her lifetime, working men and women stood little chance of improving themselves. A man had to be wealthy to enter the professions or to be a Member of Parliament, clergyman, Army or Naval officer or to go to law. Change did not come quickly and the opinionated and interfering little woman who almost drove her prime ministers mad with her meddling in state business sometimes believed herself to be an absolute, instead of constitutional, monarch.

Indeed, the list of things she *could* do as Queen makes interesting reading.

In his *English Constitution*, Walter Bagehot lists some of the many things that Queen Victoria, by exercising her Prerogative, was legally entitled to do, *without consulting her Parliament*:

> She could disband the army (by law she cannot engage more than a certain number of men, but she is not obliged to engage any men); she could dismiss all the officers, from the General commanding-in-chief downwards; she could dismiss all the sailors too; she could

> sell off all our ships of war and all our naval stores; she could make a peace by the sacrifice of Cornwall or begin a war for the conquest of Brittany. She could make every citizen in the United Kingdom, male or female, a peer; she could make every parish in the United Kingdom a 'university'; she could dismiss most of the Civil Servants; she could pardon all offenders. In a word, the Queen could, by prerogative, upset all the action of civil government, by disbanding our forces, whether land or sea, leave us defenceless against foreign nations.

She never accepted the telephone but allowed two of them to be installed in Buckingham Palace so that her guests could order their carriages. Nor did she care much for that new invention, the motor car: 'I'm told that they smell exceedingly nasty and are very shaky and disagreeable conveyances altogether.' And as for the hairstyles of the 1880s she wrote: 'The present fashion of a fringe and frizzle in front is frightful.'

Oddly enough, although she had given birth to nine children, she did not really care for babies and once said: 'An ugly baby is a very nasty object and the prettiest is frightful.' She never breast-fed her children and once when she saw her daughter, Princess Alice, suckling one of her brood of seven, the Queen had a cow in the royal dairies named Princess Alice.

It seems that she became bored with the matter of procreation, once she was past child-bearing at which point (and even after nine children) she was so ignorant of sexual matters she asked her doctor: 'Oh, doctor, can I have no more fun in bed?' Years later when she heard about yet another grandchild (she had over thirty) she is alleged to have remarked: '... it seems to me to go on like the rabbits in Windsor Park!'

Many people think that the Queen was neither amused nor entertained; that she spent forty years of widowhood seeing almost no one and doing almost nothing except interfering with the machinery of state. In fact, she entertained on a massive scale and was herself entertained by companies as varied as the Royal Opera and the Eton College Musical Society; from Welsh male-voice choirs to professional soloists and orchestras; from West End theatre companies to entertainments presented by her servants, Household and children.

The amateur entertainments were often led, or inspired, by the Hon. Sir Alick Yorke the unofficial court jester and it was to Sir Alick that she declared: 'We are *not* amused' after she once made him repeat a risqué joke which she had missed.

The Queen also engaged the D'Oyly Carte Opera Company to sing songs from the operettas of W. S. Gilbert and her great friend Sir Arthur Sullivan.

All these events followed one of the beautifully cooked and served dinners prepared by her brilliant chef. There were servants behind every chair and, of course, the Queen often dined from gold plates in private and her guests regularly dined from gold plate. The Queen liked gold. She often breakfasted in the garden under a tent with a green-fringed parasol. Everything on the table, including her egg cup, was of solid gold, except her cup and saucer!

Another commonly held belief is that Queen Victoria never laughed or smiled, even though her last surviving granddaughter, Her late Royal Highness the Princess Alice, Countess of Athlone, speaking of her grandmother, said: 'Oh, but my grandmother *was* amused. She was amused by so many things. She loved to be entertained and she *did* laugh. I remember her rocking with laughter.'

A more notorious grandchild also vividly remembered his grandmother laughing. This was Kaiser Wilhelm II of Germany, son of Queen Victoria's eldest daugher, the Princess Royal who became the Empress Frederick of Germany. The Kaiser said he

Prince George, Duke of York, and Princess May of Teck after their wedding ceremony at St James's Palace on July 6, 1893, a detail from the painting by Forestier.

The Queen with her grandson, Prince William of Prussia – the future Kaiser. She worried about his impulsiveness even as a child.

particularly remembered an incident after his grandmother had asked Admiral Foley to tell her all about the sinking of the *Eurydice*.

After the old Admiral had told her, the Queen changed the subject and asked after his sister who was a friend of hers. The Admiral, who was very deaf, and believing that the Queen was still speaking of the ship, said in a loud voice: 'Well, Ma'am, I'm going to have her turned over and take a good look at her bottom and have it well scraped.' 'The effect of this answer was stupendous,' wrote the Kaiser. 'My grandmother put down her knife and fork, hid her face in her handkerchief and shook and heaved with laughter until the tears rolled down her face.'

Queen Victoria's sense of humour is also displayed in this story she often told. When she was seventy, she was spending the night at Windsor Castle. It was a beautiful, starlit night and the Queen opened a window to look out. A sentry, probably mistaking her for a young maid began to flirt with her outrageously. The Queen, laughing aloud said that she backed away from the window and closed it, but confessed to her family that she laughed at the incident and was 'thrilled' by it.

She also told the story of an incident during the wedding reception for the couple who became King George V and Queen Mary (her grandson Prince George and Princess May of Teck) in 1893. Dawson-Damer was drunk and went up to the Queen and said 'Gad, how glad I am to see you! How well you're looking. But, I say, do forgive me, but I can't for the life of me recall your name.' Queen Victoria said that she smiled at him and said: 'Oh, never mind my name. I'm very glad to see you. Sit down and tell me all about yourself.'

Her friend Lord Edward Pelham-Clinton would have witnessed the Queen's sense of humour at first hand. He also witnessed the Queen's final years and writes in his private diary of her last days. He was as close to the Queen as was anyone—even her family—during those years and at her interment, her son (King Edward VII), a friend of Lord Edward's since their youth, asked him to scatter earth upon his mother's coffin.

Later, writing in his diary, Lord Edward described it as 'The last, the very last act that could be performed for the Queen.'

VICTORIA, by the Grace of God of the United Kingdom of Great Britain and Northern Ireland, QUEEN, Defender of the Faith, EMPRESS OF INDIA. Her Majesty was born at Kensington Palace on May 24, 1819, the daughter of TRH The Duke and Duchess of Kent. She ascended the throne at the decease of her uncle, HM King William IV on June 20, 1837 and was crowned in Westminster Abbey on June 28, 1838. Was proclaimed EMPRESS OF INDIA at Delhi on January 1, 1877. The Queen married, at the Chapel Royal, St James's Palace on February 10, 1840, HRH Prince Albert, the Prince Consort (the title and dignity of Prince Consort were conferred on His Royal Highness by Letters-Patent under the Great Seal of England on June 25, 1857). He was also Duke of Saxony, Prince of Saxe-Coburg and Gotha and a Knight of the Garter, a Knight of the Thistle and a Knight of St Patrick. He held the Grand Cross of the Order of St Michael and St George; he was Great Master of the Order of the Bath; Extra Knight of the Order of the Star of India; Knight of the Golden Fleece of Spain; Knight of the Seraphim of Sweden; a Privy Councillor and held doctorates, *honoris causa* from several universities. He was a Field-Marshal in the Army and was the second son of Ernest I, Reigning Duke of Saxe-Coburg. His Royal Highness was born at Rosenau Castle near Coburg on August 26, 1819 and died at Windsor Castle, Berkshire on December 14, 1861. HER MAJESTY QUEEN VICTORIA, EMPRESS OF INDIA, died of a cerebral haemorrhage at Osborne House, Isle of Wight on January 22, 1901, in her eighty-second year having reigned for sixty-three years and seven months—when the Crown devolved on her eldest son, HRH Albert Edward, Prince of Wales who became HM King Edward VII, EMPEROR OF INDIA.

COLONEL THE LORD EDWARD (WILLIAM) PELHAM-CLINTON, GCVO, KCB, Grand Cross Saxe Ernestine Order (1897); Grand Cross of the Crown of Prussia (1901); Divisional Lieutenant. Born in London on August 11, 1836 second son of the 5th Duke of Newcastle and his wife who was the daughter of the 10th Duke of Hamilton. Married Matilda, daughter of Sir William Craddock Hartopp, 3rd Baronet, who died in 1892. Educated at Eton. Ensign in the Rifle Brigade in 1854. Was in the Crimea after the fall of Sebastopol and promoted Captain in 1857. In Canada from 1861–1865. Member of Parliament for North Nottinghamshire 1865–1868 and a member of the Sherwood Rangers Yeoman Cavalry from 1865–1868. Promoted to Lieutenant-Colonel in 1878 and retired from the army in 1880 visiting India in the same year. Commanded the London Volunteer Rifle Brigade from 1881–1890. GROOM-IN-WAITING to Queen Victoria from 1881 to 1894. MASTER OF THE HOUSEHOLD (for Queen Victoria) from 1894 to January, 1901. MASTER OF THE HOUSEHOLD (for King Edward VII) from January, 1901 to July 22, 1901. Then, GROOM-IN-WAITING until his death in 1907. Residences: 81, Eccleston Square, Belgrave Road, London, SW1 and The Heights, Witley, Surrey. Clubs: Army and Navy; Wellington.

THE CHILDREN OF QUEEN VICTORIA AND PRINCE ALBERT

PRINCESS VICTORIA (Vicky) 1840–1901	The Princess Royal. She married, in 1859 Prince Frederick William of Prussia (1831–88: Fritz). Later Crown Princess of Prussia and Empress Frederick of Germany. They had eight children, the eldest of whom became Kaiser Wilhelm II (1859–1941: Willy).
PRINCE ALBERT EDWARD (Bertie) 1841–1910	The Prince of Wales. He married, in 1863, Princess Alexandra of Denmark (1844–1925: Alix). They had five children including Prince Albert Victor, Duke of Clarence (1864–92: Eddy); Prince George (1865–1936), who married Princess May of Teck (King George V and Queen Mary), and three daughters: Louise (1867–1931) who married the Duke of Fife (1840–1912); Princess Victoria (1868–1935) who did not marry and Princess Maud (1869–1938) who married King Haakon VII of Norway (1872–1957). Prince Albert Edward acceded to the throne as King Edward VII on January 22, 1901 on the death of his mother.
PRINCESS ALICE 1843–78	Married, in 1862, Louis IV, the Grand Duke of Hesse-Darmstadt (1837–92) and they had two sons and five daughters.
PRINCE ALFRED (Affie) 1844–1900	The Duke of Edinburgh and Saxe-Coburg-Gotha who married in 1874 the Grand Duchess Marie of Russia (1853–1920). They had one son (young Affie: 1874–99) and four daughters, one of whom, Marie (1875–1938: Mossy) married King Ferdinand of Rumania.

PRINCESS HELENA (Lenchen) 1846–1923	Married, in 1866, Prince Christian of Schleswig-Holstein (1831–1917) and had four children: Prince Christian Victor (1867–1900); Prince Albert (1869–1931); Princess Helena Victoria (1870–1948) and probably their best known daughter, Princess Marie-Louise (1872–1956) whose marriage to Prince Aribert of Anhalt was dissolved.
PRINCESS LOUISE 1848–1939	Married in 1871, the Marquis of Lorne, later 9th Duke of Argyll (1849–1914). They had no children.
PRINCE ARTHUR 1850–1942	Duke of Connaught. Married in 1879, Princess Louise of Prussia (1860–1917: Louischen). They had one son and two daughters.
PRINCE LEOPOLD 1853–84	Duke of Albany. Married in 1882 Princess Helena of Waldeck-Pyrmont (1861–1922). Prince Leopold died of haemophilia. His mother was a carrier of this disease. They had one son and a daughter (HRH Princess Alice, Countess of Athlone).
PRINCESS BEATRICE 1857–1944	She married Prince Henry of Battenberg (1858–96: Liko) in 1885 and they had three sons and one daughter, Victoria Eugénie (Ena) who became Queen Ena of Spain (1887–1941) having converted to Roman Catholicism in March 1906 two months before her marriage to HM Don Alfonso XIII.

HRH Princess Victoria, the Princess Royal, eldest child of Queen Victoria and the Prince Consort, at the time of her marriage to Crown Prince Frederick of Prussia in 1858.

TRH the Prince and Princess of Wales with their family aboard the Royal Yacht Osborne *in 1880.*

HRH Princess Alice with her husband, Prince Louis of Hesse, and their children.

HRH Prince Alfred, Duke of Edinburgh.

HRH Princess Helena.

On Parade.
Out Walking.
Arthur.
At home.

MARCH 26th

ABOVE: *HRH Prince Leopold, Duke of Albany, aged about two years old, by Winterhalter. His birth was the first at which Queen Victoria was given chloroform.*

ABOVE LEFT: *Sketches by Queen Victoria of HRH Prince Arthur, Duke of Connaught, aged about three years old.*

FAR LEFT: *HRH Princess Louise, aged about thirteen.*

LEFT: *The Queen's youngest child, HRH Princess Beatrice, aged about seven.*

QUEEN VICTORIA'S PRIME MINISTERS AND THEIR TERMS OF OFFICE

TOOK OFFICE		REMAINED IN OFFICE
April, 1835	**Viscount Melbourne**	6yrs 141 days
September, 1841	**Sir Robert Peel**	4yrs 303 days
July, 1846	**Lord John Russell**	5yrs 236 days
February, 1852	**Earl of Derby**	– 305 days
December, 1852	**Earl of Aberdeen**	2yrs 44 days
February, 1855	**Lord Palmerston**	3yrs 15 days
February, 1858	**Earl of Derby**	1yr 113 days
June, 1859	**Lord Palmerston**	6yrs 141 days
November, 1865	**Earl Russell**	– 242 days
July, 1866	**Earl of Derby**	1yr 236 days
February, 1868	**Benjamin Disraeli**	– 286 days
December, 1868	**W. E. Gladstone**	5yrs 74 days
February, 1874	**Earl of Beaconsfield** (Benjamin Disraeli)	6yrs 67 days
April 1880	**W. E. Gladstone**	5yrs 57 days
June, 1885	**Marquis of Salisbury**	– 227 days
February, 1886	**W. E. Gladstone**	– 178 days
August, 1886	**Marquis of Salisbury**	6yrs 15 days
August, 1892	**W. E. Gladstone**	1yr 197 days
March, 1894	**Earl of Rosebery**	1yr 121 days
July 1895–July 1902	**Marquis of Salisbury**	6yrs

Lord Palmerston (Henry John Temple, 3rd Viscount Palmerston), born 1784 and died in 1865. He was Prime Minister twice: from February, 1855, to February, 1858; and then from June, 1859, to October, 1865.

Lord John Russell, afterwards 1st Earl Russell, born 1798 and died 1878, He was Prime Minister twice: from July, 1846, to February, 1852; and then from October, 1865, to June, 1866.

Earl of Derby (Edward George Geoffrey Smith Stanley, 14th Earl of Derby), born 1799 and died 1869. He was Prime Minister three times: from February to December 1852; from February, 1858, to June, 1859; and then from June, 1866, to December, 1868.

Mr Benjamin Disraeli (1st Earl of Beaconsfield), born 1804 and died 1881.
He was Prime Minister twice, after being Chancellor of the Exchequer in all three Derby administrations: from February, 1868, to December, 1868; and then from February, 1874, to April, 1880.

ABOVE: *Lord Salisbury (Robert Arthur Talbot Gascoyne-Cecil, 3rd Marquis of Salisbury), born 1830 and died 1903. He was Prime Minister and Foreign Secretary three times and then Prime Minister. Prime Minister and Foreign Secretary: July, 1885, to February, 1886; August, 1886, to August, 1892; and from June, 1895, to November, 1900. Prime Minister from November, 1900, to July, 1902.*

ABOVE LEFT: *The Rt Hon. William Ewart Gladstone, born 1809 and died 1898. He was Prime Minister four times: 1868 to 1874; 1880 to 1885; 1886; and then from 1892 to 1894.*

LEFT: *Lord Rosebery (Archibald John Philip Primrose, 5th Earl of Rosebery), born 1847 and died 1929. He was Prime Minister from 1894 to 1895 after being Foreign Secretary in the third and fourth Gladstone administrations.*

The 5th Duke of Newcastle, father of Lord Edward Pelham-Clinton.

THE PELHAM-CLINTONS

LORD EDWARD PELHAM-CLINTON and his father, the 5th Duke of Newcastle, were both severe men leading austere lives. The Duke was said to have no sense of humour; Lord Edward always looked melancholic.

The Duke had been Secretary of State for War during the Crimea and was a great friend of Queen Victoria and of Prince Albert. They selected him as one of the gentlemen who would accompany their son, the Prince of Wales on what became an enormously successful visit to Canada and the USA in 1860.

He sent glowing and enthusiastic reports back to the Queen and Prince and was completely overwhelmed by the warmth of the reception given for the Prince of Wales by the New Yorkers. There is no doubt that the severe and unsmiling Duke managed to unbend a little during this royal tour.

There was, in fact, at least one excuse for his demeanour: his wife (a daughter of the 10th Duke of Hamilton) had suddenly run away with a Belgian courier in 1850. Ten years later—the year of the royal tour—the Duke's daughter, Lady Susan Pelham-Clinton (Lord Edward's sister) shocked everyone by deciding to marry Lord Adolphus Vane-Tempest, son of Lord and Lady Londonderry. The problem was that Lord Adolphus was insane.

The Duke was so annoyed that he refused to give her away; he refused her a dowry; he refused even to loan her his carriage to take her to church.

In one of her many gossipy letters to her daughter, the Crown Princess of Prussia, whose bridesmaid Lady Susan had been in 1858, Queen Victoria wrote: '... She told the Duke she would marry Lord Adolphus when she (Lady Susan) was of age! So she did ... she was given away by her (eldest) brother, Lord Lincoln who is very worthless, I fear. It is most sad ... Susan will pay dearly for it. Lord Adolphus is a good creature, but between his natural tendancy to madness, there is a sad prospect for Susan.'

How right the Queen was in her prediction.

After a terrible marriage, which lasted only four years, Lord Adolphus died after, it was reported, having had some kind of 'struggle' with his four keepers. It is also said that he tried to kill Lady Susan and their child!

Three years later in 1867, a sadder and wiser widowed Lady Susan met the Prince of Wales and she became his occasional mistress for about the next four years. By mid-1871 they had drifted apart a little and in the late summer of that year, the Prince was told that Lady Susan was expecting his child.

He was very annoyed that she had not told him immediately. In fact, it now seems that Lady Susan had not told him because she did not wish to worry one she 'loved and honoured' so much, and also because she felt she could have an abortion. Only when this failed did she enlist the Prince's help. The Prince told her to go to his doctor, Dr Oscar Clayton who was, it seems, a 'confidential practitioner' in these matters. History does not record what happened to the child, if it was not aborted and lived, but it does record that Lady Susan became very ill and was too ill to attend the thanksgiving service for the recovery of the Prince of Wales in January, 1872.

She died in 1875 and it was discovered years later that the Prince had kept her love letters for forty years, so great was his affection for her.

Since the 5th Duke, the father of Lord Edward and Lady Susan, there have been four more and the family (which has also added Hope to its name: Pelham-Clinton-Hope) is now led by Wing-Commander Henry Edward Hugh Pelham-Clinton-Hope, OBE, His Grace the 9th Duke of Newcastle. The Duke inherited the title from his father, the 8th Duke in 1941. His heir is his cousin, Edward Charles Pelham-Clinton.

PRINCIPAL EVENTS

1861–70

1861: Death of Prince Albert (December 14).
Outbreak of American Civil War.
William Morris began producing wallpapers and tapestries.
Louis Pasteur, French pioneer of bacteriology, developed germ theory of disease.

1862: Second great International Exhibition opened by the Duke of Cambridge (May 1).
Verdi's opera, *La Forza del Destino* first performed.
Marriage of Princess Alice to Louis of Hesse (July 1).
Legendary French tragedienne, Sarah Bernhardt made her acting debut in Paris.
Remains of the Prince Consort transferred to the mausoleum at Frogmore (December 18).

1863: The Prince of Wales married Princess Alexandra of Denmark (March 10).
Inauguration of the Great Exhibition memorial to the Prince Consort in the Horticultural Gardens, London (June 11).
Football Association formed.
Death of novelist William Thackeray, aged fifty-two (December 24).

1864: Birth of Prince Albert-Victor of Wales (January 8).
Louis Pasteur first demonstrated 'pasteurization'.
Giuseppe Garibaldi visited England (April 3–27).
Geneva Convention establishing the International Red Cross held.

Louis Pasteur, the French bacteriologist.

A. Gardner took this photograph of Abraham Lincoln on April 10, 1865. It was the President's last sitting. He was assassinated five days later.

The marriage of HRH Princess Alice to HRH Prince Louis of Hesse in the drawing room at Osborne House, Isle of Wight, on July 1, 1862.

1865: Abraham Lincoln assassinated by J. W. Booth (April 14).
Prince George of Wales born (June 3).
Earl Russell Prime Minister for 242 days (from November 6).
Joseph Lister pioneered antiseptic surgery.
English fleet visited Cherbourg (August 15).
French fleet visited Portsmouth (August 29).
Lord Palmerston died (October 18).
American Civil War ended.

1866: Marriage of Princess Helena to Prince Christian of Schleswig-Holstein (July 5).
Earl of Derby Prime Minister, in office for 1 year and 236 days (from July 6).
Austria at war with Prussia and Italy.
Dr Barnado's first East End Juvenile Mission founded.
Riots in Ireland.

Doctor Thomas Barnardo, founder of the Barnardo Homes, c. 1905.

1867: Queen Victoria laid foundation stone of the Royal Albert Hall (May 20).
Dominion of Canada established.
Second Reform Bill (August 15).

1868: Benjamin Disraeli Prime Minister for 286 days (from February 27).
Extreme summer temperatures caused over 20,000 deaths (July 1–September 30).
William Gladstone Prime Minister for five years and 74 days (from December 9).
Richard Wagner's opera *Die Meistersinger von Nürnberg* first performed.

1869: The Earl of Derby, former Prime Minister, died aged 70 (October 23).
Suez Canal officially opened by Empress Eugénie (November 17).
Irish Church disestablished.

1870: Charles Dickens died (June 9).
Franco–German War (July 19).
Elementary Education Act.
Dogma of Papal Infallibility.
Richard Wagner's *Die Walküre* first performed.
Queen Victoria consented to the marriage of Princess Louise to the Marquis of Lorne (October 24).

SELECTIONS FROM THE JOURNALS OF QUEEN VICTORIA

Osborne House, Isle of Wight, 1850, by W. Leitch.

OSBORNE, January 1st, 1862

HAVE BEEN UNABLE TO WRITE my Journal since the day my beloved one left us, and with what a heavy broken heart I enter on a new year without him! My dreadful and overwhelming calamity gives me so much to do, that I must henceforth merely keep notes of my sad and solitary life. This day last year found us so perfectly happy, and now! Last year music woke us; little gifts, new year's wishes, brought in by maid, and then given to dearest Albert, the children waiting with their gifts in the next room—all these recollections were pouring in on my mind in an overpowering manner. Alice slept in my room, and dear baby [*Princess Beatrice*] came down early. Felt as if living in a dreadful dream. Dear Alice much affected when she got up and kissed me. Arthur gave me a nosegay, and the girls, drawings done by them for their dear father and me. Could hardly touch my breakfast.

When dressed saw Dr. Jenner, [*afterwards Sir William Jenner, and Physician-in-Ordinary to the Queen*] Mr. Ruland, [*Librarian at Windsor*] and Augusta Bruce [*daughter of 7th Earl of Elgin; Resident Bedchamber Woman to the Queen; afterwards Lady Augusta Stanley*]. Went down to see the sketch for a statue of my beloved Albert in Highland dress, which promises to be good. Then out with Lenchen, [*Princess Helena, afterwards Princess Christian*] Toward [*the Land Steward at Osborne, who assisted the Prince Consort to lay out the grounds*] always following and pointing out trees and everything. When I came in, saw the Duke of Newcastle [*father of Lord Edward Pelham-Clinton*] in dear Albert's room, where *all* remains the same. Talking for long of him, of his great goodness, and purity, quite unlike anyone else. Saw Sir J. Clark, [*Physician-in-Ordinary to the Queen*] Sir C. Phipps, [*Keeper of HM Privy Purse*] and then dear, kind Uncle Leopold [*The King of the Belgians*]. Dined with dear Marie [*Princess Ernest Leiningen, wife of her half-nephew*] and went over to Feodore's [*Queen Victoria's half-sister, Princess of Hohenlohe-Langenburg*] room. Dear Uncle came upstairs to see me for a short while, also Bertie [*The Prince of Wales, afterwards King Edward VII*]. Alice gave me my beloved Albert's Christmas present, so precious, and so sad.

OSBORNE, January 21st, 1862

THE EXPRESSIONS OF UNIVERSAL ADMIRATION and appreciation of beloved Albert are most striking, and show how he was beloved and how his worth was recognised. Even the poor people in small villages, who don't know me, are shedding tears for me, as if it were their own private sorrow.

Saw General Grey and then Lord Elgin, who goes as Governor-General to India. We talked of India. General Grey was to show him the papers with my beloved Albert's views on India, in which he took so great an interest, as in all that concerned it.

OSBORNE, January 29th, 1862

AFTER LUNCHEON saw [*the Prime Minister*] Lord Palmerston (who has been very ill). It made me very nervous seeing him for the first time since my great misfortune, but I felt it was right not to put it off any longer. He seemed very nervous himself. Spoke of Uncle, whom he had been to see, and of my remaining here for the present. He could in fact hardly speak for emotion. It showed me how much he felt my terrible loss, and he said what a dreadful calamity it was. Then he spoke about Bertie [*her eldest son, the Prince of Wales*], and the desirability for his travelling, which would be such a good thing for him. I repeated that it had been his Father's wish he should do so; and Lord Palmerston said it was most important he should marry. I observed that he was a very good and dutiful son, but that for him, just at his age, the loss of his Father was terrible, which Lord Palmerston thoroughly understands and feels keenly. Everything was quiet, he thought there would be no trouble, but '*the* difficulty of the moment' was Bertie. I felt the same, and would hardly have given Lord Palmerston credit for entering so entirely into my anxieties. He alluded to Princess Alexandra [*of Denmark, who became Princess of Wales, and later Queen Alexandra*] and thought the political objections must not be minded, as they did not affect *this* country. I did not speak as if there were any certainty, but praised the young lady. With America he hoped matters would go well. He was most anxious to facilitate things for me.

WINDSOR CASTLE, March 19th, 1862

SAW SIR C. PHIPPS, who had been speaking with Mr. Gladstone about money matters. I feel very anxious about a provision for Bertie and his wife, in the event of his marrying; a provision for my younger sons on their coming of age and marrying; and a provision for the younger children under age, in case of my death. He showed me a very satisfactory paper from Mr. Gladstone on the subject. Then saw Mr. Gladstone for a little while, who was very kind and feeling. We talked of the state of the country. He spoke with such unbounded admiration and appreciation of my beloved Albert, saying no one could ever replace him.

WINDSOR CASTLE, June 14th, 1862

HEARD OF BERTIE'S LANDING, [*on his return from his visit to the Near East*] after a boisterous crossing. The good General [*Major-General Bruce*] none the worse for it. Bertie arrived at half past five, looking extremely well. I was much upset at seeing him, and feeling his beloved father was not there to welcome him back. He would have been so pleased to see him so improved, and looking so bright and healthy. Dear Bertie was most affectionate, and the tears came into his eyes when he saw me. Drove with Alice and Augusta B[*ruce*]. Saw Sir C. Phipps, who had seen General Bruce, and said he required the greatest quiet, and was hardly to be recognised with his white beard, so thin and haggard, and not able to walk alone. After dinner saw good Dr. Minter, who gave me an account of Bertie, and of the General's illness. Then Dr. Stanley came, and I thanked him for all he had done for our boy. He was so kind and full of sympathy, which I shall not easily forget. He spoke most kindly of Bertie, and thanked me for having asked his sister here to meet him. Remained some time talking with him.

LAEKEN [*King Leopold's Palace at Brussels*]
September 3rd, 1862

AT HALF PAST I WENT DOWN TO LUNCHEON with the girls, going first to the Drawing-room where Marie B[*rabant*] [*wife of the Duke of Brabant, King Leopold's elder son, afterwards King Leopold II*] and Mrs. Paget [*wife of the Minister at Copenhagen*] introduced Princess Christian, who presented her two daughters Alexandra and Dagmar, [*afterwards Empress of Russia and later Ex-Empress Marie*] and Prince Christian [*Princess Alexandra's father who succeeded in the late autumn of 1863 to the throne of Denmark*]. I had seen him last 24 years ago. The Brabants and Philip [*Count of Flanders, younger son of King Leopold*] were also there. Alexandra is lovely, such a beautiful refined profile, and quiet ladylike manner, which made a most favourable impression. Dagmar is quite different, with fine brown eyes. Princess Christian must have been quite good-looking. She is unfortunately very deaf. Uncle [*King Leopold*] soon came in, and after a rather stiff visit they all (excepting myself) went to luncheon. I spoke to Mrs. Paget in the next room and told her I was favourably impressed. Baby [*Princess Beatrice*] lunched with me.

Afterwards Marie B. brought Prince and Princess Christian upstairs, leaving them with me. Now came the terribly trying moment for me. *I* had *alone* to say and do what, under other, former happy circumstances, had devolved on us both together. It was not without much emotion that I was able to express what I did to the Princess: my belief that they knew what we wished and hoped, which was terrible for me to say *alone*. I said that I trusted their dear daughter would feel, should she accept our son, that she was doing so with her whole heart and will. They assured me that Bertie *might hope* she would do so, and that they trusted *he* also felt a real inclination, adding that they hoped God would give their dear child strength to do what she ought, and that she might be able to pour some comfort into my poor heart, that they were sure she would become quickly attached to me, and be a good wife to Bertie. I replied I would do all I could to be a *real* mother to her, but I feared she was entering a very sad house. This ended this most trying meeting. Feodore afterwards came to my room and I told her all. She spoke with great admiration of the young Princess.

Dined as yesterday, and afterwards Prince and Princess Christian and Princess Alexandra came upstairs. She looked lovely, in a black dress, nothing in her hair, and curls on either side, which hung over her shoulders, her hair turned back off her beautiful forehead. Her whole appearance was one of the greatest charm, combined with simplicity and perfect dignity. I gave her a little piece of white heather which Bertie gave me at Balmoral, and I told her I hoped it would bring her luck. Dear Uncle Leopold, who sat near me, was charmed with her. Very tired, and felt low and agitated.

WINDSOR CASTLE, December 9th, 1862

SAW LORD RUSSELL [*John Russell: a past and future Prime Minister*], who talked of Bertie's Marriage Treaty, then of the very important decision of the Cabinet to recommend me to give up the Protectorate of the Ionian Islands, and to give them to Greece. It would be a boon to them, and it was hoped would ensure their not attacking Turkey. How I did miss beloved Albert, his advice, his opinion! These are such important events, and he is not here any more to share the responsibility with me. But dear Albert would certainly have agreed and approved . . .

December 14th

[*the first anniversary of the Prince Consort's death*]

OH! THIS DREADFUL, DREADFUL DAY! At 10 we went into the dear room (all the children but

The wedding of the Prince of Wales to Princess Alexandra of Denmark at St George's Chape

sor. *In this painting by Frith the Queen can be seen watching the ceremony from the gallery.*

baby there) and Dr. Stanley most kindly held a little service for us, reading Prayers and some portions of the 14th and 16th Chapters of St. John, and spoke a few and most comforting and beautiful words. The room was full of flowers, and the sun shining in so brightly, emblems of his happiness and glory, which comforted me. I said it seemed like a birthday, and Dr. Stanley answered, 'It *is* a birthday in a new world.' Oh! to think of my beginning another year alone! Went with Alice and Louis to Frogmore, and into the Mausoleum, then drove a little afterwards. Lunched alone with Baby. Out with Augusta B[*ruce*].

WINDSOR CASTLE, December 18th, 1862

WOKE VERY OFTEN DURING THE NIGHT, thinking of the sacred work to be carried out at 7 o'clock. At that hour the precious earthly Remains were to be carried with all love and peace to their final resting-place by our three sons (for little Leopold had earnestly begged to go too). Dear Louis, Sir C. Phipps, Col. Biddulph, General Grey, as well as Löhlein and Maget (dear Albert's two valets), were there too. I cannot say more. I got some sleep during that time, and later Alice came to tell me all had been peacefully and lovingly accomplished. Dull, raining, and mild. Took half an hour's drive with Alice, and at quarter to 1 we all drove down as yesterday to Frogmore, taking Baby with us. Waited a little while in the house, and then walked to the Mausoleum, entering it, preceded only by the Dean [*The Very Reverend & Hon. Dr Gerald Wellesley, Dean of Windsor*]. It seemed so like the day at Frogmore, when Albert was so dear and loving. Everyone entered, each carrying a wreath. The Dean, with a faltering voice, read some most appropriate Prayers. We were all much overcome when we knelt round the beloved tomb. When everybody had gone out, we returned again and gazed on the great beauty and peace of the beautiful statue. What a comfort it will be to have that near me!

WINDSOR CASTLE, March 10th, 1863

ALL IS OVER and this (to me) most trying day is past, as a dream, for all seems like a dream now and leaves hardly any impression upon my poor mind and broken heart! Here I sit lonely and desolate, who so need love and tenderness, while our two daughters have each their loving husbands, and Bertie has taken his lovely, pure, sweet Bride to Osborne, such a jewel whom he is indeed lucky to have obtained. How I pray God may ever bless them! Oh! what I suffered in the Chapel, where all that was joy, pride, and happiness on January 25th, '58 [*when the Princess Royal was married in the Chapel Royal, St James's Palace*], was repeated *without* the principal figure of all, the guardian angel of the family, being there. It was indescribable. At one moment, when I first heard the flourish of trumpets, which brought back to my mind my whole life of 20 years at *his* dear side, safe, proud, secure, and happy, I felt as if I should faint. Only by a violent effort could I succeed in mastering my emotion!

But now I must return to the beginning of the day. Directly after breakfast went over to the State Rooms, to embrace darling Alix, and give her my blessing. Her mother was much affected. Went with her into Alix's bedroom, where she was in her dressing-gown, and very *émotionnée*. Then I went back to my room and could see from my windows all the crowds of people assembling and arriving. Cold from nervousness and agitation, I dressed, wearing my weeds, but a silk gown with crape, a long veil to my cap, and, for the first time since December '61, the ribbon, star, and badge of the Order of the Garter, the latter being one my beloved one had worn, also the Victoria and Albert Order, on which I have had dearest Albert's head put above mine, and a brooch containing a miniature of him set round with diamonds, which I have worn ever since '40.

Drove with the Duchess of Sutherland [*wife of the 2nd Duke; Mistress of the Robes*] and Jane Churchill, [*wife of the 2nd Baron; Lady of the Bedchamber*] Katherine Bruce and Lord Methuen [*the 2nd Baron; ADC and afterwards Lord-in-Waiting to the Queen*] following in another carriage. We started from the usual door, going on to the North Terrace, where we got out and went through a covered way down the small stairs, quite quietly, up into the Deanery. A Guard of Honour was mounted in the Quadrangle. Before I had left I had seen Lenchen in her pretty dress and train, lilac and white, and Louise and sweet baby, the same colours. Louise wore the pearls belonging to dearest Albert's mother, which he had

A family group on the Prince of Wales's wedding day.
The Prince and Princess of Wales stand behind the Queen, Princess Helena is on her right and Princess Beatrice on her left. Prince and Princess Louis of Hesse stand behind Crown Princess Frederick of Prussia, and Prince Arthur kneels beside her.

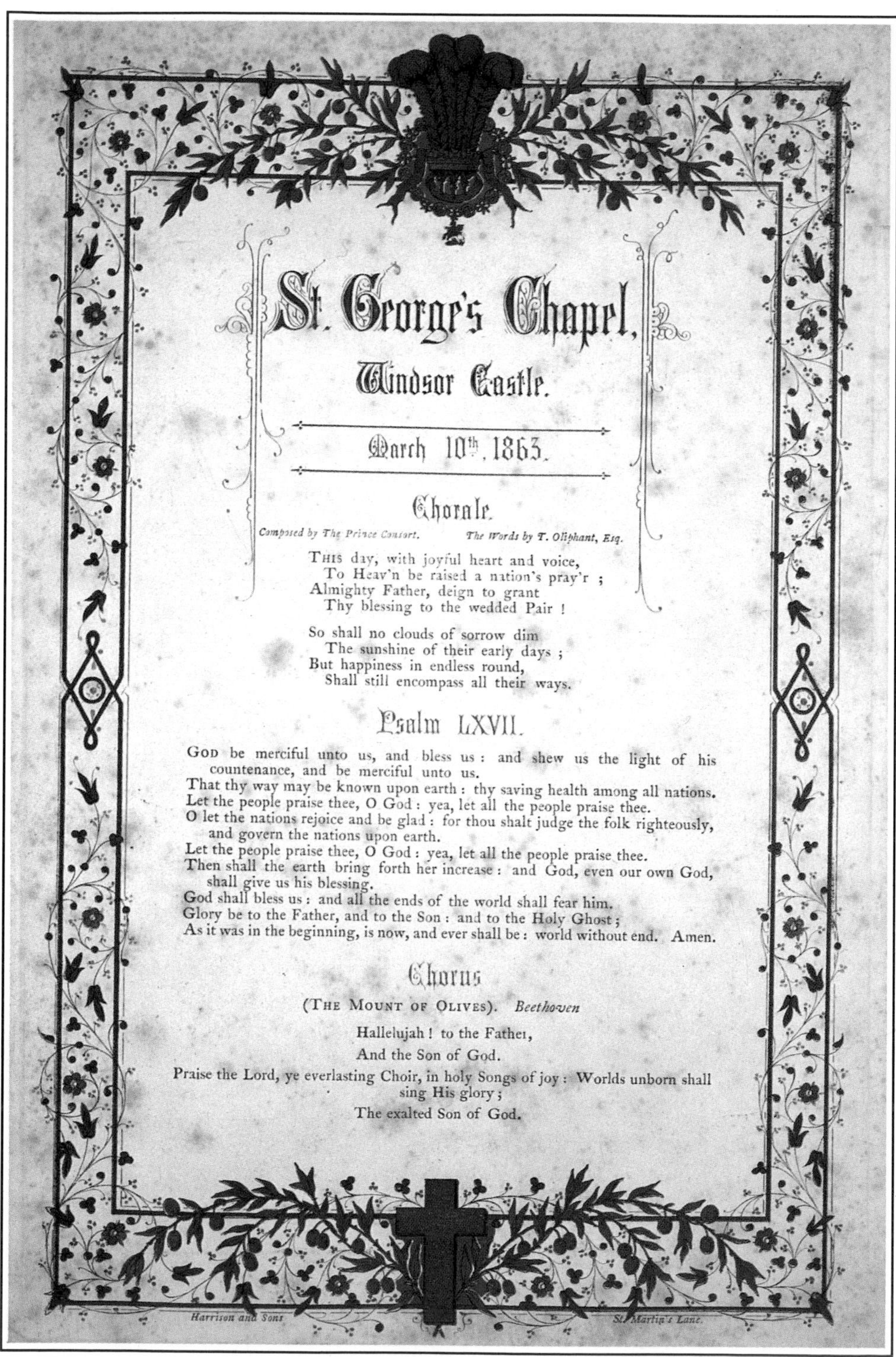

St. George's Chapel,

Windsor Castle.

March 10th, 1863.

Chorale.

Composed by The Prince Consort. *The Words by T. Oliphant, Esq.*

THIS day, with joyful heart and voice,
To Heav'n be raised a nation's pray'r ;
Almighty Father, deign to grant
Thy blessing to the wedded Pair !

So shall no clouds of sorrow dim
The sunshine of their early days ;
But happiness in endless round,
Shall still encompass all their ways.

Psalm LXVII.

GOD be merciful unto us, and bless us : and shew us the light of his countenance, and be merciful unto us.
That thy way may be known upon earth : thy saving health among all nations.
Let the people praise thee, O God : yea, let all the people praise thee.
O let the nations rejoice and be glad : for thou shalt judge the folk righteously, and govern the nations upon earth.
Let the people praise thee, O God : yea, let all the people praise thee.
Then shall the earth bring forth her increase : and God, even our own God, shall give us his blessing.
God shall bless us : and all the ends of the world shall fear him.
Glory be to the Father, and to the Son : and to the Holy Ghost ;
As it was in the beginning, is now, and ever shall be : world without end. Amen.

Chorus

(THE MOUNT OF OLIVES). *Beethoven*

Hallelujah ! to the Father,
And the Son of God.
Praise the Lord, ye everlasting Choir, in holy Songs of joy : Worlds unborn shall sing His glory ;
The exalted Son of God.

Harrison and Sons *St. Martin's Lane.*

A section of the beautifully designed and printed service sheet for the marriage of HRH the Prince of Wales to Princess Alexandra of Denmark. The service included the chorale, 'This day, with joyful heart and voice' to music by the groom's late father, the Prince Consort.

always intended to give her. To see them go alone was dreadful. We waited a short while in the Deanery, and then went along a covered way prepared over the leads, which brought us into the Royal Closet. The divisions had been removed, and, when I stepped up to the window, the Chapel full of smartly dressed people, the Knights of the Garter in their robes, the waving banners, the beautiful window, altar, and reredos to my beloved one's memory, with the bells ringing outside, quite had the effect of a scene in a play.

Sat down feeling strange and bewildered. When the procession entered to the playing of the March in *Athalie*, and after Aunt Cambridge, [*the Duchess of Cambridge*] Mary, [*the Duchess of Cambridge's daughter, afterwards Duchess of Teck, and mother of Queen Mary*] and our five fatherless children (the three girls and two little boys) came into view, the latter without either parent (at Vicky's wedding they walked before, behind, and near me), I felt terribly overcome. I could not take my eyes off precious little Baby, [*Princess Beatrice*] with her golden hair and large nosegay, and smiled at her as she made a beautiful curtsey. Everyone bowed to me. I quite overlooked Alice coming in, looking extremely well in a violet dress, covered with her wedding lace, and a violet velvet train, from the shoulders trimmed with the miniver beloved Mama had worn at Vicky's wedding, Louis in the Garter robes leading her. Last came dear Vicky (leading little William), in a white satin dress trimmed with ermine, etc. When she caught sight of me, coming up the Choir, she made a very low curtsey, with an inexpressible look of love and respect, which had a most touching effect. There was a pause, and then the trumpets sounded again, and our boy, supported by Ernest C[*oburg*] and Fritz, [*the Crown Prince of Prussia, afterwards the Emperor Frederick II*] all in Garter robes, entered; Bertie looking pale and nervous. He bowed to me, and during the long wait for his Bride kept constantly looking up at me, with an anxious, clinging look, which touched me much. At length she appeared, the band playing Handel's Processional March, with her eight bridesmaids, looking very lovely. She was trembling and very pale. Dearest Albert's Chorale was sung, which affected me much, and then the service proceeded. When it was over, the young couple looked up at me, and I gave them an affectionate nod and kissed my hand to sweet Alix. They left together, immediately followed by *all* the others, Beethoven's 'Hallelujah Chorus' (from *The Mount of Olives*) being played.

I went back to the Castle, getting out at the North Terrace, and went upstairs for a few minutes. Then hearing the couple were coming, I hastened down the Grand Staircase (the first time since my misfortune), where all the Beefeaters were drawn up. My *only* thought was that of welcoming *our children*, and I stepped out and embraced both dear Bertie and Alix most warmly, walking upstairs next to them and past several of the guests, who had already arrived. We went into the ante-room, next the Rubens Room, and here, soon after, Prince Christian, George, [*the Duke of Cambridge*] Ernest C., and Fritz joined us. Went then with Alice over to the Dining-room, and afterwards to the White Drawing-room, where the young couple and *all* the others came, for the signing of the Register, which took a very long time. A family luncheon of thirty-eight followed, in the Dining-room, the Joinvilles and daughter, Aumales, and Nemours and Marguerite [*Orléans Princes and Princesses*] having come for that. Edward Weimar [*Prince Edward of Saxe-Weimar*] and the Maharajah [*Prince Duleep Singh*] were also included. *I* lunched alone with baby.

WINDSOR CASTLE, June 16th, 1864

AFTER LUNCHEON SAW MR. GLADSTONE, who told me what had passed at the Cabinet. Lord Russell had read my letter, upon which the Cabinet all at once said they had never authorised him to inform me that they had decided on offering arbitration, which if not accepted by Denmark, and refused by Germany, would entail England's giving material aid to Denmark. It was very serious and disagreeable for me to receive on repeated occasions such unauthorised decisions from Lord Russell, and ones of such magnitude. The Cabinet all felt that the moment had not yet come to consider whether material aid should be given, and certainly not until an answer had been received from Denmark, saying whether arbitration would be accepted if proposed.

Here the Queen was referring to the Schleswig–Holstein problem. The duchies of Schleswig and Holstein had been held by the kings of Denmark from 1460—but were not part of their kingdom. Some of the inhabitants were German and Holstein was a member of the German Confederation formed in 1815. Ownership of the duchies had long been disputed by Prussia and when the King of Denmark died without an heir in 1863, Prussia, supported by Austria, fought and defeated the Danes in 1864. Two years later Prussia annexed the duchies. It was not until 1920 that a plebiscite gave the northern part of Schleswig to Denmark. The rest of Schleswig, with Holstein, stayed part of Germany.

WINDSOR CASTLE, June 21st, 1864

SAW LORD PALMERSTON [*the Prime Minister*] as soon as I arrived, and found him very sensible, wonderfully clear-headed, and fully alive to the extreme dangers of the situation. Showed him a telegram from Copenhagen, which made it clear that the Danes were not inclined, at any rate, to accept arbitration in its complete form, which of course would

Prince Otto Von Bismarck, the 'Iron Chancellor'.
He was the creator of the German Empire and waged war against Denmark in 1864 for possession of Schleswig-Holstein, against Austria in 1866, and against France in 1870.

render it useless. He did not apprehend the great danger of the whole of Germany being united as one man against us, though he thought matters most serious. The greatest danger he saw from France joining us was dragging us into a war, in which she would claim the Rhine, and possibly revolutionise the whole of Italy. He also entirely agreed with me that it was very doubtful whether we could do anything, for nothing but naval assistance could be given, and that only for three months. Would *that* not therefore be more humiliating for England than doing nothing at all? He felt this very strongly and said the Danes were the most obstinate people he knew; 'they are not an intelligent race and very *borné*.' He had told Quaade again and again that they were going on to their own destruction, for no one would help them. The very outside of any assistance they could get from here would be by sea, and that was very doubtful. He still hoped that matters might be arranged peaceably, the difference being so very small, and no stone should be left unturned to effect this.

WINDSOR CASTLE, July 2nd, 1864

LORD CLARENDON [*Diplomat and Liberal politician. Foreign Secretary 1865–6 and 1868–70*] dined with Lenchen, Louise, Janie E. [*the Dowager Marchioness of Ely*], and me. He was full of mischievous stories. After dinner he talked long and much of the state of affairs. His great fear was the recklessness of Bismarck leading the Prussians to do something which would again rouse the excitement of the people here. Lord Palmerston had entirely spoilt the end of his speech by the allusion to Copenhagen, 'for when one has untied one's hands, one does not tie them again.' But we had had a very great escape, for, if the Danes had accepted, after what Lord Russell had said, we should have been in a very awkward position, the danger of which could not be overrated. The French had been only waiting to see us well engaged and then would have most likely dragged us into a regular European war, going themselves to the Rhine. I said I quite shuddered at what might have happened.

OSBORNE, February 12th, 1865

The Queen is worried about the effects of the American Civil War.

SAW SIR C. WOOD about a 2nd or 3rd class of the Star of India, which is to be established, and which he says is quite in consonance with what dearest Albert wished. Then talked of my statue for Bombay and one of him, which they wish to have in the museum there. Also talked of America and the danger, which seems approaching, of our having a war with her, as soon as she makes peace; of the impossibility of our being able to hold Canada, but we must struggle for it; and far the best would be to let it go as an independent kingdom, under an English Prince! But can we stave this off, and who could be chosen? I told Sir C. Wood that dearest Albert had often thought of the Colonies for our sons, but that I had disliked the idea. However, now I felt, once knowing the serious reasons put before me, I could not but entertain the thought, though for Alfred it would not do. For Arthur it might be different.

The American Civil War (1861–5) was fought between eleven of the Southern States (North and South Carolina; Mississippi, Florida, Alabama, Georgia, Louisiana, Texas, Virginia,

Arkansas and Tennessee)—the Confederate States—which wished to maintain their 'states rights' in particular Negro slaves, and the Northern States. The Confederate States claimed the right to secede from the Union; the Northern, or Federal States, fought to maintain the Union and elected President Lincoln as their leader. The Confederates elected Jefferson Davis. At first, the Confederates were successful, but they suffered a series of spectacular defeats and on April 9, 1865, General Robert E. Lee surrendered to General Grant and about a month later, the war was over. There were over 600,000 casualties. Slavery was abolished. Queen Victoria's fears about being drawn into a war with America were groundless as were her fears about 'being able to hold Canada'. Confederation of Upper and Lower Canada (now Ontario and Quebec), Nova Scotia and New Brunswick was achieved by the British North America Act which came into force on July 1, 1867—a mere two years after Queen Victoria's 'doubts'.

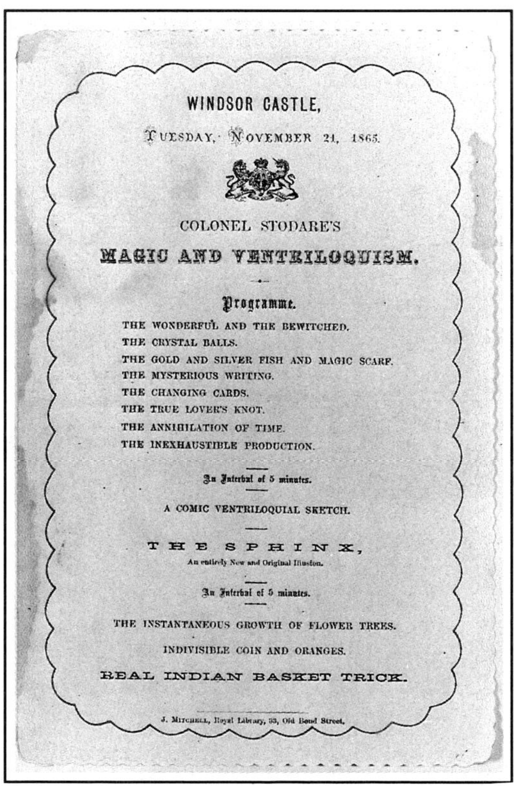

WINDSOR CASTLE,

TUESDAY, NOVEMBER 21, 1865.

COLONEL STODARE'S

MAGIC AND VENTRILOQUISM.

Programme.

THE WONDERFUL AND THE BEWITCHED.
THE CRYSTAL BALLS.
THE GOLD AND SILVER FISH AND MAGIC SCARF.
THE MYSTERIOUS WRITING.
THE CHANGING CARDS.
THE TRUE LOVER'S KNOT.
THE ANNIHILATION OF TIME.
THE INEXHAUSTIBLE PRODUCTION.

An Interval of 5 minutes.

A COMIC VENTRILOQUIAL SKETCH.

THE SPHINX,
An entirely New and Original Illusion.

An Interval of 5 minutes.

THE INSTANTANEOUS GROWTH OF FLOWER TREES.

INDIVISIBLE COIN AND ORANGES.

REAL INDIAN BASKET TRICK.

J. Mitchell, Royal Library, 33, Old Bond Street.

Colonel Stodare's Magic and Ventriloquism show in November, 1865, was among the first entertainments presented at Windsor after the death of the Prince Consort.

WINDSOR CASTLE, February 6th, 1866

Queen Victoria goes in state to open Parliament for the first time since Prince Albert's death.

A FINE MORNING. Terribly nervous and agitated. At ½ past 10 left Windsor for London, with the children, ladies, and gentlemen. Great crowds out, and so I had (for the first time since my great misfortune) an escort. Dressing after luncheon, which I could hardly touch. Wore my ordinary evening dress, only trimmed with miniver, and my cap with a long flowing tulle veil, a small diamond and sapphire coronet rather at the back, and diamonds outlining the front of my cap.

It was a fearful moment for me when I entered the carriage *alone*, and the band played; also when all the crowds cheered, and I had great difficulty in repressing my tears. But our two dear affectionate girls [*Princesses Helena and Louise, who faced Her Majesty in the carriage*] were a true help and support to me, and they so thoroughly realised all I was going through. The crowds were most enthusiastic, and the people seemed to look at me with sympathy. We had both windows open, in spite of a very high wind.

When I entered the House [*of Lords*], which was very full, I felt as if I should faint. All was silent and all eyes fixed upon me, and there I sat alone. I was greatly relieved when all was over, and I stepped down from the throne . . .

So thankful that the great ordeal of to-day was well over, and that I was enabled to get through it.

WINDSOR CASTLE, July 5th, 1866

WAS AWOKE BY THE SOUND OF THE MARRIAGE BELLS, but felt very sad and agitated.—Breakfasted alone with dear Lenchen [*her daughter, Princess Helena*]. All hustle & excitement. Lenchen dressed in my bedroom, cleared out for the occasion; I wore a black moire antique dress, interwoven with silver, my long veil surmounted by a diamond diadem & the rest of my jewels diamonds.—Lenchen's wedding dress was of white satin, trimmed with one superb flounce of Honiton lace, originally chosen for me, by dearest Albert, & sprays of orange flowers & myrtles, & a very long train, trimmed with the same lace & flowers. We sat waiting in my room for ever so long, Bertie coming in & out, & being very kind & amiable. At length at 20. m. to 1 the Bride's procession moved, Ly. Caroline Lennox (a nice girl) coming in, to carry Lenchen's train. She presented her with

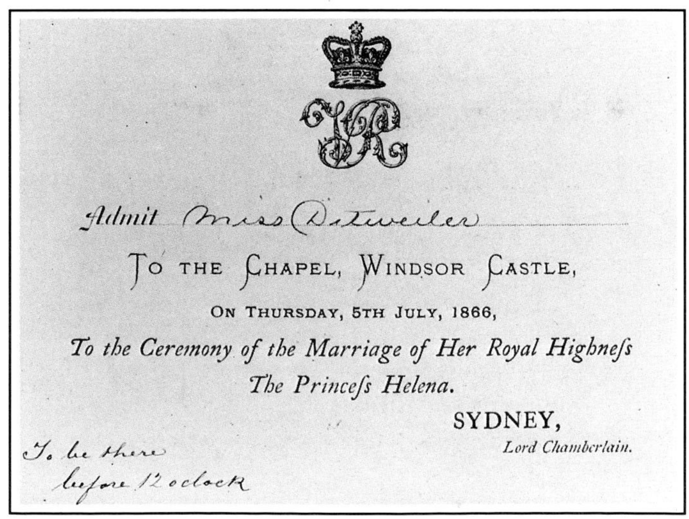
Admit Miss Ditweiler

TO THE CHAPEL, WINDSOR CASTLE,

ON THURSDAY, 5TH JULY, 1866,

To the Ceremony of the Marriage of Her Royal Highness The Princess Helena.

SYDNEY,
Lord Chamberlain.

To be there before 12 oclock

An invitation to Princess Helena's wedding addressed to Miss Ditweiler, who was Queen Victoria's dresser and friend for thirty-three years from 1859 to her death on August 25, 1892.

The marriage of Princess Helena and Prince Christian of Schleswig-Holstein was celebrated in the Private Chapel at Windsor Castle on July 5, 1866.

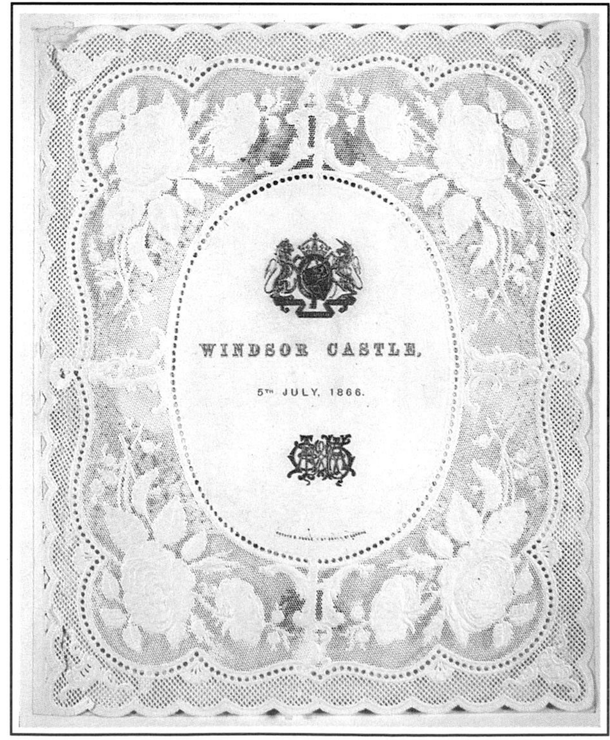

A beautiful lace cover from the service sheet for Princess Helena's wedding.

a splendid pendent of different coloured diamonds, the gift of all the Bridesmaids, who were: Ly. Margaret Scott, Ly. Laura Phipps, Lady Mary Fitzwilliam, Ly. Muriel Campbell, Lady Caroline Lennox, Ly. Albertha Hamilton, Lady Alexandrina Murray, & Ly. Ernestine Edgcumbe. The Bridesmaids wore white dresses & veils, trimmed with forget-me-nots, blush roses & white heather. The corridor was full of our servants & their wives, &c. I led Lenchen, who walked between Bertie & me, & I gave her away. The Ceremony, which was performed by the Archbishop of Canterbury, was short, without the exhortation. I could not see dear Lenchen's face, as I stood a little behind her. At the conclusion of the service she embraced me warmly, & I did the same to Christian, whose countenance showed the deepest emotion. The Register was signed in the White Drawingroom, the Ld. Chancellor, Ld. Granville, Ld. Russell & Ld. Clarendon, coming in to sign, as well as the Archbishop, the Bishop of London, the Bishop of Oxford, the Bishop of Worcester [*Clerk of the Closet*] & the Bishop of Winchester. This over we went with the dear Couple into the Green Drawingroom, where, as well as in the Red Drawingroom, all the guests were assembled, who came by. We then went in to luncheon, the Bridal pair going in first, then Bertie & Marie B. & Leopold & me, &c—Leopold in a few kind words, in very good English, gave out the healths of the Bride & Bridegroom. After luncheon we all separated & Lenchen & Christian came for a little while to my room, & I gave him the Garter. He was much overcome when I told him with what confidence I gave our darling good Child to him. Then they changed their clothes, Lenchen reappearing in a pretty white muslin & lace dress, with a white bonnet trimmed with orange flowers. At 4, went with them into the Corridor, where the whole family were assembled and we again waited a little while. Then came the moment of parting, which both dear Lenchen & I dreaded. I went to the bottom of the stairs and kissed her again. Numbers of people crowded to see her go, & all the ladies & gentlemen were in the Quadrangle. Quantities of rice & shoes were thrown, as the carriage drove away with an Escort. Crowds were on the Hill, also the Eton Boys. I ran back to my room to get a distant view of the dear Couple driving away, loudly cheered. Dear Marie Leiningen remained a few minutes with me, then I rested feeling terribly tired & sad. So many conflicting emotions filled my heart.—At 6 drove down to Frogmore with Baby & took tea in the Colonade, as it was very windy.—Wished all good night before dinner, & dined alone with Leopold, Baby & the good Dss of Roxburghe, who was all kindness & sympathy. She remained some little time with me & read to me, after which I sat sadly alone with my thoughts!—

WINDSOR CASTLE, November 14th, 1866

BEFORE LUNCHEON saw, with Lenchen, Mr. Theodore Martin, the gentleman who Mr. Helps [*the Royal Librarian*] wishes should be entrusted with the *Life*, [*of the Prince Consort*] as General Grey cannot continue it, and Mr. Helps himself has no time. He was too ill to bring Mr. Martin, who is very pleasing, clever, quiet, and *sympathique*. He is also well known to Augusta Stanley.

The Queen travels to Wolverhampton (then in Staffordshire) to unveil a statue to Prince Albert.

WINDSOR CASTLE, November 30th, 1866

A BRIGHT MORNING, though very cold. Shortly before 10 started by train for Wolverhampton, with Lenchen, Louise, Christian, etc. . . .

With a sinking heart and trembling knees got out of the train, amidst great cheering, bands playing, troops presenting arms, etc. Was received by Lord Lichfield, Lord Lieutenant of the County (who presented the Mayor), and Lady Lichfield, looking so young and handsome, who was standing with Lady Waterpark. When we were told all was ready entered our carriages, I driving with my daughters and Christian, with an escort of the 8th Hussars. The postilions wore the Ascot livery. Lord A. Paget and General Grey rode just behind the carriage. All along the three or four miles we drove, the town was beautifully decorated, with flags, wreaths of flowers, and endless kind inscriptions. There were also many arches. It seemed so strange being amongst so many, yet feeling so *alone*, without my beloved husband! Everything so like former great functions, and yet so unlike! I felt much moved, and nearly broke down when I saw the dear name and the following inscriptions—'Honour to the memory of Albert the Good,' 'the good Prince,' 'His works follow him,' and so many quotations from Tennyson. There were barriers all along, so that there was no overcrowding, and many Volunteers with bands were stationed at different points.

The arrangements on the spot where the statue stood were extremely good and the decorations very pretty. There were high galleries all round, and a covered daïs for me, but the cold wind made it fearfully draughty. The Prayers and Address were both long, and trying to many. I made several very deep curtsies when I got out of the carriage and stepped forward. The enthusiasm was very great.

The Mayor was completely taken by surprise when I knighted him, and seemed quite bewildered, and hardly to understand it when Lord Derby told him. There was some slight delay in the uncovering of the statue, but it [*the covering sheet*] fell well and slowly, amidst shouts and the playing of the dear old Coburg March by the band. How I could bear up, I hardly know, but I remained firm throughout.

WINDSOR, April 10th, 1867

AT THREE, THE KING OF DENMARK [*the King and Queen of Denmark had been staying for some time at Marlborough House, to which they had been summoned owing to the very serious illness of their daughter, the Princess of Wales. The illness, though still severe, was by 10 April no longer critical; but it lasted for several months*] came to wish me good-bye, and paid me a short visit. Received him on the staircase, and took him to the Audience Room. He seemed low and unhappy about his daughter. It had been agreed that he and Christian should meet, so at half past three, he, Lenchen, and the others came in, and the King spoke very kindly to Christian, saying that he had had a similar misfortune to his, in losing his dear mother. Christian asked after Alix, and the King went away, shaking hands with him. Am most thankful for this meeting, which must do good. [*The point of the meeting was in the former relations of both men to the Duchies of Schleswig and Holstein, at this time, by right of conquest, a part of Prussia.*]

The foundation stone of the Royal Albert Hall was laid by the Queen on May 20, 1867, and the first brick was laid by Mrs Henry Cole on November 7, 1867. Henry Cole, who had become Chairman of the Society of Arts in 1851, was absolutely determined that a great hall

The opening of the Royal Albert Hall by Queen Victoria on March 29, 1871. An engraving from The Illustrated London News.

would be built '... the finest in Europe for hearing, seeing and convenience. It will afford ample sitting room for about 12,000 persons ... the access and egress shall be most ample ...'

When the Queen arrived to lay the foundation stone, she found 7000 people packed inside, eager to get a glimpse of her. Many of them had not seen her since the death of the Prince six years earlier. Her Majesty was almost entirely in black although she wore a white 'Mary Queen of Scots' cap and a white lace collar on her gown. She was obviously under great emotional strain when she spoke: 'I thank you for your affectionate and dutiful address. It has been with a struggle that I have nerved myself to a compliance with the wish that I should take part in this day's ceremony; but I have been sustained by the thought that I should assist by my presence in promoting the accomplishment of his great designs to whose memory the gratitude and affection of the country is now rearing a noble monument which I trust may look down on such a centre of institutions for the promotion of art and science as it was his fond hope to establish here. It is my wish that this hall should bear his name to whom it will have owed its existence, and be called "The Royal Albert Hall of Arts and Sciences".'

In his book, *London, Vol II* in *The Buildings of England* series (Penguin), the late Professor Sir Nikolaus Pevsner describes the hall as 'a vast circular building, seating 8000 within its circumference of 735ft. ... The exterior is a domed brick cylinder with four porches and very little decoration in terra-cotta and mosaic, especially bold a frieze of the Triumph of Art and Letters running all round by Armitage, Pickersgill, Marks and Poynter.' Pevsner described the area with its great hall, colleges of art, music and science and proposed museums as 'An accumulation of cultural institutions as compact and as varied as exists in the sixth of a square mile between the Albert Memorial and the Victoria and Albert Museum is probably unparalleled anywhere, and certainly was unparalleled when the buildings were first planned.'

The opening ceremony was held on March 29, 1871, and the Queen entered this grandest

The Royal Albert Hall today.

of halls, followed by the Prince and Princess of Wales and several of her children including the Duke of Saxe-Coburg and Gotha, Prince Arthur, Princess Louise and her husband the Marquis of Lorne and Princes Leopold and Christian.

It is reported that the Queen's youngest daughter, Princess Beatrice wore 'the fashionable green' but Her Majesty was again in black. A black silk dress trimmed with black fur, black bonnet but with white and black strings and white flowers. She looked tired and old, but was only fifty-two. She was cheered to the echo (and *what* an echo in that amazing building) by the 10,000 people in the hall, and the band and grand organ struck up the National Anthem.

The organ, described by one critic as 'qualifying in its own way as an eighth wonder of the world' was built by the master organ builder, Henry Willis, who also built the organ in St George's Hall, Windsor Castle.

After Her Majesty had sat down, the Prince of Wales read a welcoming address in a voice that could be heard in all parts of the hall: twice, in some places, because of the acoustics.

In a distinct but soft voice, his mother answered: 'In handing you this answer, I have to

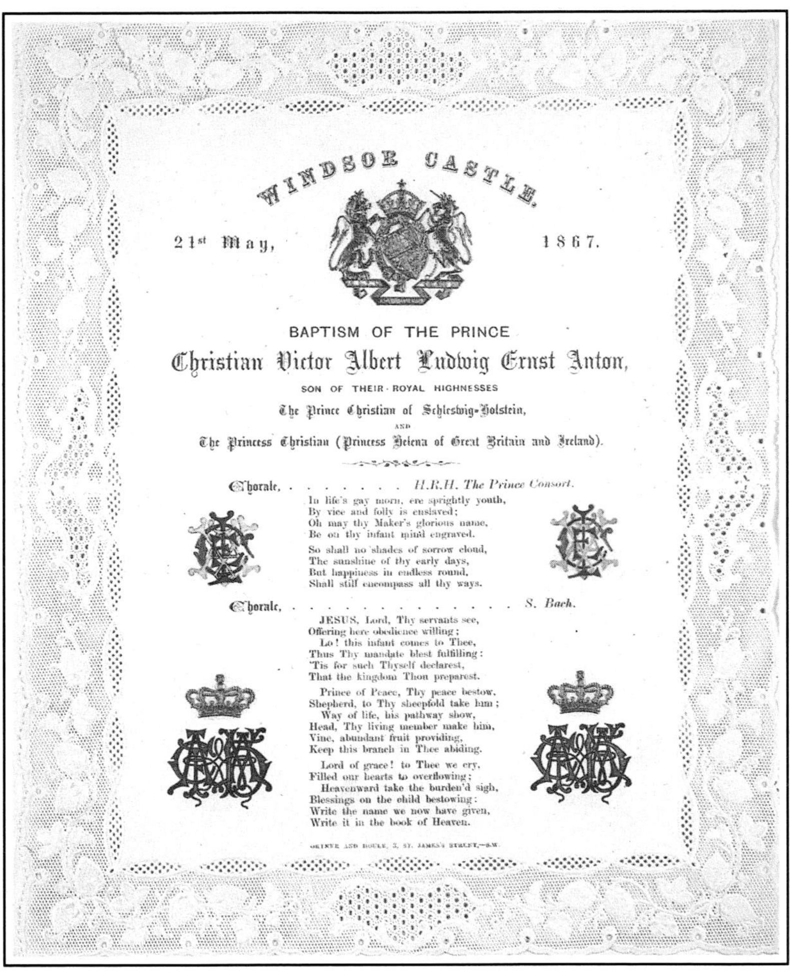

WINDSOR CASTLE,

21st May, 1867.

BAPTISM OF THE PRINCE

Christian Victor Albert Ludwig Ernst Anton,

SON OF THEIR ROYAL HIGHNESSES

The Prince Christian of Schleswig-Holstein,

AND

The Princess Christian (Princess Helena of Great Britain and Ireland).

Chorale, ... *H.R.H. The Prince Consort.*

In life's gay morn, ere sprightly youth,
By vice and folly is enslaved;
Oh may thy Maker's glorious name,
Be on thy infant mind engraved.

So shall no shades of sorrow cloud,
The sunshine of thy early days,
But happiness in endless round,
Shall still encompass all thy ways.

Chorale, ... *S. Bach.*

JESUS, Lord, Thy servants see,
Offering here obedience willing;
Lo! this infant comes to Thee,
Thus Thy mandate blest fulfilling:
'Tis for such Thyself declarest,
That the kingdom Thou preparest.

Prince of Peace, Thy peace bestow,
Shepherd, to Thy sheepfold take him;
Way of life, his pathway show,
Head, Thy living member make him,
Vine, abundant fruit providing,
Keep this branch in Thee abiding.

Lord of grace! to Thee we cry,
Filled our hearts to overflowing;
Heavenward take the burden'd sigh,
Blessings on the child bestowing:
Write the name we now have given,
Write it in the book of Heaven.

Ten months after Princess Helena married she gave birth to her first child – a son, Christian Victor Albert Ludwig Ernst Anton. He was christened at Windsor on May 21, 1867.

express my great admiration of this beautiful hall and my earnest wishes for its complete success.'

The hall was in uproar. There were cheers, shouts and whistles of admiration and genuine appreciation only interrupted by the Lord Bishop of London offering a prayer. 'Amen' echoed through the hall.

It was here that Her Majesty was expected to declare the hall open. Instead, she called the Prince of Wales to her side and whispered something to him.

Walking to the front of the stage and in clear ringing tones, and not without a touch of pride in his voice Prince Albert and Queen Victoria's eldest son announced: 'Her Majesty the Queen declares this Hall now open.'

The Queen often drove to the Royal Mausoleum at Frogmore where her beloved Albert was buried and frequently had a picnic meal there. Her guests of the moment went with her.

WINDSOR, July 9th, 1867

A FINE, BUT VERY HOT, MORNING. Drove to Frogmore as usual, and took our last breakfast with the dear Queen [*of Prussia*]. Remained there a little while and then went up to the Castle, taking the Queen at twelve down to the station, where we took leave of her. She was quite sad at going away, and told me repeatedly how happy her visit had made her. Nothing could have been kinder or pleasanter than she was, so discreet, and not interfering in the slightest way with my mode of life. She is a true devoted friend of mine, as she was of dearest Albert. She spoke very wisely about German politics, and regretted with me much that had taken place, and the way in which things had been done. She thought it most sad and regrettable that the individualities of the different parts of Germany should have been destroyed, which ought never to have been done. Bertie accompanied the Queen to London.

OSBORNE, July 24th, 1867

A VERY FINE MORNING. Breakfasted early on the lawn, and at quarter to ten drove with the Empress [*Eugénie of France*], Alice, Louise, Arthur, Louis, etc., to the Pier, where we took leave of her [*the Empress had been on a private visit to Queen Victoria at Osborne—their first meeting since the Prince Consort's death*], Arthur and Louis accompanying her to the *Reine Hortense*, which was lying some way out. We returned at once. Nothing could have been kinder or more amiable than the Empress was. I took the opportunity of urging peace (mutually, on the side of France and Prussia), and no arming, laying all the blame on Prussia. Greatly relieved the visit was over, as I am feeling so far from well, and everything tries me so.

The Duchess of Roxburghe and Mr. Walpole dined. Talked to him afterwards of the Reform Bill. He feels, like many, that it may have gone too far, but still he had great confidence in the good sense and loyalty of the people. The upper classes and aristocracy must however 'buckle to,' or they will deservedly suffer. The lower orders are becoming so well educated that they will push on.

BALMORAL, October 14th, 1867

GEN. GREY ASKED TO SEE ME when I came in, and said he was sorry to alarm me, but must show me a telegram from Mr. Hardy, reporting that the Mayor of Manchester [*a statue of the Prince Consort, the gift of the Queen, was to be unveiled there by HM*] had informed him, having the news from a reliable source, that the Fenians had said they meant to try and seize me here, and were starting to-day or to-morrow! Too foolish!! Mr. Hardy added that special precautions should be taken, so Gen. Grey asked to be allowed to send at once for a detachment of troops from Aberdeen to be placed at Abergeldie, but letting it appear as if it were for to-morrow's ceremony. He has also asked for additional police.

BALMORAL, September 28th, 1868

TOOK LEAVE OF MR. DISRAELI, who seemed delighted with his stay and was most grateful.

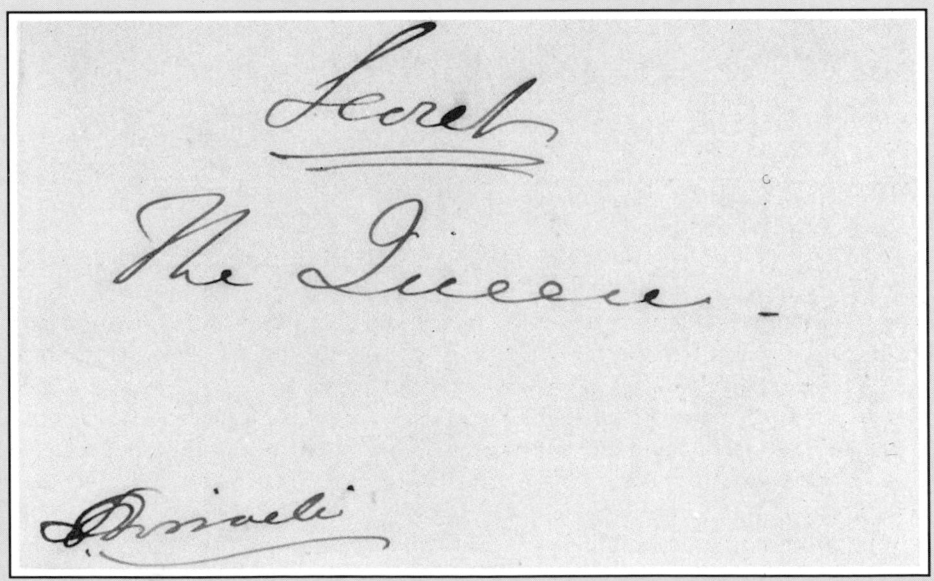
Secret

The Queen

Disraeli

Only Lord Edward Pelham-Clinton could tell us why he kept this photograph and envelope intended for the Queen from that arch-flatterer, novelist and politician Benjamin Disraeli. The envelope is clearly marked Secret, The Queen *and, in the left-hand corner* Disraeli. *It was common practice for those who knew the Queen to put their name, initials, or a special sign on the envelope when writing to her so that she would open their letters personally. Disraeli's photograph was a pin-up of its day, clearly intended for his admirers.*

Balmoral Castle in the Queen's beloved Scottish Highlands.

He certainly shows more consideration for my comfort than any of the preceding Prime Ministers since Sir Robert Peel and Lord Aberdeen.

The Queen came to adore Disraeli, later the Earl of Beaconsfield. She visited Dizzy and his wife at their home, and fell for his charm and flattery. She laughed when she heard his nickname for her ('The Faery'). He was amused when the Queen once told him: 'If only the Queen were a man, she would like to go and give those Russians, whose word one cannot believe, such a beating!'

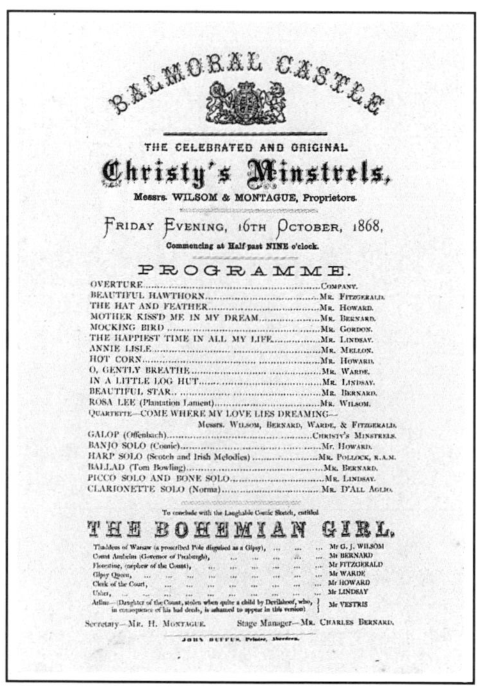

BALMORAL CASTLE

THE CELEBRATED AND ORIGINAL

Christy's Minstrels,

Messrs. WILSOM & MONTAGUE, Proprietors.

FRIDAY EVENING, 16TH OCTOBER, 1868,

Commencing at Half past NINE o'clock.

PROGRAMME.

OVERTURE....Company.
BEAUTIFUL HAWTHORN....Mr. Fitzgerald.
THE HAT AND FEATHER....Mr. Howard.
MOTHER KISS'D ME IN MY DREAM....Mr. Bernard.
MOCKING BIRD....Mr. Gordon.
THE HAPPIEST TIME IN ALL MY LIFE....Mr. Lindsay.
ANNIE LISLE....Mr. Mellon.
HOT CORN....Mr. Howard.
O, GENTLY BREATHE....Mr. Warde.
IN A LITTLE LOG HUT....Mr. Lindsay.
BEAUTIFUL STAR....Mr. Bernard.
ROSA LEE (Plantation Lament)....Mr. Wilsom.
Quartette—COME WHERE MY LOVE LIES DREAMING—
Messrs. Wilsom, Bernard, Warde, & Fitzgerald.
GALOP (Offenbach)....Christy's Minstrels.
BANJO SOLO (Comic)....Mr. Howard.
HARP SOLO (Scotch and Irish Melodies)....Mr. Pollock, R.A.M.
BALLAD (Tom Bowling)....Mr. Bernard.
PICCO SOLO AND BONE SOLO....Mr. Lindsay.
CLARIONETTE SOLO (Norma)....Mr. D'All Aglio.

To conclude with the Laughable Comic Sketch, entitled

THE BOHEMIAN GIRL.

Thaddeus of Warsaw (a proscribed Pole disguised as a Gipsy), ... Mr G. J. WILSOM
Count Arnheim (Governor of Presburgh), ... Mr BERNARD
Florestine, (nephew of the Count), ... Mr FITZGERALD
Gipsy Queen, ... Mr WARDE
Clerk of the Court, ... Mr HOWARD
Usher, ... Mr LINDSAY
Arline—(Daughter of the Count, stolen when quite a child by Devilshoof, who, in consequence of his bad deeds, is ashamed to appear in this version) Mr VESTRIS

Secretary—Mr. H. Montague. Stage Manager—Mr. Charles Bernard.

John Duffus, Printer, Aberdeen.

It was to be many years before minstrels were considered vulgar and in poor taste. The Queen adored Christy's Minstrels who performed for her and her guests after dinner on October 16, 1868. Offenbach's 'Galop' is, presumably, the famous one now known as the 'Can-Can'. It was certainly a varied programme.

BUCKINGHAM PALACE, March 4th, 1869

Drove to the deanery at Westminster, where the Dean and Augusta had invited the following celebrities to meet me: Mr. Carlyle, the historian, a strange-looking eccentric old Scotchman, who holds forth, in a drawling melancholy voice, with a broad Scotch accent, upon Scotland and upon the utter degeneration of everything; Mr. and Mrs. Grote, old acquaintances of mine from Kensington, unaltered, she very peculiar, clever and masculine, he also an historian, of the old school; Sir C. and Lady Lyell, he an old acquaintance, most agreeable, and she very pleasing; Mr. Browning, the poet, a very agreeable man. It was, at first, very shy work speaking to them, when they were all drawn up; but afterwards, when tea was being drunk, Augusta got them to come and sit near me, and they were very agreeable and talked very entertainingly.

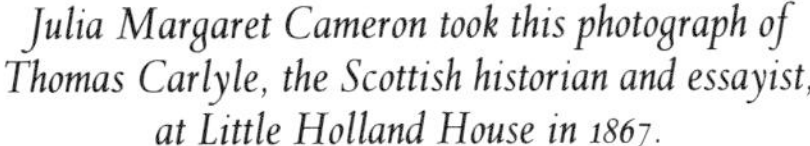

Julia Margaret Cameron took this photograph of Thomas Carlyle, the Scottish historian and essayist, at Little Holland House in 1867.

Robert Browning, the English poet.

OSBORNE, June 20th, 1869

MY ACCESSION DAY, already 32 years ago. May God help me in my solitary path, for the good of my dear people, and the world at large. He has given me a very difficult task, one for which I feel myself in many ways unfit, from inclination and want of power. He gave me great happiness, and He took it away, no doubt for a wise purpose and for the happiness of my beloved one, leaving me alone to bear the heavy burden in very trying and troubled times. Help I have been given, and for this I humbly thank Him; but the trials are great and many.

The Queen opens Blackfriars Bridge.

WINDSOR, November 6th, 1869

I AM AFRAID I CAN ONLY GIVE a very imperfect account of this most successful and gratifying progress and ceremony. Drove from Paddington Station the same way we usually do, going to Buckingham Palace and from there down the Mall and up to Westminster Palace. Everywhere great crowds of people and many amongst them well-dressed, all cheering and bowing and in the best of humour. Crossed Westminster Bridge, going up Stamford Street, all the time at a gentle trot, the streets admirably kept. From here the crowds became more and more dense, the decorations commenced, and the enthusiasm was very great—not a window empty and people up to the very tops of the houses, flags and here and there inscriptions, everyone with most friendly faces. The day was cold, but quite fine, no fog and, though no real sunshine, there were occasional glimpses of it.

At 12 o'clock we reached Blackfriars Bridge, the first portion of which was entirely covered in; here on a platform with raised seats and many people, stood the Lord Mayor, who presented the sword, which I merely touched, and he introduced the engineer, Mr. Cubitt (son of the eminent engineer Sir William Cubitt, well known to my dearest Albert) and another gentleman. I was presented with an Address and a fine illuminated book describing the whole. The Bridge was then considered opened, but neither I nor the Lord Mayor said so. This however has not been found out ... Everywhere dense crowds. I never saw more enthusiastic, loyal or friendly ones, and there were numbers of the very lowest. This, in the very heart of London, at a time when people were said to be intending to do something, and were full of all sorts of ideas, is very remarkable.

Felt so pleased and relieved that all had gone off so well. Nothing could have been more gratifying. But it was a hard trial for me *all alone* with my children in an open carriage amongst such thousands!

BUCKINGHAM PALACE, March 9th, 1870

I SAW MR. HELPS THIS EVENING at half past six, who brought and introduced Mr. Dickens, the celebrated author. He is very agreeable, with a pleasant voice and manner. He talked of his latest works, of America, the strangeness of the people there, of the division of classes in England, which he hoped would get better in time. He felt sure that it would come gradually.

Charles Dickens reading with his wife and sister.

BALMORAL, June 11th, 1870

I OMITTED POSTING IN, on the day I received it, a notice of the death of C. Dickens [*Dickens died on 9 June*]. Mr. Helps telegraphed it. He is a very great loss. He had a large, loving mind and the strongest sympathy with the poorer classes. He felt sure that a better feeling, and much greater union of classes would take place in time. And I pray earnestly it may.

WINDSOR CASTLE, June 27th, 1870

JUST AS WE GOT INTO THE CARRIAGE to drive down to Frogmore, Janie E[*ly*] came with a telegram from Constance Stanley, saying that Lord Clarendon had died at six this morning. This shocked us very much. I had feared the worst, knowing that he had been in a bad state of health for the last year, but never expected so rapid an end. He is in many ways a great loss, for he was very clever, had great experience and knowledge of foreign affairs and countries, and was very conciliatory. He was very satirical, and could be irritable and hasty, but he was much attached to me, was warm-hearted and an excellent husband and father, being adored by his family, for whom I feel deeply.

June 29th

HEARD THAT OUR BELOVED SIR JAMES CLARK [*the Queen's doctor, whom she had visited two days earlier*] had passed away quite peacefully this afternoon at three! I cannot realise it! He too gone, that dear kind intimate friend of thirty-five years, who had been with me when my nine children were born, and was with us at Frogmore, in the room, when beloved Mama died. How he supported and kept me up when dearest Albert was ill, and was in the room when all ended. He to whom I could say almost anything, who was so wise, so discreet, is also taken from me. Really this has been a dreadful year and most fatal to those connected with me. How thankful I am I went to see dear Sir James.

BALMORAL, September 5th, 1870

HEARD THAT THE MOB AT PARIS had rushed into the Senate and proclaimed the downfall of the dynasty, proclaiming a Republic! This was received with acclamation and the proclamation was made from the Hôtel de Ville. Not one voice was raised in favour of the unfortunate Emperor! How ungrateful! It was agreed that the following message should be conveyed to the Empress, viz: that 'I was not insensible to the heavy blow which had fallen on her, nor forgetful of former days.' No one knows where she is!

BALMORAL, September 12th, 1870

OMITTED TO MENTION that my dearest kindest friend, dear old Lehzen, [*Baroness Lehzen, the Queen's governess*] expired quite quietly and peacefully on the 9th. For two years she had been quite bedridden, from the results of breaking her hip. Though latterly her mind had not been clear, still there were days when she constantly spoke of me, whom she had

Emperor Napoleon II and Empress Eugénie of France at the Crystal Palace in 1855, during their visit to England. The Queen recalled this visit, and her own visit to France with the Prince Consort, when the Emperor and Empress were forced into exile in England.

Baroness Lehzen, the Queen's governess, from a sketch made by Princess Victoria before her accession.

known from the age of six months. She had devoted her life to me, from my fifth to my eighteenth year, with the most wonderful self-abnegation, never even taking one day's leave! After I came to the throne she got to be rather trying and especially so after my marriage, but never from any evil intention, only from a mistaken idea of duty and affection for me. She was an admirable governess, and I adored her, though I also feared her. I feel much that she too is gone. Within seven months I have lost the dear Countess Blücher, General Grey, Sir James Clark, and her!

The Queen visits her friend, the Empress Eugénie of France and her son, the Prince Imperial, who had fled from Paris. Empress Eugénie (1826–1920) was a daughter of a Spanish nobleman, the Count of Montijo. In 1853 she married Louis Napoleon soon after he became the French Emperor, Napoleon III (1808–73). The Emperor aroused the mistrust of Europe and isolated France after he attempted to found a vassal empire in Mexico (1863–7). In France, his regime was notoriously corrupt and he had to fight very strong opposition from socialists and republicans alike. Napoleon subsequently made concessions to a parliamentary government. However, in 1870, Prince Bismarck manoeuvred him into war with Prussia. Napoleon was forced to surrender at Sedan whereupon his Empire collapsed. The Imperial family fled to England living first at Chislehurst where the Emperor died. Their son, the Prince Imperial (1856–79), was killed fighting with the British Army against the Zulus. The widowed Eugénie later lived at Farnborough (Hampshire) where she built a magnificent mausoleum within the Roman Catholic Church, now known as Farnborough Abbey, for the tombs of the Imperial family.

WINDSOR CASTLE, November 30th, 1870

Dull, raw, and cold. At quarter to eleven, started with Beatrice and Janie Ely (who had come down on purpose) and Lord C. FitzRoy, for Chislehurst, in Kent, where the poor Empress Eugénie is staying.

At the door of Camden Place stood the poor Empress, in black, the Prince Imperial, and, a little behind, the Ladies and Gentlemen. The Empress at once led me through a sort of corridor or vestibule and an ante-room into a drawing-room with a bow window. Everything was like a French house and many pretty things about. The Empress and Prince Imperial alone came in, and she asked me to sit down near her on the sofa. She looks very thin and pale, but still very handsome. There is an expression of deep sadness in her face, and she frequently had tears in her eyes. She was dressed in the plainest possible way, without any jewels or ornaments, and her hair simply done, in a net, at the back. She showed the greatest tact in avoiding everything which might be awkward, and enquired after Vicky and Alice, asked if I had had any news, saying, 'Oh! si seulement l'on pouvait avoir le paix.' Then she said how much had happened since we had met at Paris and that she could not forget the dreadful impressions of her departure from there. She had remained as long as she could, but once General Trochu had allowed the Chambers to be taken possession of by the populace, there was nothing to be done but to go away. The garden had been already full of people who were entering the Tuileries, and there had been no troops to resist them. The night before she had lain down fully dressed, on her bed. The crossing had been fearful. Afterwards she talked of other things. The Prince Imperial is a nice little boy, but rather short and stumpy. His eyes are rather like those of his mother, but otherwise I think him more like the Emperor. Beatrice brought the Empress a nosegay from Louise. We stayed about half an hour and then left. The Empress again most kindly came to the door. It was a sad visit and seemed like a strange dream.

Principal Events

1871–80

1871: Wedding of Princess Louise and the Marquis of Lorne (March 21).
Royal Albert Hall opened (March 29).
Abolition of religious tests at Oxford and Cambridge.
Sir Henry Morton Stanley's famous meeting with Dr David Livingstone.
Bank holidays established.
The Prince of Wales seriously ill with typhoid (December).

1872: Thanksgiving for the recovery of the Prince of Wales (January 21).
The Queen, Prince and Princess of Wales, Court and Parliament went in state to St Paul's Cathedral for national thanksgiving service (February 27).
Eighteen-year-old Arthur O'Connor fired blanks at Queen Victoria as Her Majesty entered Buckingham Palace (February 29).
Arthur O'Connor tried; pleaded guilty and sentenced to imprisonment and flogging (April 9).
Edison's telegraph introduced.

1873: Death of Emperor Napoleon III (January 9).

Sir Arthur Sullivan was one of the Queen's favourite composers. She adored his music, although she thought that he should devote his time and talents to writing more church music.

PRECEDING PAGES: *The wedding of Princess Louise to the Marquis of Lorne, eldest son of the Duke of Argyll, in St George's Chapel, Windsor Castle, March 21, 1871.*

Proposed marriage of the Duke of Edinburgh to Grand Duchess Marie of Russia announced by the Queen (July 17). Annuity bill for the Duke passed (August 5).
Tolstoy's *Anna Karenina* published.

1874: Marriage of the Duke and Duchess of Edinburgh (January 2).
Sir Garnet Wolseley returned from successful expedition against the Ashantis (March 21).
Benjamin Disraeli, Earl of Beaconsfield, Prime Minister for six years and 67 days (from February 21).
Thomas Hardy's *Far From the Madding Crowd* published.
Verdi's *Requiem* first performed.
A testimonial of gratitude for British assistance during the war received by Queen Victoria from the French nation (December 3).

1875: Prince of Wales departed for India (May 1).
Britain bought Suez Canal shares (November 1).
Bizet's opera *Carmen* first performed.
Gilbert and Sullivan partnership established in their first operetta *Trial by Jury*.

1876: Queen Victoria proclaimed Empress of India (May 1) in England.
Prince of Wales returned from India, arriving at Portsmouth (May 11).
Remmington typewriters introduced.

1877: Thomas Alva Edison invented the phonograph.
Russo–Turkish War; conference at Constantinople.
Queen Victoria solemnly proclaimed Empress of India in Delhi.
English fleet sent to Bosphorus.

1878: Earl Russell, former Prime Minister, died aged 85 (May 28).
Salvation Army founded by General Booth.
London first lit by electric street lighting.
Tchaikovsky's ballet *Swan Lake* first performed in London.
Eddystone lighthouse (fourth structure) built.
Death of Princess Alice from diptheria at Darmstadt (December 14).

1879: Death of the Prince Imperial of France (June 19).
Marriage of the Duke and Duchess of Connaught at Windsor (March 13).
London's first telephone exchange opened.
Ibsen's *Doll's House* first performed.

1880: William Gladstone Prime Minister again for five years and 57 days (from April 28).
Benjamin Disraeli's *Endymion* published.
Tchaikovsky's *1812 Overture* first performed.

WINDSOR CASTLE, February 8th, 1871

AFTER LUNCHEON SAW MR. GLADSTONE, who looks upon the future very gloomily, but thinks there will be peace. [*The Queen was referring to the Franco–Prussian War (1870–71) at the end of which the French Emperor Napoleon III, was defeated.*] I urged strongly the necessity for great prudence and for not departing from our neutral position. The only thing I thought, which might possibly justify combined action on the part of all the neutrals, would be if a recommencement of hostilities seemed imminent. We might all protest and insist on both belligerents giving way, but it would never do for us to take action alone, in which Mr. Gladstone quite agreed . . .

February 9th

LEFT AT TEN FOR LONDON, with Louise, Beatrice, Leopold, Jane C., and the two Equerries. Lunched before one, and dressed for the opening of Parliament. Wore a dress trimmed with ermine and my new small diamond Crown, over a veil, on my head. Louise and Beatrice drove with me in the carriage. There was a great crowd and much cheering and enthusiasm. Got out at the same entrance as last time. Louise and Beatrice stood on the steps of the throne, and Arthur to my right, near Bertie. Alix, Lenchen, and Mary Teck sat on the Woolsack. The Commons took a long time coming in. The Speech was extremely long, was read very well by the Lord Chancellor, in a fine powerful voice. More cheering on the way back. Reached Buckingham Palace at three. Had rather a bad headache, so I kept quiet and at five returned to Windsor. The park was immensely crowded, when I drove to the station.

The French Emperor, Napoleon III, is received by the Queen.

WINDSOR CASTLE, March 27th, 1871

AT A LITTLE BEFORE THREE, went down with our children and Ladies and Gentlemen to receive the Emperor Napoleon. I went to the door with Louise and embraced the Emperor 'comme de rigueur.' It was a moving moment, when I thought of the last time he came here in '55, in perfect triumph, dearest Albert bringing him from Dover, the whole country mad to receive him, and now! He seemed much depressed and had tears in his eyes, but he controlled himself and said, 'Il y a bien longtemps que je n'ai vu votre Majesté.' He led me upstairs and we went into the Audience Room. He is grown very stout and grey and his moustaches are no longer curled or waxed as formerly, but otherwise there was the same pleasing, gentle, and gracious manner. My children came in with us. The Emperor at once spoke of the dreadful and disgraceful state of France, and how all that had passed during the last few months had greatly lowered the French character, the officers breaking their parole included. There seemed to be 'point d'énergie.' He was dreadfully shocked at 'tout ce qui se passe à Paris.' He said he had been most kindly treated at Wilhelmshöhe, and that he had kept well all through the winter. He expressed renewed admiration of England and spoke of its being sixteen years since he came to Windsor.

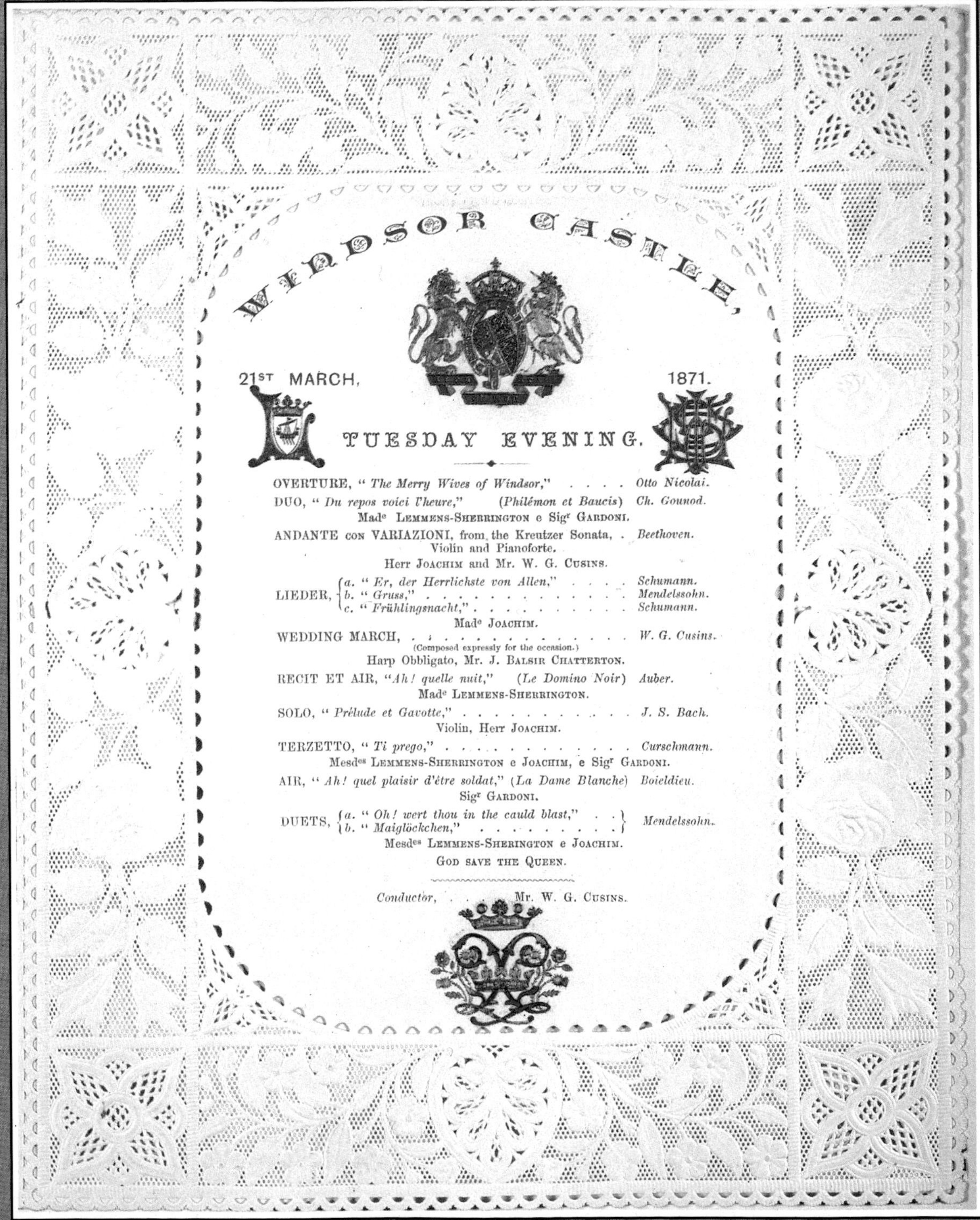

WINDSOR CASTLE,

21ST MARCH, 1871.

TUESDAY EVENING.

OVERTURE, "*The Merry Wives of Windsor,*" . . . . *Otto Nicolai.*
DUO, "*Du repos voici l'heure,*" (*Philémon et Baucis*) *Ch. Gounod.*
Mad^e^ LEMMENS-SHERRINGTON e Sig^r^ GARDONI.
ANDANTE CON VARIAZIONI, from the Kreutzer Sonata, . *Beethoven.*
Violin and Pianoforte.
Herr JOACHIM and Mr. W. G. CUSINS.
LIEDER, { *a.* "*Er, der Herrlichste von Allen,*" . . . . *Schumann.*
b. "*Gruss,*" . . . . *Mendelssohn.*
c. "*Frühlingsnacht,*" . . . . *Schumann.*
Mad^e^ JOACHIM.
WEDDING MARCH, ... *W. G. Cusins.*
(Composed expressly for the occasion.)
Harp Obbligato, Mr. J. BALSIR CHATTERTON.
RECIT ET AIR, "*Ah! quelle nuit,*" (*Le Domino Noir*) *Auber.*
Mad^e^ LEMMENS-SHERRINGTON.
SOLO, "*Prélude et Gavotte,*" . . . . *J. S. Bach.*
Violin, Herr JOACHIM.
TERZETTO, "*Ti prego,*" . . . . *Curschmann.*
Mesd^es^ LEMMENS-SHERRINGTON e JOACHIM, e Sig^r^ GARDONI.
AIR, "*Ah! quel plaisir d'être soldat,*" (*La Dame Blanche*) *Boieldieu.*
Sig^r^ GARDONI.
DUETS, { *a.* "*Oh! wert thou in the cauld blast,*" . . } *Mendelssohn.*
b. "*Maiglöckchen,*" . . . . }
Mesd^es^ LEMMENS-SHERINGTON e JOACHIM.
GOD SAVE THE QUEEN.

Conductor, . . . Mr. W. G. CUSINS.

A programme printed on lace for a concert given in Windsor Castle on March 21, 1871, in honour of the wedding that day of the Queen's daughter Princess Louise to the Marquis of Lorne.

BALMORAL, August 22nd, 1871

HAD A GOOD NIGHT. Feeling better. Never since a girl, when I had typhoid fever at Ramsgate in '35, have I felt so ill. Got up late, and took a short drive. Able to take a little luncheon. Remained quietly in my room.

September 3rd

ANOTHER SUNDAY UNABLE TO GO TO THE KIRK or have service in the house. A very fine day. Had a bad night and got up quite late. Sat in the tent. Slept a little after my luncheon, then saw Dr. Marshall, who examined my poor arm and begged I should let some other surgeon, for instance Professor Lister, [*the famous surgeon, afterwards Lord Lister*] see it, as he felt the responsibility too great. I rather demurred, but said I would think the matter over. Finally I consented to Professor Lister being telegraphed for. Went a little in the garden chair, after five, Beatrice walking.

Joseph Lister, the surgeon, who travelled to Balmoral to operate on the abscess on the Queen's arm.

On August 14, the Queen had an acute sore throat and consequently, took her meals in private. It was not until August 20 that she wrote in her Journal 'suffering tortures until something seemed to give way in the throat and the choking sensations with violent spasms ceased'. It was subsequently discovered that the Queen had a very serious abscess in her arm, which was lanced by Professor Lister. Her third medical problem at this time was rheumatism in one of her feet.

September 4th

IN THE AFTERNOON took a little turn in the garden chair. It was so fine. On coming in heard Mr. Lister had arrived. Sir William Jenner explained everything about my arm to him, but he naturally said he could do nothing or give any opinion till he had made an examination. I had to wait nearly half an hour before Mr. Lister and Dr. Marshall appeared! In a few minutes he had ascertained all and went out again with the others. Sir William Jenner returned saying Mr. Lister thought the swelling ought to be cut: he could wait twenty-four hours, but it would be better not. I felt dreadfully nervous, as I bear pain so badly. I shall be given chloroform, but not very much, as I am so far from well otherwise, so I begged the part might be frozen, which was agreed on. Everything was got ready and the three doctors came in. Sir William Jenner gave me some whiffs of chloroform, whilst Mr. Lister froze the place, Dr. Marshall holding my arm. The abscess, which was six inches in diameter, was very quickly cut and I hardly felt anything excepting the last touch, when I was given a little more chloroform. In an instant there was relief. I was then tightly bandaged, and rested on my bed. Quite late saw Beatrice and Affie for a moment, after Mr. Lister had been in to see me. Felt very shaken and exhausted.

September 11th

THANKFUL AND HAPPY to be relieved of my bandages. To-day I have been very miserable from a violent attack of rheumatism or even rheumatic gout, which has settled in my left ankle, completely crippling me and causing me dreadful pain. I am quite disheartened, as this makes almost a *third* Illness. Mr. Lister took his leave this morning, and Dr. Marshall dressed the wound and put on the bandage. It made him a little nervous, but he did it very well.

September 18th

UP BY NINE AFTER A RATHER BAD NIGHT. My foot much swollen, and I could hardly walk a step. The doctors, after looking at it, pronounced it to be severe rheumatic gout, and I was not to walk, indeed I could not. How distressing and disappointing! Was rolled into my sitting-room, where Alice came to see me, much shocked and grieved. Was carried downstairs and took a little drive. The rest of the day I remained in my room. By degrees agonies of pain came on which continued almost without intermission, the foot swelling tremendously. Sir William Jenner tried to encourage me as to its not lasting long. Dear Alice was in and out constantly, and very affectionate and kind, helping my maids in moving me. Was very depressed.

She learns that her son, Bertie, the Prince of Wales has 'mild typhoid fever', but it becomes much more serious.

BALMORAL, November 22nd, 1871

BREAKFASTED FOR THE FIRST TIME AGAIN with my children, and felt it was a step forward and I was returning to ordinary life. Heard dear Bertie had 'mild typhoid fever' and I at once determined to send off Sir William Jenner to Sandringham. This was gratefully accepted by Alix. Felt very anxious. This fearful fever, and at this very time of the year! Everyone much distressed.

WINDSOR CASTLE, November 27th

At eight a telegram arrived. The report not good, a restless night and incessant wandering. We are all in the greatest anxiety. The alarm in London great. Immense sympathy all over the country. Heard from Sir William Jenner, who had returned to Sandringham, that, though Bertie was certainly very ill, he had found him less alarmingly so than he had expected. Though quite delirious, he knew people quite well.

SANDRINGHAM, November 29th, 1871

Better accounts. Quieter, mind clearer. Nourishment taken well. I was nervous and agitated at the thought of this sad journey, weak as I still am. At eleven I left with the Duchess of Roxburghe and Colonel Ponsonby. Reached Wolferton after three. Affie, Sir William Knollys, and Colonel Ellis met me there, and a quarter of an hour's drive brought us to Sandringham. The road lay between commons, and plantations of fir trees, rather wild-looking, flat, bleak country. The house, rather near the high-road, a handsome, quite newly built Elizabethan building, was only completed last autumn. Dear Alix and Alice met me at the door, the former looking thin and anxious, and with tears in her eyes. She took me at once through the great hall upstairs to my rooms, three in number.

I took off my things and went over to Bertie's room, and was allowed to step in from behind a screen to see him sleeping or dozing. The room was dark and only one lamp burning, so that I could not see him well. He was lying rather flat on his back, breathing very rapidly and loudly. Of course the watching is constant, and dear Alix does a great deal herself. Two nurses and Gillet, the valet, take turns in the nursing. How all reminded me so vividly and sadly of my dearest Albert's illness!

SANDRINGHAM, December 8th, 1871

Was dreadfully alarmed, though, I own, hardly unprepared for a less good report. The telegram [*The Queen received the telegram at Windsor where she had spent the earlier part of the day*] I received at quarter past eight said: 'The Prince passed a very unquiet night. Not so well. Temperature risen to 104. Respirations more rapid. Dr. Gull and I are both very anxious.' . . . It was decided to send for Leopold and Beatrice, as the danger seemed so great. Went over again to the dressing-room. The fearful breathing continued, but dear Bertie was not worse. Alix and Alice still with him.

December 10th

The feeling shown by the whole nation is quite marvellous and most touching and striking, showing how really sound and truly loyal the people really are. Letters and telegrams pour in and no end of recommendations of remedies of the most mad kind. Receive the kindest letters full of sympathy from the Ministers, my own people and friends.

December 11th

THIS HAS BEEN A TERRIBLE DAY. At half past five I was woken by a message from Sir William Jenner saying dear Bertie had had a very severe spasm, which had alarmed them very much, though it was over now. I had scarcely got the message, before Sir William returned saying there had been another. I saw him at once, and he told me the spasm had been so severe, that at any moment dear Bertie might go off, so that I had better come at once. I hurriedly got up, put on my dressing-gown, and went to the room, where I found Alix and Alice by the bedside, and Dr. Gull and the two devoted nurses. It was dark, the candles burning, and most dreary. Poor dear Bertie was lying there breathing heavily, and as if he must choke at any moment. I remained sitting behind the screen. Louise and her three brothers came into the dressing-room. Everything was done that could be thought of to give a little relief. After a little while he seemed easier, so the doctors advised us to go away, and I went back to my room, breakfasted, and dressed.

I went backwards and forwards continually. Dined with Leopold and Beatrice. He behaves so well and shows so much feeling. Went back to see after dear Bertie the last thing before going to bed. The talking was incessant, without a moment's sleep. Dr. Gull said he was much alarmed. Went away with a very heavy heart and dreading further trouble. Felt quite exhausted.

Mr. Gladstone to Queen Victoria
CARLTON H. TERRACE, December 11th, 1871: . . . Mr. Gladstone received to-day your Majesty's commands for copies of the forms of Prayer prepared by the Archbishop, and despatched them to Sandringham.

He knows not how either to touch, or to leave untouched, the painful subject, which in the very street seems to absorb the mind of every passer-by, and which is now pressing with such fearful weight on your Majesty. It is heart-rending to look back upon that picture of youth and health, and of vigour seemingly inexhaustible, which but a few weeks ago was before his eyes; and to remember that singular combination of warmth and kindliness with unaffected and unfailing dignity, which is now all laid low on the bed of sickness and of suffering. Mr. Gladstone will not mock the sorrow of this moment by assurances which, even when sincere, must seem so poor and hollow; but he earnestly commends the sufferer and all the afflicted round him, most of all the Mother and the Wife, to Him who alone is able either to heal or to console, and who turns into mercies the darkest of all His dispensations.

SANDRINGHAM, December 13th, 1871

THIS REALLY HAS BEEN THE WORST DAY of all, and coming as it has so close to the sad 14th, filled us and, I believe, the whole country with anxious forebodings and the greatest alarm . . .

December 14th

THIS DREADFUL ANNIVERSARY, the 10th, returned again. It seems impossible to believe all that time has passed. Felt painfully having to spend the day away from Windsor, but the one great anxiety seems to absorb everything else. Instead of this date dawning upon another deathbed, which I had felt almost certain of, it brought the cheering news that dear Bertie had slept quietly at intervals, and really soundly from four to quarter to six; the respirations much easier, and food taken well . . . It seemed hardly possible to realise the day and to feel that on this *very* day our dear Bertie is getting better instead of worse!

WINDSOR CASTLE, December 21st, 1871

A GOOD TELEGRAM FROM SANDRINGHAM. Bertie slept all through the night, no cough, temperature normal. Directly after luncheon saw Mr. Gladstone, who spoke very feelingly about dear Bertie's illness, his present condition, and the wonderful feeling and sympathy which had been evinced on this occasion. I consulted Mr. Gladstone as to what could be done to express my sense of gratitude. After some discussion it was agreed that I should write him a letter, expressive of my deep feeling of the sympathy and loyalty shown.

SANDRINGHAM, December 31st, 1871

[*THE PRINCE HAD A SERIOUS RELAPSE on 27 December*] Could hardly believe it was the last day in the old year, which has really been a most trying one. Ever since the beginning of August we have been in trouble of one kind or another, culminating in this dreadful illness of poor dear Bertie's. But I thank God for His great mercy, for amidst all dangers, trials, and sufferings, He has always protected us and brought us through the 'fiery furnace'. May I ever prove grateful for it! Went over once more to Bertie's room. He was quiet, thank God. How I pray the New Year may see him safely on the road to recovery!

SANDRINGHAM, January 1st, 1872

NEVER BEFORE HAVE I SPENT NEW YEAR'S DAY away from home, and never did I think to spend it here, with poor Bertie so ill in bed, though, thank, God! no longer in danger, at any rate not in any immediate danger. May our Heavenly Father restore him and let this heavy trial be for his good in every way! May sweet, darling Alix be preserved and blessed, and may the dear children grow up to be a blessing to their parents, to their country, and to me!

Gave my photographs framed to the two excellent nurses, and Bertie's valet, etc. Writing telegrams in quantities. Then went over to Bertie, who kissed me and gave me a nosegay, which he had specially ordered, and which touched me very much, as well as his being able to wish me a happy New Year. What a blessed beginning after such dreadful anxiety!

BUCKINGHAM PALACE, February 27th, 1872

LUCKILY A FINE MORNING . . . Went to dress, and wore a black silk dress and jacket, trimmed with miniver, and a bonnet with white flowers and a white feather. Beatrice looked very nice in mauve, trimmed with swan's down. Bertie was very lame and did not

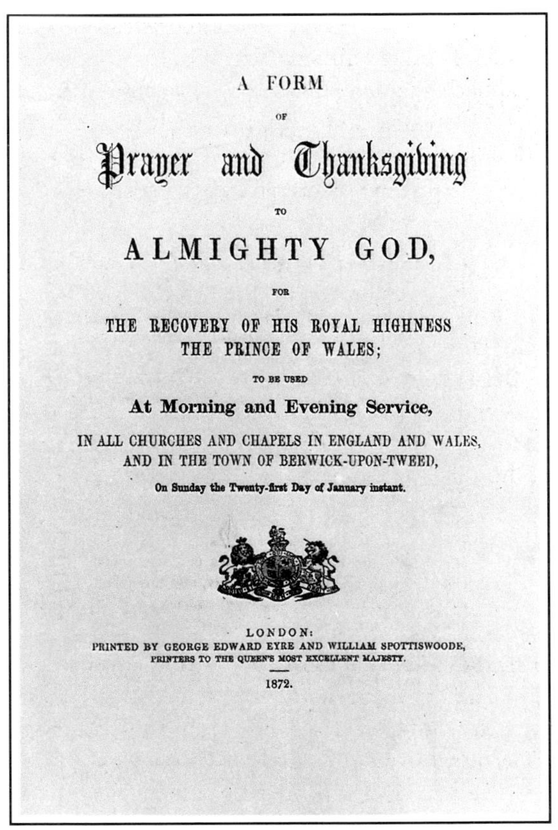

A FORM

OF

Prayer and Thanksgiving

TO

ALMIGHTY GOD,

FOR

THE RECOVERY OF HIS ROYAL HIGHNESS
THE PRINCE OF WALES;

TO BE USED

At Morning and Evening Service,

IN ALL CHURCHES AND CHAPELS IN ENGLAND AND WALES,
AND IN THE TOWN OF BERWICK-UPON-TWEED,

On Sunday the Twenty-first Day of January instant.

LONDON:
PRINTED BY GEORGE EDWARD EYRE AND WILLIAM SPOTTISWOODE,
PRINTERS TO THE QUEEN'S MOST EXCELLENT MAJESTY.

1872.

The period approaching Christmas, 1871, was very worrying for the Queen as her Journals show. Great was her relief when the Prince of Wales recovered, and she was delighted to sanction this Prayer and Thanksgiving service to be used in 'all churches and chapels in England and Wales, and in the town of Berwick-upon-Tweed' on Sunday, January 21, 1872. Berwick, held alternately by the English and the Scots, was made a neutral town in 1551, hence its special mention in such documents.

look at all well, I grieved to see. My three other sons were there, and the poor Emperor Napoleon and Empress Eugénie, who were anxious to see the procession quietly, and whom I had specially invited to come to the Palace. The boys with little George [*later King George V*] went on and got into an open carriage and four, with Lord Ailesbury, and in a few minutes I followed, taking poor Bertie's arm, for he could only walk very slowly, down to the Grand Entrance. We entered an open State landau with six horses, ridden by three postilions. Alix (in blue velvet and sable) sat next to me, and Bertie opposite, with Beatrice, and little Eddy [*Prince Albert Victor*] between them. We had a Sovereign's escort, as on all State occasions. Seven open dress carriages with a pair of horses went in front of us, and *immediately* in front, the Lord Chancellor in his carriage, and the Speaker in his strange quaint old one.

I have no time to describe at length the long progress, the millions out, the beautiful decorations, the wonderful enthusiasm and astounding affectionate loyalty shown. The deafening cheers never ceased the whole way, and the most wonderful order was preserved. We seemed to be passing through a sea of people, as we went along the Mall. Our course going to St. Paul's was down the Mall, by Pall Mall, Trafalgar Square, straight up the Strand, Fleet Street, and Temple Bar, which was handsomely decorated. There

Landseer's painting of the Queen at Osborne House with her Highland Servant, John Brown, in attendance, 1865.

were stands and platforms in front of the Clubs, etc., full of well-dressed people, and no end of nice and touching inscriptions. At the corner of Marlborough House there was a stand on which stood Bertie's dear little girls, who waved their handkerchiefs . . . reached St. Paul's by five minutes to one. The large inscription put on the top was, 'I was glad when they said unto me, I will go into the House of the Lord.' . . .

I thought that the interior fell rather flat after the exterior. The Cathedral itself is so dull, cold, dreary, and dingy. It so badly lacks decoration and colour . . .

Got back to the Grand Entrance of Buckingham Palace at twenty minutes to four, and Bertie and Alix, with their boys, took leave in the hall, going straight home. I went upstairs and stepped out on the balcony with Beatrice and my three sons, being loudly cheered. Rested on the sofa after taking some tea. Could think and talk of little else, but to-day's wonderful demonstration of loyalty and affection, from the very highest to the lowest. Felt tired by all the emotion, but it is a day that can never be forgotten!

An attack is made on the Queen's life; the attacker is caught by her Highland servant, John Brown.

BUCKINGHAM PALACE, February 29th, 1872

At half past four drove in the open landau and four with Arthur, Leopold, and Jane C., the Equerries riding. We drove round Hyde and Regent's Parks, returning by Constitution Hill, and when at the Garden Entrance a dreadful thing happened, which God in His mercy averted having any evil consequences. It is difficult for me to describe, as my impression was a great fright, and all was over in a minute. How it all happened I knew nothing of. The Equerries had dismounted, Brown [*John Brown: the Queen's Highland Servant*] had got down to let down the steps, and Jane C. was just getting out, when suddenly someone appeared at my side, whom I at first imagined was a footman, going to lift off the wrapper. Then I perceived that it was someone unknown, peering above the carriage door, with an uplifted hand and a strange voice, at the same time the boys calling out and moving forward. Involuntarily, in a terrible fright, I threw myself over Jane C., calling out, 'Save me,' and heard a scuffle and voices! I soon recovered myself sufficiently to stand up and turn round, when I saw Brown holding a young man tightly, who was struggling, Arthur, the Equerries, etc., also near him. They laid the man on the ground and Brown kept hold of him till several of the police came in. All turned and asked if I was hurt, and I said, 'Not at all.' Then Lord Charles FitzRoy, General Hardinge, and Arthur came up, saying they thought the man had dropped something. We looked, but could find nothing, when Cannon, the postilion, called out, 'There it is,' and looking down I then did see shining on the ground a small pistol! This filled us with horror. All were as white as sheets, Jane C. almost crying, and Leopold looked as if he were going to faint.

It is to good Brown and to his wonderful presence of mind that I greatly owe my safety, for he alone saw the boy rush round and followed him! When I was standing in the hall, General Hardinge came in, bringing an extraordinary document which this boy had intended making me sign! It was in connection with the Fenian prisoners! Sir T. Biddulph came running, greatly horrified. Then the boy was taken away by the police and made no attempt to escape . . .

WINDSOR CASTLE, March 1st, 1872

NUMBERS OF PEOPLE CALLED last night and wrote their names down, also a great many this morning. The wretched boy O'Connor was to be examined this morning at the Police Court, where the Equerries as well as Brown would probably have to go . . . On returning saw Mr. Gladstone, who was dreadfully shocked at what [*had*] happened, and to whom I recounted the whole thing. It is so sad that such an occurrence should have come to mar the splendid effect of the 27th. It is this which distresses him so much, for it is so hard on the millions of loyal people. There was an Act for misdemeanour which he thought would meet the case; if not, it must be further altered. I said, when O'Connor's sentence had expired, he ought not to be allowed to remain in the country.

Could it have been because he was supposed to be a medium and was able to put Queen Victoria in touch with the spirit of Prince Albert that John Brown, the Queen's Highland Servant was so popular with Her Majesty?

Or could it be that the Queen and Brown were actually having some kind of love affair? Or had they been married in a Church of Scotland ceremony? Or was the Queen mad and Brown her keeper?

There is some evidence for the first theory, but no evidence at all to support the love, marriage or madness theories.

John Brown was a handsome, hard-drinking Highlander who had worked as a gillie for the Prince Consort at Balmoral. He had often attended the Queen and Prince on their rambles and they were delighted by his blunt way of speaking to them and his honesty. Eventually, he became a combination of groom, attendant, footman, maid, and constant companion, even to the extent of sleeping in a bedroom very near the Queen's.

Members of the Royal Family and Court loathed him and there were frequent rows and disagreements involving him. But he captivated and delighted the Queen who showered special privileges on him and, after he died, even had a special memorial in his honour placed in the royal mausoleum at Frogmore.

On February 3, 1865, she wrote in her Journal: 'I have decided that Brown should remain permanently and make himself useful in other ways besides leading my pony as he is very dependable.'

There was much gossip and speculation about the nature of their relationship, especially in the 'highest' circles. The Queen was even nicknamed 'Mrs John Brown' by many in fashionable London society and was libelled in the *Lausanne Gazette* which actually dared to print the 'marriage' rumour as a fact.

The Queen did not help matters. She refused to contradict rumours and continued to make sure that her private life was so strictly private that the few who were close to her either knew little of her private life, or were simply not prepared to discuss the Queen. Further, she *did* see a great deal of Brown and to many it seemed that it was more important pleasing him than pleasing certain members of her family.

By the time Brown died in 1883, the majority of the Queen's family, her Household and Court had (grudgingly) accepted him. That cleverest of prime ministers, Benjamin Disraeli, often asked after him in letters to the Queen. He was quick to realize that for whatever reasons, the Queen was besotted with Brown and that he was a person of great consequence in the royal household.

When he died, not only did she herself write his obituary notice for *The Times*, but had designed a 'John Brown Memorial Broach' made in gold with Brown's head on one side and the royal monogram on the other.

The Prince of Wales detested Brown, and after his mother died he took great delight in

Adelina Patti as Juliet in 1867. She charmed the Queen when she sang at Windsor in July, 1872.

personally smashing the statuettes of the gillie which he found scattered around the royal residences.

Perhaps King Edward was the only person to know the truth about his mother and John Brown.

WINDSOR CASTLE, July 4th, 1872

... HAD SOME MUSIC in the Red Drawing-room, to which my three children, Lenchen, and the ladies and some of the gentlemen came. Adelina Patti, the famous prima donna, now the favourite, since the last six years, Messrs. Faure and Capoul, sang, Mr. Cusins accompanying them on the piano. I was charmed with Patti, who has a very sweet voice and wonderful facility and execution. She sings very quietly and is a very pretty ladylike little thing. The duet with Faure was quite lovely, and her rendering of 'Home, Sweet Home' was touching beyond measure, and quite brought tears to one's eyes. Faure has a very fine baritone voice. Capoul, tenor, I cared less for.

OSBORNE, July 23rd, 1872

THERE IS A CURIOUS LAW in the Isle of Man, by which I am obliged to sign the order for the execution of criminals, which the Sovereign never does in England. I have had to sign

Sir George Gilbert Scott, architect of the Albert Memorial.

this warrant for the first and I hope last time in my life. The case is that of a man—John Kewish by name who had killed his father.

The Queen was determined that her capital should have at least one memorial to her beloved husband.

It was decided to hold a design competition. The competition attracted international interest and there were, in addition, all kinds of extraordinary schemes proposed by, no doubt, well meaning, but artistically and structurally ignorant people.

For example, one engineer suggested that the committee should consider erecting an iron structure 500 feet high. Someone else suggested an enormous monolith and the Duke of Argyll, owner of the Ross of Mull quarries, offered a piece of granite 114 feet in length. But experts doubted whether it was strong enough.

The Queen's artistic wishes were not clear in her mind, but she was quite definite as to the type of memorial: it was to have a portrait statue of Prince Albert and it had to be in the open air.

The most spectacular design was the unsolicited one from the architect, Alexander 'Greek' Thompson whose Greek revival style of architecture can still be seen in several Glasgow churches.

Eventually, the eminent architect, Sir George Gilbert Scott was appointed by the trustees. He was given full control over the work and his Gothic Revival building which is

such a familiar sight in Kensington Gore opposite the Royal Albert Hall incorporates the work of eleven distinguished sculptors.

The memorial is 175 feet high and has 175 life-size (or larger-than-life-size) figures; each figure hewn out of the solid mass of the base of the memorial. It consists of a canopy raised on twenty-four steps, the columns of which are hewn from the Duke of Argyll's piece of granite. Beneath the canopy is a fourteen-foot high bronze statue of the Prince by J. H. Foley. The base of the memorial is surrounded by statues illustrating Astronomy, Chemistry, Rhetoric, Medicine, Geometry, Geology, Physiology and Philosophy. There are also statues of the Virtues: Prudence, Humility, Justice, Fortitude, Temperance, Faith, Hope and Charity and of mourning and exultant angels. At the four corners of the perimeter are groups representing the Continents, Engineering, Manufacturing and Agriculture.

The Fine Arts are represented by over a hundred sculptures. Those of poets and musicians include Auber, Rameau, Josquin des Pres, Monteverdi, Virgil, Dante, Pythogaras, Homer, Chaucer, Shakespeare, Purcell, Mendelssohn, Handel, Mozart, Arne, Tallis and Orlando Gibbons.

Painters include Turner, Reynolds, Gainsborough, Hogarth, Rembrandt, Holbein,

GREAT NORTH OF SCOTLAND RAILWAY.

ARRANGEMENT OF CARRIAGES

COMPOSING

Her Majesty's Train,

FROM BALLATER TO GOLSPIE,

On Friday, 6th September, 1872.

Break.	Queen's Fourgon.	Servants.	Servants.	Lady Churchill. — Miss Bauer.	Personal Servants. — Queen's Dressers.	Her Majesty and Princess Beatrice.	Prince Leopold. — Sir W. Jenner. Mr. Collins.	Earl Granville. — Colonel Ponsonby.	Directors.	Break.	Engine.
	Carriage Truck.	First Class Carriage.	First Class Carriage.	Double Saloon.	Royal	Saloons.	Double Saloon.	Double Saloon.	First Class Carriage.		

G. CORNWALL AND SONS, PRINTERS, ABERDEEN.

ABOVE: *The Queen travelled throughout Britain and part of Europe by rail, but the train's greatest advantage for her was that it could speed her from Southampton or Windsor to Balmoral. Once there, she often made other train journeys. This particular train was travelling only a short distance (from Ballater to Golspie) but nevertheless it carried a large number of servants, members of the Royal Household, including a doctor, and members of the Great North of Scotland Railway Company.*

LEFT: *The Albert Memorial today.*

Durer, Rubens, Fra Angelico, Raphael, Michaelangelo, Titian, Tintoretto, Correggio, Velasquez, Murillo and Delacroix.

Architects include A. W. Pugin, Charles Barry, Scott himself, Inigo Jones, Palladio, William of Sens and Delorme.

Among the sculptors represented are: Giovanni di Bologna, Peter Vischer, Bandinello, Cellini, Baccio d'Agnolo; Jean Goujon, Pierre Puget, Grinling Gibbons, Francis Bird, Nicholas Stone and Bernini.

Queen Victoria went to see the memorial in July, 1872 declaring it to be 'really magnificent'. Prince Albert's statue was not put in its place of honour until 1875, but the memorial was informally opened to the public in August, 1872. Thousands visited it and three years later when Albert's statue was finally put in its place, the workmen were almost prevented from doing their work, so great was the crush.

In 1882, a writer described it as 'being beyond question the finest monumental structure in Europe'.

The Queen hears of the death of Emperor Napoleon III.

OSBORNE, January 9th, 1873

HAD ENQUIRED BUT WAS SURPRISED at getting no news from Chislehurst, and soon after I came home, Janie E. came into my room with a telegram in her hand, saying, 'It is all over,' which I could not believe, so impossible it seemed. The telegram was from M. Piétri, the Emperor's Secretary [*nephew of the former Minister of Police*], begging her to communicate to me the sad news that 'l'Empereur a cessé de souffrir à 11 heures moins ¼. L'Impératrice est dans les larmes.' Was quite upset. Had a great regard for the Emperor, who was so amiable and kind, and had borne his terrible misfortunes with such meekness, dignity, and patience. He had been such a faithful ally to England, and I could [*not*] but think of the wonderful position he had, after being a poor, insignificant exile, of the magnificent reception given him in England in 1855, and his agreeable visit here in '57, and ours to Paris in '55!

WINDSOR CASTLE, February 20th, 1873

A VERY FOGGY, RAW DAY. At quarter past ten, left Windsor for Chislehurst, by the South-Western, Beatrice, Jane C., and Colonel Maude accompanying me. We passed through London, which was wrapped in a thick yellow fog. Drove straight from the station in a closed landau . . .

From thence drove to Camden House, where at the door, instead of his poor father, who had always received me so kindly, was the Prince Imperial, looking very pale and sad. A few steps further on, in the deepest mourning, looking very ill, very handsome, and the picture of sorrow, was the poor dear Empress, who had insisted on coming down to receive me. Silently we embraced each other and she took my arm in hers, but could not speak for emotion. She led me upstairs to her boudoir, which is very small and full of the souvenirs which she had been able to save. She cried a good deal, but quietly and gently, and that sweet face, always a sad one, looked inexpressibly pathetic. She described the poor Emperor's death, and how terribly sudden it had been at the last.

The Queen opens Victoria Park in Hackney which, even today, is one of the nicest parts of the East End of London.

BUCKINGHAM PALACE, April 2nd, 1873

. . . AT THE ENTRANCE OF VICTORIA PARK there were troops, Life Guards and Foot Guards, who kept the Park, and were under the command of Edward S[*axe*] W[*eimar*]. We stopped under an awning, where addresses were handed into the carriage by the members, Mr. Reed and Mr. Holms, to which I answered, expressing my gratification at my kind reception and the pleasure it gave me to visit the Park. Another bouquet and an address from the parishes of Hackney, Bethnal Green, and Shoreditch were presented. We had driven at a gentle trot through the streets, but went at a foots-pace round the Park. There were many kind expressions of 'God bless you,' 'Come again,' and nothing could have been more hearty or cordial than my reception by those poorest of the poor. It was really touching. The Park is a large one and a great boon to the poor people. We returned by Bethnal Green, passing the celebrated Museum, Hackney Road, Shoreditch (the very

The Queen visited Victoria Park in the East End of London in April, 1873. She was very gratified at the success of her visit.

worst part of London), Bishopsgate Street, Threadneedle Street, fearfully narrow and crowded with clerks, past the Bank, Mansion House, on the balcony of which stood the Lord Mayor in his robes, bowing! The crowds in the City were very great and enthusiastic, and many nosegays were given me. We drove along the Embankment, which is very fine, and through the Horse Guards home. It was a very fine warm day. Got home shortly before one, very gratified and pleased with the most successful morning.

WINDSOR CASTLE, June 20th, 1873

My accession day, thirty-six years ago, which seems almost impossible. May God guide me further and enable me to do what is right!

Felt nervous and agitated at the great event of the day, the Shah's visit. All great bustle and excitement. The guns were fired and bells ringing for my Accession Day, and the latter also for the Shah. The Beefeaters were taking up their places, pages walking about, in full dress, etc. Arthur arrived, crowds appeared near the gates, the Guard of Honour and Band marched into the Quadrangle, and then I dressed in a smart morning dress, with my large pearls, and the Star and Ribbon of the Garter, the Victoria and Albert Order, etc . . .

I stepped forward and gave him my hand, which he shook, expressing to the Grand Vizier my great satisfaction at making the Shah's acquaintance. Then took his arm and walked slowly upstairs, and along the Corridor, the Grand Vizier close behind, and the

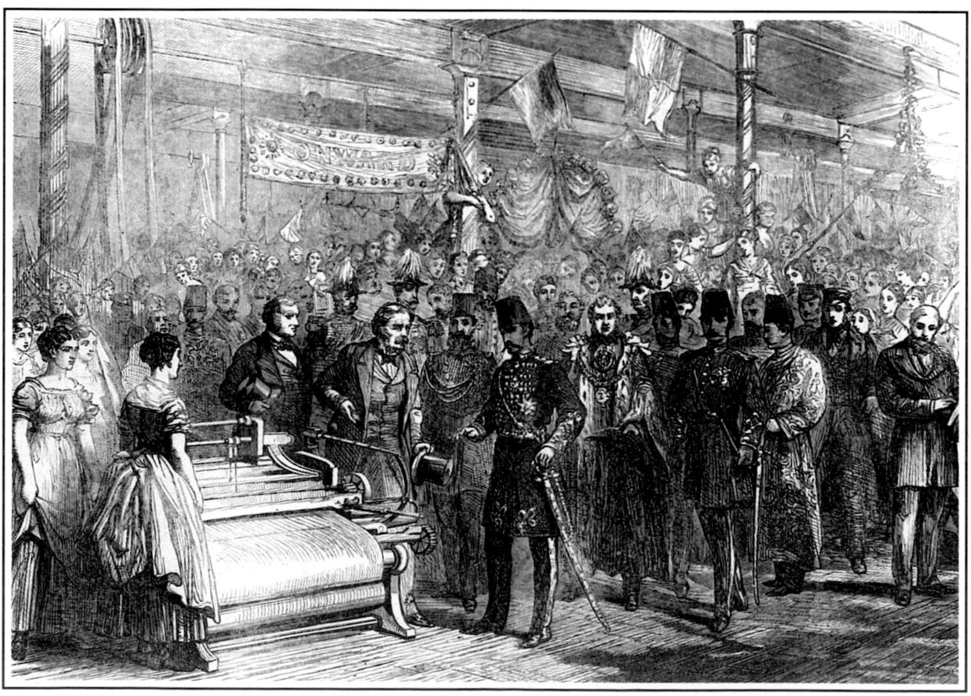

*The Shah of Persia visited Queen Victoria in 1873.
He was taken to cities outside London, including Portsmouth, Liverpool, Crewe and Manchester. This engraving from* The Illustrated London News *records his visit to the weaving-room at Haworth's Mills, Manchester.*

Princes and Princesses, including all the Persian ones, the ladies, etc., following, to the White Drawing-room. The Shah is fairly tall, and not fat, has a fine countenance and is very animated. He wore a plain coat (a tunic) full in the skirt and covered with very fine jewels, enormous rubies as buttons, and diamond ornaments, the sword belt and epaulettes made entirely of diamonds, with an enormous emerald in the centre of each. The sword-hilt and scabbard were richly adorned with jewels, and in the high black astrakan cap was a aigrette of diamonds. I asked various questions through the Grand Vizier, but the Shah understands French perfectly and speaks short, detached sentences.

BALMORAL, October 1st, 1873

After luncheon heard that the great artist and kind old friend, Sir Edwin Landseer had died peacefully at 11. A merciful release, as for the last three years he had been in a most distressing state, half out of his mind, yet not entirely so. The last time I ever saw him was at Chiswick, at Bertie's garden party, two years ago, when he was hardly fit to be about, and looked quite dreadful. He was a great genius in his day, and one of the most popular of English artists. It is strange that both he and Winterhalter, our personal, attached friends of more than thirty years' standing, should have gone within three or four months of each other! I cannot at all realise it. How many an incident do I remember, connected with Landseer! He kindly had shown me how to draw stags' heads, and how to draw in chalks, but I never could manage that well. I possess 39 oil paintings of his, 16 chalk drawings, two frescos, and many sketches.

Sir Edwin Landseer sculpting the lions for Trafalgar Square.

WINDSOR CASTLE, March 9th, 1874

A VERY RAINY MORNING.—Took leave of Victor & Liko after breakfast.—Could not go out.—Went over to St. George's Hall to see the preparations for the big dinner. [*In honour of the Duke and Duchess of Edinburgh who had been married on January 2 in Russia.*]—Resting on the sofa, for I was rather tired.—It cleared and the afternoon became fine, though cold.—Drove with Beatrice in the Phaeton.—Bertie & Alix arrived—he remained talking with me some time. Louise also arrived.—Joined all the family in the Corridor. Marie wore a white silk dress trimmed with beautiful narrow point d'Alençon & her fine ruby 'parure', including a diadem. All the Princesses wore their 'Grand Cordons', & the Princes (those who had them) Russian orders. I had mine on. Went over to the Drawingrooms & North Corridor to the Reception Room, where the guests were assembled. The Princes & Gentlemen were all in uniform. We went at once in to dinner in St. George's Hall, without talking to any one, Affie & Marie going in first. I sat between him & her. It seemed all like a strange dream, to be in that Hall, where I had not dined since June '60 & not had a State Dinner since '55, when the King of Sardinia was here, & now without *him* who was my all in all, & directed everything. The gold plate looked very handsome. The Band played well, & I felt more & more relieved, as I saw how well everything went. Three Toasts were given out, first Affie & Marie's, then mine & the Empr., & Empress of Russia. After dinner I presented some of the Ladies to Marie, who was wonderfully self possessed, & then slipped away.—The greater part of the guests returned to London. So thankful all had gone off so well for after 14 years doing nothing of the kind & alone, without *him* who used to direct all, it was very trying!—

WINDSOR CASTLE, May 13th, 1874

ON GETTING UP, RECEIVED A TELEGRAM FROM AFFIE saying that the Emperor of Russia's yacht had gone aground and could not be got off till the tide rose. He would land at Dover, but could not arrive till half past 7! What a *contretemps*! Everybody had to be put off till later, for he was to have arrived at half past 1! Drove in the afternoon with Louise and Beatrice in the Park, which is in such beauty, and it was so warm and lovely.

When we came in, Lord A. Paget met me, saying the Emperor could not be here till 9 or possibly 10! Alix arrived. We decided to take a little refreshment about half past 8. Then came a telegram saying they would not be here till 9.50. We began to dress, and at half past 9 went over to the State Rooms with Alix, Lenchen, Louise, Beatrice, and the two Duchesses. Alix had a very bad cold. Lord Hertford met us and we sat waiting in the Waterloo Gallery. The Grand Staircase looked beautiful with all the flowers and the Yeomen of the Guard lining it. The Great Officers of State as well as the Ladies and Gentlemen were all there, everyone *en gala* . . . I stepped out to greet the Emperor . . . I presented my three daughters and then we walked upstairs, and went into the Rubens Room (the Emperor's drawing-room), where, soon after, Affie and the Grand Duke Alexis joined us. Then the Emperor presented his immense suite to me in the Waterloo Gallery. I wore my Russian Order.

We only sat down to dinner, in fact supper, at quarter to 11.

RIGHT: *Franz Winterhalter, the German artist who painted many portraits of the Queen and her family.*

BELOW: *The wedding of the Queen's son, Prince Alfred, the Duke of Edinburgh, to* HIH *the Grand Duchess Marie, only daughter of Czar Alexander II of Russia, took place in the Church of St Peter and St Paul in St Petersburg on January 2, 1874. Here the bride receives holy water before the ceremony.*

The avenue leading from the Home Park to the south front of Windsor Castle.

WINDSOR CASTLE, June 28th, 1875

RAINY MORNING, but we went down all the same to Frogmore, and breakfasted in the Garden Cottage. We noticed an immense number of little frogs, hardly bigger than a bluebottle fly, hopping and crawling all over the grass and paths, which seemed to increase. I observed it first, yesterday, but much more to-day and especially near the Cottage—quite disgusting.

WINDSOR CASTLE, November 24th, 1875

RECEIVED A BOX FROM Mr. Disraeli, with the very important news that the Government has purchased the Viceroy of Egypt's shares in the Suez Canal for £4,000,000, which gives us complete security for India, and altogether places us in a very safe position! An immense thing. It is entirely Mr. Disraeli's doing. Only three or four days ago I heard of the offer and at once supported and encouraged him, when at that moment it seemed doubtful, and then to-day all has been satisfactorily settled.

November 25th

AT A LITTLE AFTER SIX SAW MR. DISRAELI, who remained for an hour, and was full of his great success. He said that at first Lord Derby had been much against the plan, also Sir S. Northcote, but that Lord Salisbury had supported him, and that my support had been a great help. It is of course a great step, and may have far-reaching consequences.

ABOVE: *Queen Victoria described richard Wagner's countenance as 'not pleasing'.*

LEFT: *A special programme for a command performance at the Royal Albert Hall on February 25, 1876. By this date, the hall had been open for five years.*

WINDSOR CASTLE, April 25th, 1876

SAW MR. DISRAELI AT ONE. He was much annoyed at what had occurred about the Titles Bill, which certainly seemed inexplicable. Speaking of the Proclamation, he explained that it had been most carefully considered that the title was not to be used in writs and other legal matters in England, or in ordinary translations, but would be for commissions in the Army, as officers served in India as well as in England, also in all foreign treaties and communications with foriegn Sovereigns. In these cases I should have to sign 'Victoria R. & I.'

WINDSOR CASTLE, December 19th 1876

WALKED WITH BEATRICE down to the Mausoleum and back. She has been very busy these last days sorting old music of mine, amongst which treasures have been found. After my dreadful misfortune in '61, everything was left untouched, and I could not bear to look at what my darling one and I used to play daily together. Only within the last five or six years have I looked at my music again, and only quite lately re-opened my duet books and others. The past has seemed to rush in upon me in a strange and marvellous manner. Those notes and sounds bring back memories and scenes which seemed effaced.

WINDSOR CASTLE, January 1st, 1877

NEVER SINCE MY BELOVED MOTHER AND HUSBAND were taken from me have I spent this day here. May God bless this new year to us all, long preserve my dear ones, and help me to improve and do my duty! Gave and received many cards. My thoughts much taken up with the great event at Delhi to-day, and in India generally, where I am being proclaimed Empress of India, also with the grave anxieties about the Eastern question. I have for the first time to-day signed myself as V. R. & I.

WINDSOR CASTLE, May 17th, 1877

AFTER LUNCHEON THE GREAT COMPOSER WAGNER, about whom the people in Germany are really a little mad, was brought into the corridor by Mr. Cusins. I had seen him with dearest Albert in '55, when he directed at the Philharmonic Concert. He has grown old and stout, and has a clever, but not pleasing countenance.

OSBORNE, August 11th, 1877

. . . WE LANDED AGAIN AT OSBORNE PIER, and waited a little while in the carriage to see the *Thunderer* steam away to Cowes. She is very ugly-looking, more like a floating bridge or lighthouse, than a ship. Lady Ailesbury (Maria Marchioness), Lord and Lady Wilton (he looking dreadfully ill), Captain Wilson, Lord C. Beresford, Lady Waterpark, and General Ponsonby dined. Captain Wilson, in speaking of the *Thunderer*, said he was not afraid of her at sea, only she must not be pressed, as she is a dead weight, without elasticity. Lord Charles Beresford is very funny, beaming with fun and a trifle cracky, but clever, and a good officer.

WINDSOR CASTLE, December 15th, 1877

... AT HALF PAST TWELVE left with Beatrice (who was better), Janie E., General Ponsonby, and Colonel du Plat for Hughenden, going by train to High Wycombe, which we reached in about three-quarters of an hour, and where Lord Beaconsfield with the Mayor received us on the platform. There was a great crowd. An Address was handed by the Mayor, in answer to which Lord Beaconsfield said a few words, and the daughter gave me a bouquet ...

It took us hardly quarter of an hour to reach Hughenden, which stands in a park, rather high, and has a fine view. Lord Beaconsfield met me at the door, and led me into the library, which opens on to the terrace and a pretty Italian garden, laid out by himself. We went out at once, and Beatrice and I planted each a tree, then I went back into the library and he gave me an account of yesterday's Cabinet, which had been very stormy.

OSBORNE, January 14th, 1878

AFTER DINNER we went to the Council Room and saw the telephone. A Professor Bell explained the whole process, which is most extraordinary. It had been put in communication with Osborne Cottage, and we talked with Sir Thomas and Mary Biddulph, also heard some singing quite plainly. But it is rather faint, and one must hold the tube close to one's ear.

BALMORAL, May 29th, 1878

HEARD OLD LORD RUSSELL WAS DEAD, having died last night. He had been ill for the last three weeks, and his memory quite gone. He was nearly 86. A man of much talent, who leaves a name behind him, kind and good, with a great knowledge of the constitution, who behaved very well on many trying occasions; but he was impulsive, very selfish (as shown on many occasions, especially during Lord Aberdeen's administration), vain, and often reckless and imprudent. He was a link with the past, and was one of my first Ministers forty-one years ago.

WINDSOR CASTLE, December 14th, 1878

THIS TERRIBLE DAY COME ROUND AGAIN! Slept tolerably, but woke very often, constantly seeing darling Alice before me. When I woke in the morning, was not for a moment aware of all our terrible anxiety. And then it all burst upon me. I asked for news, but nothing had come. Then got up and went, as I always do on this day, to the Blue Room, and prayed there.

OSBORNE, January 1st, 1879

WHAT A SAD BEGINNING to the New Year! What sadness, what grief on so many sides! Our darling precious Alice, [*the Grand Duchess of Hesse died a fortnight earlier*] one of my beloved

Benjamin Disraeli, Lord Beaconsfield, with the Queen at High Wycombe railway station during her visit to him in December 1877.

Alexander Graham Bell, inventor of the telephone.

five daughters, gone, after but six days' illness, gone for ever from this world, which is not, thank God, our permanent home! What misery in her once dear, bright, happy home! And my poor dear Loosy far away in a distant land, in another quarter of the globe! [*Princess Louise was in Canada, with her husband Lord Lorne, who was the Governor-General.*]

OSBORNE, January 8th, 1879

HEARD FROM LORD BEACONSFIELD [*formerly Benjamin Disraeli*], that there would be nothing to prevent my going to the North of Italy [*He had written on 6th January: 'Italy is probably one of the safest places in Europe. It would appear that there are no British members of the International, and it is said that the Society itself is scrupulous in not permitting foreigners to accomplish* [*its*] *behests.'*] in the latter part of March, which I am very anxious to do, as I feel it an absolute necessity for my nerves and health, to have a complete change of scene. Germany I could not bear to go to this spring, Switzerland was too cold, and Italy I have long desired to see.

OSBORNE, January 17th, 1879

BEFORE LUNCHEON I received the Chinese Minister's wife, Madame Kuo, who was presented by Lady Waterpark. She is small, and wears the usual Chinese dress, only with a large sort of tippet over it, entirely lined with fur, which she kept on all the time in the house, only a few little ornaments on her head, but nothing else, and no additional wraps for going in the open carriage! She had the celebrated small squashed feet.

OSBORNE, February 11th, 1879

DIRECTLY AFTER BREAKFAST THERE CAME A TELEGRAM from Colonel Stanley to General Ponsonby, telling of a great and most unfortunate disaster at the Cape, or rather more Natal, the Zulus having defeated our troops with great loss, and Lord Chelmsford [*the General in Command in South Africa*] obliged to retire [*the rout by Zulu warriors of the British forces at Iswandlhara*]. How this could happen we cannot yet imagine. A Cabinet was to be called at once, and large reinforcements ordered out. Thirty officers, 70 non-commissioned officers, and 500 men have fallen. It is fearful. The Zulus lost more than 3,000. I sent the telegram over to Bertie, who soon came over to me, and remained talking a long time.

Zululand in South-East Africa was eventually annexed to Natal. In 1876, King Cetewayo opposed missionaries in his country and organised armed resistance against the British. For the next few years, the British fought the Zulus. The King was captured by the British in August, 1879 and the war was settled by treaty a month later. It was reported in July, 1881 that the cost of the war had been £4,922,141. However, there were many subsequent problems, with mini-wars waged between the various chiefs and even a further rebellion in 1906.

The Lord Steward
has received Her Majesty's commands
to invite Lieut-Col. Lord Edward Clinton.
(Rifle Brigade) and Lady Edward Clinton.
to Dinner at Windsor Castle on
Monday 8th March and to remain
until the next day.

Windsor Castle.
7th March 1880.

See other side.

March 8. 1880

Windsor Castle.

We are invited to dine & sleep

Dinner Party

Her Majesty - The Queen
R H. Princess Beatrice
His R H. Prince Leopold
The Maharajah Duleep Singh
General Sir Thomas Steele
The Duchess of Athol
Marchioness of Ely.
Lord Torrington
Colonel McNeil.
} in waiting

TOP: *Lord and Lady Edward Pelham-Clinton received the Queen's Command to 'dine and sleep' at Windsor Castle on Monday, March 8, 1880.*

ABOVE: *Lord Edward made a note of the other guests, and also the names of those in waiting on a piece of Windsor Castle writing paper.*

OVERLEAF: *The rout of Lord Chelmsford's forces at Iswandlhara was followed by the most famous battle of the Zulu War, the attack on the garrison at Rorke's Drift. This painting by A. De Neuville commemorates the defence of the post by Lieutenant Chard of the Royal Engineers and Lieutenant Bromhead with eighty men of the 24th Regiment. They were attacked by 4000 Zulu warriors, who gained a foothold within the defences on six occasions during the night and succeeded in burning the hospital. The garrison repulsed these attacks at bayonet point and when they were relieved the following morning 351 Zulus lay dead around the entrenchments.*

WINDSOR CASTLE, May 12th, 1879

RECEIVED THE NEWS THAT CHARLOTTE, the eldest daughter of the Crown Princess of Prussia, who had married the Hereditary Prince of Saxe-Meiningen had been safely delivered of a little girl, [*Princess Feodora of Saxe-Meiningen, who married Prince Henry of Reuss*] all doing quite well, and I have thus become a great-grandmother! Quite an event.

BALMORAL, June 19th, 1879

AFTER DINNER LEILA ERROLL READ, and I was writing, when, just before 11, a telegram was given me with the message that it contained bad news. When I, in alarm, asked what, I was told it was that the Prince Imperial [*of France*] had been killed. I feel a thrill of horror in even writing it. I kept on saying 'No, no, it can't be!' To die in such an awful way is too shocking! Poor dear Empress! her only child, her *all*, gone! I am really in despair. He was such an amiable, good young man, who would have made such a good Emperor for France one day. It is a real misfortune. The more one thinks of it the worse it becomes. Got to bed very late, it was just dawning! and little sleep did I get.

WINDSOR CASTLE, March 8th, 1880

THE MAHARAJAH DULEEP SINGH [*His Highness the Maharajah Duleep Singh's territory was annexed by the British after the Second Sikh War. He was brought up in England and in 1863 he bought Elveden Hall, a mansion in Norfolk, and transformed it into an Indian Palace. He was a great favourite of the Queen.*], looking very well, only too fat, the Dss. of Athole, Ld. & Ly. Edward Clinton (he is particularly nice, & commands the Rifles) Sir J. Steele, Janie Ely, Ld. Torrington, Col: McNeill & Col: Liddell dined.

OSBORNE, August 18th, 1880

JUST 25 YEARS AGO that we arrived in state and splendour at Paris and St. Cloud, so kindly received by the Emperor and Empress, and now! she, at Osborne, a widow, childless, and an exile! Terrible! After breakfast, went up to the dear Empress, and brought her back the letters and parcel she had entrusted to me, when she went away, and which I carried about with me everywhere. She asked me to keep the small packet, which I was only to open after her death, and then said, would I perhaps like to open it and 'de l'avoir de mon vivant,' which I said I would, and she undid the parcel, and took out a most splendid emerald cross, cut out of one stone, without any joins, and set at the points in fine diamonds, with two magnificent large ones at the top. It had been given her by the King of Spain when she married. When I asked her if she would not still wear it, she answered, 'non, non, jamais plus de pareilles choses,' that it was one of the few things she had kept and reserved for the future wife of her dear son. Alas! she gives everything away now, and I think it too kind of her to have given me this precious souvenir.

August 19th

TALKED OF LADY BURDETT COUTTS' extraordinary and dreadful idea of marrying a young Mr. Bartlett, who is only 29, and she 66! It is positively distressing and ridiculous, and will do her much harm by lowering her in people's eyes, and taking away their respect for her. [*Baroness Burdett-Coutts (1814–1906), who was a partner in Coutts and Co., the royal bankers, married Mr William Lehman Ashmead Bartlett in 1881. He assumed the additional surnames of Burdett-Coutts and was Conservative MP for Westminister from 1885 for over twenty years, taking a very active part in public affairs.*]

Angela Burdett-Coutts from a watercolour by Hartray, 1883. She was a philanthropist and a partner in Coutts and Co., the royal bankers.

IN THE TRAIN, November 23rd, 1880

FINISHED *JANE EYRE*, which is really a wonderful book, very peculiar in parts, but so powerfully and admirably written, such a fine tone in it, such fine religious feeling, and such beautiful writing. The description of the mysterious maniac's nightly appearances awfully thrilling, Mr. Rochester's character a very remarkable one, and Jane Eyre's herself a beautiful one. The end is very touching, when Jane Eyre returns to him and finds him blind, with one hand gone from injuries during the fire in his house, which was caused by his mad wife.

During Queen Victoria's reign it was the ambition of every well born person to be presented at Court—and it was usually possible.

Even those not so well born but rich, or with rich parents, could usually find some distinguished relation or 'connection' who would agree to sponsor them for presentation. There were also cases of people actually paying 'sponsors' to present them just as people were duped into paying for honours which they never received.

Apart from the social cachet, presentation usually meant that you had arrived in 'society' if you were not in it by right of birth.

There were two main routes to presentation: at a Drawing Room or at a Levée, both formal functions and not to be confused with social events presented by the Royal Family.

Drawing Rooms were ceremonial receptions presided over by Queen Victoria, or, in her absence, the Princess of Wales or the princess next in precedence. They were always held in the Throne Room of Buckingham Palace at 3pm, and there were several every year.

Ladies (often debutantes) wishing to be presented could only obtain the honour through a relation, friend or acquaintance who had previously been presented. The lady who made the presentation had to appear with the lady she presented. In addition, both must have unblemished characters. Their conduct must be *sans reproche*.

At the first Drawing Room of the season, the whole of the *corps diplomatique* attended, but at subsequent ones, only Chefs de Mission with their wives, the first secretaries of Embassies and any members of their legations or other distinguished foreigners were expected to attend.

Different entrances had to be used depending on status. For example, the Mistress of the Robes, the Master of the Horse, the Women of the Bedchamber-in-Waiting and the Pages-of-Honour-in-Waiting were set down at the Grand Entrance.

The Garden Entrance was reserved exclusively for members of the Royal Family who were received there by White Staves (ex-officers) and the Groom and Equerry-in-Waiting and taken, as they arrived into the Council Room to await the Queen's readiness.

When all the members of the Royal Family expected had arrived, the Queen would be warned, the Lord Steward, the White Staves and others having taken their places in the Throne Room. On the right of the throne would be positioned the Lord Steward, the Master of the Horse, the Vice-Chamberlain, the Gold and Silver Sticks and the Captains of the Gentlemen-at-Arms and Yeomen of the Guard. On the left of the throne, the Treasurer and Comptroller of the Household. In the space above the Throne, the Women of the Bedchamber; the Maids-of-Honour and the Ladies-in-Waiting on the royal princesses. In the circle opposite the Queen, members of the Cabinet; members of the Royal Household, including the Master of the Household and the Gentleman Ushers who would form a line in front of the Queen. The Field Officer in Brigade Waiting with the Captain of the Guard remained in the Picture Gallery near the door. The Lord Chamberlain met the Queen in the corridor by Her Majesty's private apartments with the Pages of Honour, and conducted HM to the ante-room to the Council Room where HM would greet the Royal Family.

Queen Victoria then entered the Throne Room, conducted by the Lord Chamberlain, her train being carried by the Pages-of-Honour, attended by the Mistress of the Robes and the Lady of the Bedchamber-in-Waiting who stood close behind her. HM was followed by the Royal Family who took their places near her in strict order of precedence. The Queen then took her place at the throne, and the presentations began, first the diplomatic presentations. In some cases, ambassadors' ladies who had already been presented, after being named by the Lord Chamberlain, made obeisance to the Queen and then retired. Ladies who were to be presented, kissed the Queen's hand, but peeresses, the wives of eldest sons of peers, the daughters of peers of the rank of duke, marquis, and earl were kissed by the Queen on presentation. Foreign ladies who were presented did not kiss the Queen's hand, but simply made their obeisance. After being named or presented, all ladies or gentlemen (for some gentlemen were presented by ambassadors) were expected to pass out

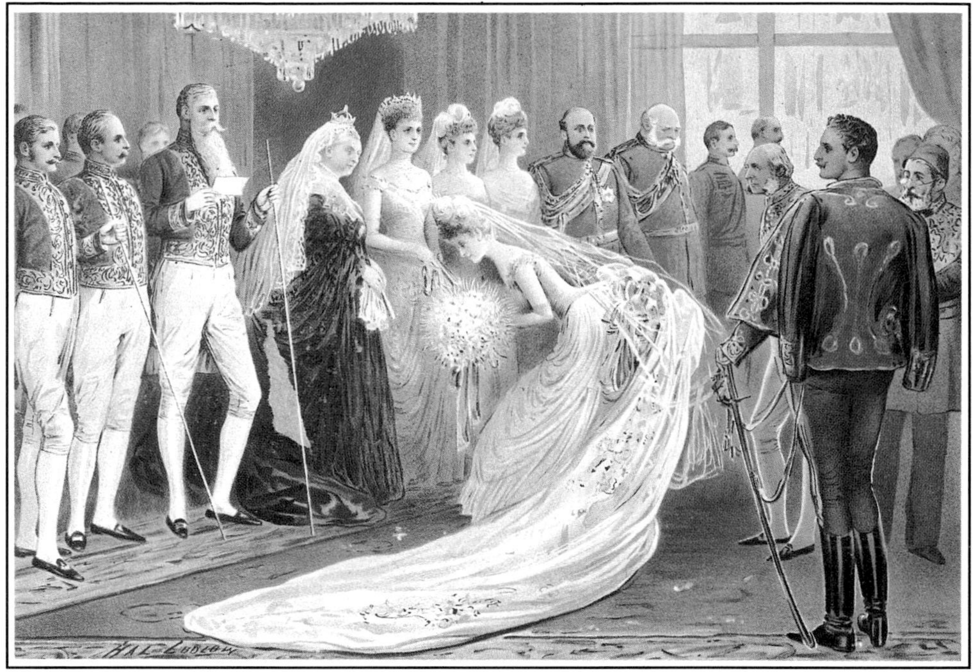

A lady kisses the Queen's hand at the Jubilee Drawing Room, May 17, 1887. The Lord Chamberlain holds the lady's card from which he reads her name to the Queen. On the Queen's left are the Princess of Wales, Princess Beatrice, Princess Louise of Wales, the Prince of Wales, the Duke of Cambridge and the Duke of Teck. Sir S. Ponsonby Fane, Comptroller of the Household, is behind the lady being presented.

of the room in to the Green Drawing Room and thence to their carriages.

During the Drawing Room silence was expected to be kept and a selection of music was played by a band of the Foot Guards in the quadrangle, while the Life Guards' Band played in the front of the palace.

Full Dress uniforms were worn by those entitled to them, and other gentlemen wore full Court dress. Ladies were always magnificently dressed in their full Court dress with feathers and trains. The Court dress of the ladies consisted of a petticoat, bodice and train. The train was up to about four yards long and was carried on the left arm folded until the lady arrived at the door of the Throne Room when it was spread on the ground. The head-dress consisted of feathers and a veil of white tulle. Diamond coronets were worn and the veil was often kept in place by diamonds or precious stones. Gloves, shoes and fans had to be white and all except royal ladies carried bouquets. Young ladies had to wear white but it was permissable to line the train with a colour. Three plumes were worn, generally set forward.

Levées were held by HRH the Prince of Wales on behalf of the Queen. Originally, levées were formal receptions held by a sovereign, just after rising from bed. But they later came to be public court receptions for men held in the Throne Room of St James's Palace. The doors were opened at 1.30 when all officers of the Household were present. The procedure was broadly similar in pomp and circumstance to the Drawing Rooms. As soon as the Prince had taken his place, the Secretary of State for Foreign Affairs was warned by the Comptroller of the Lord Chamberlain's Department to stand on the right hand of the Prince while the Members of the *corps diplomatique* were introduced. The Ambassadors, Ministers and Chargés d'Affaires with their Secretaries and Attachés passed by in order of precedence. The Ambassadors and Chefs de Mission named to the Prince any distinguished foreigners or members of their suite who were to be presented. The Ambassadors remained standing to the left of the throne, and the others took their places in a circle in front of the Prince. Gentlemen who were to be presented were named by the Lord Chamberlain. They bowed and passed by. Only the members of the Cabinet, the *corps diplomatique*, Keeper of the Privy Purse, the Private Secretary, the Master of the Household and other officers on duty had the privilege of remaining in the Throne Room after passing the Prince. The State Pages requested all others to leave the room.

State Balls held by TRH the Prince and Princess of Wales on behalf of the Queen were held at Buckingham Palace. The Lord Chamberlain usually issued invitations for about 2000 guests from lists approved by the Queen for 10.30pm. Invitation cards were accompanied by carriage tickets. The Yeomen of the Guard and the Exon-in-Waiting were on duty and the Master of Ceremonies, with his assitants received the distinguished members of the *corps diplomatique* and showed them to their seats on the left of the dais. When their Royal Highnesses had taken their seats, the Lord Chamberlain, at a command from the Prince of Wales, gave the signal to the conductor of the band or orchestra and a State Quadrille was formed. The Royal Family only danced at the top and bottom of the Ballroom and distinguished persons at the side. The space in front of the dais was kept clear by Gentlemen Ushers.

Quadrilles and waltzes were afterwards usually played alternately.

When supper was ready, it was announced to the Prince and Princess of Wales by the Lord Steward and they were conducted—as on entering—to the supper room. The supper was served at a buffet and the Prince and Princess, and other members of the Royal Family took that opportunity to meet and talk to various guests who were presented to them by the Lord Chamberlain. In the supper room, the Gentlemen Ushers formed a circle around the Royal Family. The Royal Family returned to the ballroom in procession and as they entered and left, the National Anthem was played.

At State Concerts held by the Prince and Princess of Wales on behalf of the Queen at Buckingham Palace, about 1000 guests were invited and the arrival and reception of the guests was exactly as at Levées and State Balls.

Semi-State Investitures of the Orders of Knighthood were held by the Queen at both Windsor Castle and Osborne. Carriages were reserved from London to Windsor by the Great Western Railway Company and Officers of the Royal Household were summoned to attend. Those to be invested were given luncheon on arrival at Windsor and later were marshalled in order by Garter, Principal King of Arms and then shown in to Her Majesty who was usually assisted by one of the Princes. If a gentleman had not been knighted, then the Queen would take the sword from Gold Stick and confer the honour of Knighthood upon him by touching him on each shoulder with a sword and naming him as 'Sir' with his Christian name. The new Knight kissed the Queen's hand, and again after being invested with the Insignia. The Knight then bowed, and walked backwards out of HM's presence. An identical procedure was adopted at Osborne on the Isle of Wight, except that to reach Southampton, a special train left London at 10am, and often HM's Yacht, *Alberta* took those to be invested to East Cowes from which they were collected by carriage and taken to Osborne House. These investitures were usually confined to the higher classes of the several orders, for example to Knights Grand Cross, and to Knights Commanders.

Principal Events
1881–90

1881: Benjamin Disraeli, Earl of Beaconsfield died (April 19).
Review of 52,000 volunteers by the Queen at Windsor Castle (July 9).
Married Women's Property Act.
Independence restored to the Transvaal.
Irish Land Act.
Revised version of the New Testament published.
Offenbach's *Tales of Hoffman* first performed.

1882: The Queen shot at by twenty-seven-year-old Roderick Maclean at Windsor (March 2); Maclean committed for trial for High Treason (March 10).
Dante Gabriel Rossetti, painter and poet, died (April 9).
Biologist Charles Darwin died (April 19).
Gottlieb Daimler pioneered his petrol engine.

1883: Royal College of Music founded.
Richard Wagner, composer, died (February 13).

Prince Leopold, Duke of Albany, the youngest of the Queen's four sons, at Oxford in 1874. Left to right: A. Harcourt, A. H. Mills, the Hon. S. Herbert, the Prince, W. Stirling Dalrymple and W. J. D. Campbell. The Queen records that the Prince recovered 'from fearful illnesses and various small accidents', but he died in Cannes a few days before his thirty-first birthday. He suffered from haemophilia, of which the Queen was an unknowing carrier. Her granddaughter, Alix of Hesse, wife of Czar Nicholas II, inherited the gene for haemophilia through her mother, the Queen's daughter, Princess Alice, and passed it on to her only son the Czarevitch.

1884: Prince Leopold, Duke of Albany, died March 28; buried at Windsor on April 5, two days before his thirty-first birthday.
Third Reform Bill.

First part of Oxford English Dictionary published (completed 1928).
Mark Twain's *The Adventures of Huckleberry Finn* first published.
The Queen attended the marriage of her grand-daughter Princess Victoria of Hesse to Prince Louis of Battenburg at Darmstädt (April 30).

1885: Prince Albert Victor Edward of Wales came of age (January 8).
Marquis of Salisbury Prime Minister.
Gilbert and Sullivan's *Mikado* first performed.
Marriage of Princess Beatrice and Prince Henry of Battenburg (July 23).

1886: The Queen opened parliament (January 21).
Marquis of Salisbury's administration ended (January 27), reformed (July 26).
Gladstone Prime Minister (February 2–July 20).
The Queen opened the International Exhibition of Navigation and Commerce at Liverpool (May 11).
Thomas Hardy's *Mayor of Casterbridge* published.
Queen Victoria's Golden Jubilee Year began (June 20).

1887: The Queen attended a special Jubilee service at Westminster Abbey (June 21).
Verdi's opera *Otello* first performed.
Eleven-week drought in Britain (June–August).

1888: County Councils established.
Edward Lear, artist and writer, died (January 30).
John Boyd Dunlop's pneumatic tyre patented.
Matthew Arnold died (April 15).
Severe measles epidemic throughout winter.

1889: Great London Dock Strike.
Emperor William II of Germany visited Queen Victoria (August 1–8).
Envoys from the Sultan of Zanzibar received by the Queen at Balmoral (October 29).
George Eastman's Kodak box camera came into production.

1890: Beginnings of municipal housing.
First 'tube' railway constructed in London.
Henrik Ibsen's *Hedda Gabler* first performed.
The Queen inaugurated the Empress dock at Southampton (July 26).
Emperor William II visited the Queen at Osborne (August 4–8).

Twenty years after the Prince Consort's death the Queen writes that she has 'no one to lean on'.

OSBORNE, January 1st, 1881

ANOTHER YEAR PAST, and we begin one with heavy clouds. A poor Government, Ireland in a state of total lawlessness, and war at the Cape, of a very serious nature! I feel very anxious, and have no one to lean on.

WINDSOR CASTLE, February 28th, 1881

FINE EARLY, THEN SNOWING A LITTLE . . . Gave a dinner, in the Dining Room, in honour of William's [*Prince William of Germany, afterwards the Emperor William II*] wedding.

OSBORNE, April 19th, 1881

RECEIVED THE SAD NEWS that dear Lord Beaconsfield had passed away. I am most terribly shocked and grieved, for dear Lord Beaconsfield was one of my best, most devoted, and kindest of friends, as well as wisest of counsellors. His loss is irreparable to me and the country. To lose such a pillar of strength, at such a moment, is dreadful!

There is another attempt on the Queen's life.

WINDSOR CASTLE, March 2nd, 1882

AT 4.30 LEFT BUCKINGHAM PALACE FOR WINDSOR. Just as we were driving off from the station there, the people, or rather the Eton boys, cheered, and at the same time there was the sound of what I thought was an explosion from the engine, but in another moment I saw people rushing about and a man being violently hustled, people rushing down the street. I then realised that it was a shot, which must have been meant for me, though I was not sure, and Beatrice said nothing, the Duchess [*of Roxburghe*], who was also in the carriage, thinking it was a joke. No one gave me a sign to lead me to believe anything amiss had happened. Brown however, when he opened the carriage, said, with a greatly perturbed face, though quite calm: 'That man fired at your Majesty's carriage.' . . .

Took tea with Beatrice, and telegraphed to all my children and near relations. Brown came in to say that the revolver had been found loaded, and one chamber discharged. Superintendent Hayes, of the Police here, seized the man, who was wretchedly dressed, and had a very bad countenance. Sir H. Ponsonby [*General Sir Henry Ponsonby: Private Secretary to the Queen*] came in to tell me more. The man will be examined to-morrow. He is well spoken, and evidently an educated man. Then came Lord Bridport, who repeated the same thing, saying that the man's intentions seemed very clear. An Eton boy had rushed up, and beaten him with an umbrella. Great excitement prevails. Nothing can exceed dearest Beatrice's courage and calmness, for she saw the whole thing, the man take aim, and fire straight into the carriage, but she never said a word, observing that I was not frightened. Telegrams began arriving in numbers, in answer to mine, and one or two sent before, to enquire if the report, which spread instantly to London and all over the world, was true. Was really not shaken or frightened, so different to O'Connor's attempt in 1872, though [*this*] was infinitely more dangerous. That time I was terribly alarmed.

March 3rd

I SLEPT AS WELL AS USUAL, and never once thought of what had occurred. Telegrams, as well as letters, pouring in to that extent that I literally spent my whole day in opening and reading them. Brown brought the revolver for me to see.

Voyage de Madame la Comtesse de BALMORAL

MARCHE-ROUTE

DE

CHERBOURG A MENTON

(**Chalet des Rosiers**)

STATIONS	HEURES D'ARRIVÉE	TEMPS D'ARRÊT	HEURES DE DÉPART	STATIONS	HEURES D'ARRIVÉE	TEMPS D'ARRÊT	HEURES DE DÉPART
	H. M.	M.	H. M.		H. M.	M.	H. M.
Mercredi 15 Mars 1882.					matin	—	matin
Cherbourg	—	matin	10 »	Lyon	3 19	8	3 27
Valognes	10 47	5	10 52	Valence.	5 15	7	5 22
Montebourg.	11 2	1	11 3	Orange	6 56	5	7 1
Lison	11 52	5	11 57	Avignon.	7 30	1	7 31
Bayeux	Midi 27	5	Midi 32	Arles	8 7	4	8 11
Caen	soir 1 10	5	soir 1 15	Miramas	8 44	26	9 10
Lisieux	2 11	5	2 16	Marseille (*bifurcation*). .	9 58	5	10 3
Conches	3 30	5	3 35	Toulon	11 25	5	11 30
Mantes.	4 45	5	4 50	Les Arcs	Midi 55	25	soir 1 20
Paris { Batignolles	5 55	1	5 56	Cannes	2 33	5	2 38
Paris { Bercy	6 26	4	6 30	Nice.	3 15	8	3 23
Montereau	7 50	25	8 15	Cabbe-Roquebrune. . . .	3 59	3	4 2
Laroche.	9 23	5	9 28	**Menton**	4 9	2	4 11
Dijon	Min. 1	5	Min. 6	Chalet des Rosiers (kil. 250.100)	4 15	soir	—
Mâcon	2 3	4	2 7	*Jeudi 16 Mars 1882.*			

When Prince Charles, the present Prince of Wales, travelled as 'Charlie Chester' (he is also the Earl of Chester) he was only copying what Queen Victoria had done when she travelled to the South of France as Madame la Comtesse de Balmoral. As for being incognito, she was greeted by local mayors and the President of the Republic. Everyone knew; all pretended they did not.

OSBORNE, August 14th, 1882

AT HALF PAST I WENT DOWN TO THE DRAWING-ROOM with Beatrice, Louischen, and Helen, wearing our orders. The three ladies and the gentlemen, including Capt. Bigge, were in attendance. Lord Kimberley came in first, and then, preceded by Sir J. Cowell, Cetewayo, and the three Chiefs, Nycongcwana, Umkosana, and Ungobazana, were ushered in. Mr. Shepstone, and Mr. Dunn, as well as the native interpreter, accompanied them. Cetewayo is a very fine man, in his native costume, or rather no costume. He is tall, immensely broad, and stout, with a good-humoured countenance, and an intelligent face. Unfortunately he appeared in a hideous black frock coat and trousers, but still wearing the ring round his head, denoting that he was a married man. His companions were very black, but quite different to the ordinary negro. I said, through Mr. Shepstone, that I was glad to see him here, and that I recognised in him a great warrior, who had fought against us, but rejoiced we were now friends. He answered much the same, gesticulating a good deal as he spoke, mentioned having seen my picture, and said he was glad to see me in person.

Cetewayo, the Zulu chief who caused so much trouble with his armed rebellion against British rule in Zululand, visited England in 1882. He was presented to the Queen on August 14, at Osborne House.

King Cetewayo was restored to part of his kingdom, with various restrictions on September 1, 1882. But he constantly disagreed with the other chiefs and frequently battled against his opponents until he died of heart disease on February 8, 1884. He was succeeded by his son, Dinizulu, who, after being crowned king by the Boers, granted an amnesty and promised fidelity to the British crown. He too caused a great deal of trouble and in February, 1890 was transported to St Helena.

H.R.H. The Prince of Wales' Birthday
November, 8th, 1884.

Menu.

Soups.
Clear Mock Turtle. Artichoke.

Fish.
Boiled Turbot, Lobster and Dutch Sauce.
Fillets of Haddock, Italian Sauce.
Fried Smelts.

Dressed Dishes.
Quenelles of Chicken.
Salmis of Black Game.

Removes.
Roast Capons and Macedoine Sauce.
Saddles of Mutton.
York Hams and Spinach.
Haunches of Venison.
Presented by H.R.H. The Prince of Wales.

Game.
Wild Ducks. Partridges.

Sweets.
Dressed Tomatoes. Apple Tarts.
Noyeau Jelly.

Ice Puddings.
Banana Water Ice. Strawberry Cream.

Mclure & Macdonald Lith.rs London

A very English menu for the Prince of Wales's forty-third birthday. A feature of all the Queen's menus was the beautifully designed surround and the picture of Windsor Castle, Buckingham Palace, Osborne House or Balmoral Castle incorporated in the design. The frugal Queen often used menu cards as programmes for the various entertainments presented in her homes.

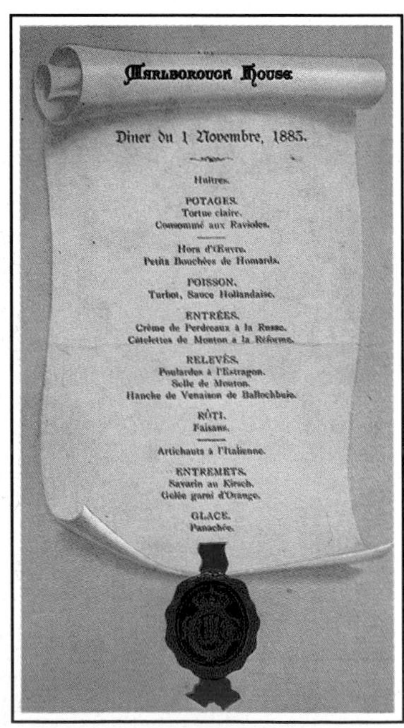

Marlborough House

Diner du 1 Novembre, 1885.

Huitres.

POTAGES.
Tortue claire.
Consommé aux Ravioles.

Hors d'Œuvre.
Petits Bouchées de Homards.

POISSON.
Turbot, Sauce Hollandaise.

ENTRÉES.
Crème de Perdreaux à la Russe.
Côtelettes de Mouton a la Réforme.

RELEVÉS.
Poulardes à l'Estragon.
Selle de Mouton.
Hanche de Venaison de Ballochbuie.

RÔTI.
Faisans.

Artichauts à l'Italienne.

ENTREMETS.
Savarin au Kirsch.
Gelée garni d'Orange.

GLACE.
Panachée.

A menu from Marlborough House showing the French influence which governed the kitchens of most large houses at the time. Marlborough House was the home of the Prince and Princess of Wales and gave its name to the Marlborough House Set, composed of friends of the Prince and Princess. The set had a reputation for high living, high spending and having a wonderful time under the leadership of the royal couple. When she became a widow, Queen Alexandra moved back into Marlborough House as did her daughter-in-law, Queen Mary, after the death of her husband, King George V. The house is now the headquarters of the Commonwealth Secretariat.

WINDSOR CASTLE, March 17th, 1883

As I was going downstairs this afternoon to go out, I missed the last steps, and came down violently on one leg, without actually falling, which caused violent pain in my knee. I could not move for a moment. Then Brown came, and helped me with great difficulty into the carriage. On coming home, however, I had to be lifted out, and supported by Brown, and Lockwood, the footman, got up to my room. Saw Dr. Reid. Tried to walk, and with great difficulty struggled in to dinner on Lenchen's arm. Afterwards went to my room and lay down on the sofa. Saw Sir Wm. Jenner and Dr. Reid, who found the knee much swollen. Getting into bed was most difficult.

The Queen is told of John Brown's death.

WINDSOR CASTLE, March 29th, 1883

Leopold came to my dressing-room, and broke the dreadful news to me that my good, faithful Brown had passed away early this morning. Am terribly upset by this loss, which removes one who was so devoted and attached to my service and who did so much for my personal comfort. It is the loss not only of a servant, but of a real friend.

OSBORNE, August 7th, 1883

After luncheon saw the great poet Tennyson, who remained nearly an hour, and most interesting it was. He is grown very old, his eyesight much impaired, and he is very shaky on his legs.

BALMORAL, November 9th, 1883

Dear Bertie's 42nd birthday. May God bless and long preserve him for the good of his country! Warm-hearted, kind, and amiable, he is always a very good son to me.

November 14th

After luncheon saw Mr. Mitford, who explained a plan of tunnelling under the Parks, from Westminster, for the underground railway, which would enable Parliament Street to be widened. I said I would only give my consent on the condition that no air-holes, or smoke, or noise, should come near the Palace, or the former be seen in the Parks.

WINDSOR CASTLE, March 28th, 1884

Another awful blow has fallen upon me and all of us to-day. My beloved Leopold, that bright, clever son, who had so many times recovered from such fearful illnesses, and from various small accidents, has been taken from us! To lose another dear child, far from me, and one who was so gifted, and such a help to me, is too dreadful!

For journeys of the Royal Family at home and abroad the art of the printer, designer and engraver were joined together to produce beautiful covers for what, after all, were only timetables.

OSBORNE, December 23rd, 1884

AFTER TEA LOUIS BATTENBERG brought his brother Liko, [*Prince Henry of Battenberg who later married her daughter, Princess Beatrice*] who has come from Berlin to spend Xmas with him and Victoria, and they three dined with us and Helen [*widow of the Queen's son, Prince Leopold, Duke of Albany, who had just died, Princess Helena lived from 1861–1922*].

OSBORNE, December 29th, 1884

RECEIVED A LETTER FROM LIKO BATTENBERG saying that my kind reception of him encouraged him to ask my consent to speaking to Beatrice, for whom, since they met in Darmstadt 8 months ago, he had felt the greatest affection! I had known for some time that she had had the same feelings towards him. They seem sincerely attached to each other, of that there can be no doubt. I let Liko know, to come up after tea, and I saw him in dear Albert's room. Then I called the dear child, and gave them my blessing. Lenchen was so delighted that all was satisfactorily settled, and poor Helen so pleased too, though it must be very trying for her.

General Charles George 'Chinese' Gordon making his last stand at Khartoum. The Queen found his Journal both 'painful and harrowing'.

WINDSOR CASTLE, July 4th, 1885

Beatrice read to me out of Gen. Gordon's most interesting Journal, which is painful and harrowing, as it shows how badly he was treated by the Government. [*General Charles George Gordon, 1833–85, went to the Sudan in 1884 to rescue English garrisons which were at the mercy of native rebels under the Mahdi, but was himself beseiged in Khartoum by the Mahdi's army. Wolseley's 'relief' expedition arrived on January 28, 1885 to find that Khartoum had been recaptured after a seige of ten months, and that General Gordon had been killed, two days earlier.*]

OSBORNE, July 23rd, 1885

Darling Beatrice's wedding day. Slept soundly, but awoke early, & could hardly realise the event that was going to take place. The day splendid, a very hot sun, but a pleasant air.—Breakfasted alone with Beatrice, under the trees. Arthur & Louischen came to speak to us, & also Liko for a few minutes, & I gave him a pin. To Beatrice, I gave a ruby half hoop ring, which my Uncle, the Duke of Sussex gave me, when I married.—Resting in my room, & Beatrice began to dress, in dearest Albert's room, in order that I might be near her. I came in, whilst her veil & wreath were being fastened on. It was *my* dear

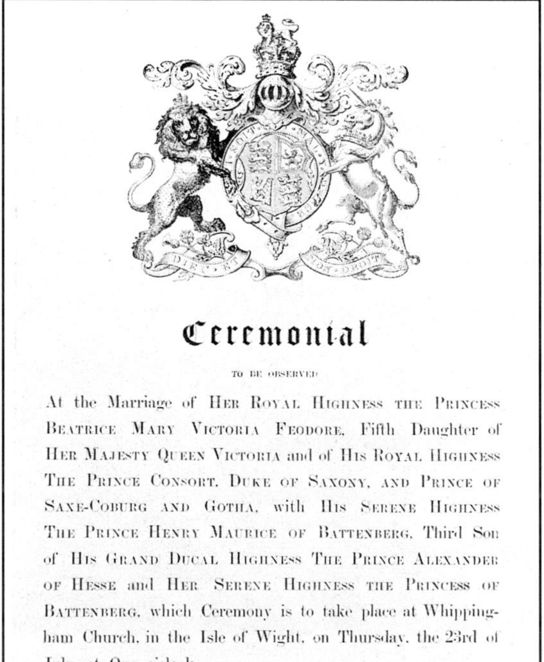

Ceremonial

TO BE OBSERVED

At the Marriage of Her Royal Highness the Princess Beatrice Mary Victoria Feodore, Fifth Daughter of Her Majesty Queen Victoria and of His Royal Highness The Prince Consort, Duke of Saxony, and Prince of Saxe-Coburg and Gotha, with His Serene Highness The Prince Henry Maurice of Battenberg, Third Son of His Grand Ducal Highness The Prince Alexander of Hesse and Her Serene Highness the Princess of Battenberg, which Ceremony is to take place at Whippingham Church, in the Isle of Wight, on Thursday, the 23rd of July, at One o'clock.

The first page of a document containing detailed instructions for the wedding of the Queen's youngest daughter and constant companion, Princess Beatrice, to Prince Henry of Battenberg (Liko) at Whippingham Church on the Isle of Wight on June 23, 1885. The Queen only permitted the marriage on the strict understanding that her daughter and prospective son-in-law would reside permanently with her. The Queen adored Liko and was devastated when he died in 1896.

wedding veil which I wore at all my Children's christenings, & the last time at dear Leopold's wedding. She wore besides, the diamond circlet with diamond stars. She was busy answering telegrams up to the last. Whilst my cap was being put on, Beatrice came in ready dressed. Her dress was quite simple, in ivory white satin, very long, trimmed with my wedding lace, & some small garlands & sprays of orange blossoms, myrtle & white heather. Her jewels were diamonds. Waited a little while downstairs, & then decided to start, driving slowly, only darling Beatrice with me, she sitting opposite to me. She did look so sweet. The 2 Equerries Sir J. McNeill and Sir H. Ewart (in uniform) rode on either side of the carriage, & Louisa Buccleuch, J. Ely, & L. Bradford, went in the carriage just before me.

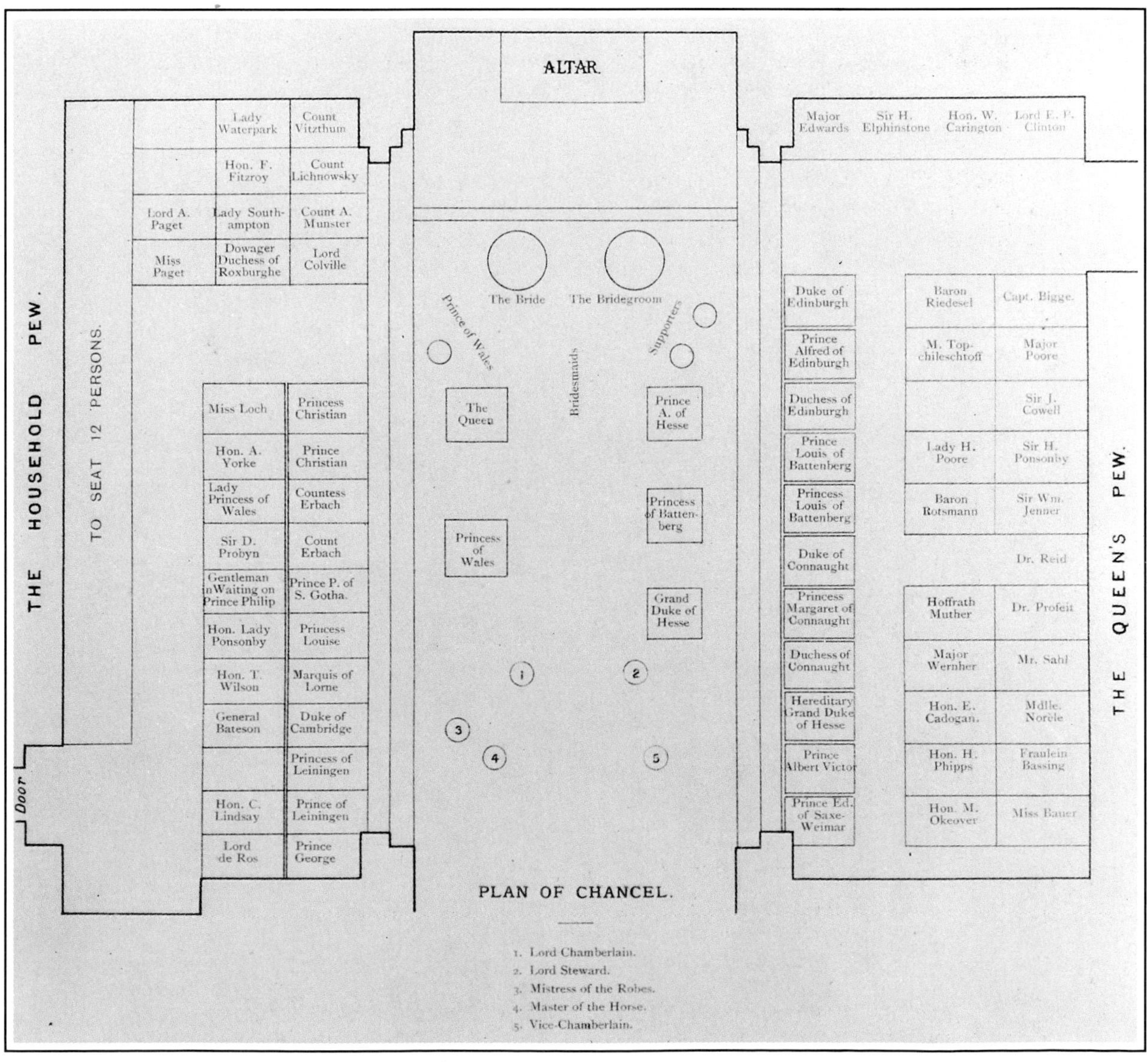

A seating plan of Whippingham Church for the wedding of Princess Beatrice and Prince Henry of Battenberg.

23RD JULY 1885

The Royal Wedding Breakfast.

THURSDAY 23RD JULY 1885.

POTAGES.

Les Quenelles au Consommé. — La Crême de Riz.

ENTRÉES CHAUDES.

Les Cotelettes d'Agneau à l'Italienne.
Les Filets de Poulets bigarrés aux Truffes.
Les Aiguilettes de Canetons aux Pois.

RELEVÉS

Les Poulardes à la Jardiniere.
Le Filet de Boeuf braisé à la Gelee.

ENTRÉES FROIDES.

Les Salades à la Parisienne.
Les Aspics de Faisans à la Belle-vue.
Les Mayonnaises de Volaille.
Les Salades de Homards

RÔTS.

Les Ortolans. Les Poulets.

RELEVÉ

Les Puddings à la Diplomate

ENTREMÊTS

Les Pois sautés au beurre.
Les Epinards au velouté. — Les Gelées Mosaique.
Les Crémes à la D' Orléans.
Les Gateaux Moka — Les Babas aux raisins.
Les Meringues à la Chantilly.
Les Gateaux Genoises au Chocolat.

Princess Beatrice on her wedding day. She wears the Queen's wedding veil held in place by a tiara of diamond stars. On her left shoulder are the insignia of the Imperial Order of the Crown of India and the Royal Order of Victoria and Albert.

Usually the Queen looked solemn when photographed. Here she is seen smiling with her daughter, Princess Beatrice, and her granddaughter, Princess Louis of Battenberg. Princess Louis of Battenberg holds her daughter, Princess Alice of Battenberg (the future Princess Andrew of Greece, mother of HRH *Prince Philip, the present Duke of Edinburgh).*

LEFT: *The beautifully designed menu for the wedding breakfast at Osborne following the marriage of Princess Beatrice and Prince Henry of Battenberg.*

BUCKINGHAM PALACE, May 4th, 1886

GOT OUT AT THE ENTRANCE TO THE EXHIBITION [*the Colonial and Indian Exhibition*] . . .

The Albert Hall was immensely full. We stood upon a large daïs under the organ, where there was an Indian chair of state, standing on an Indian carpet. The national anthem was sung, the second verse in Sanscrit, translated by Prof. Max Müller, and there was much cheering, a cheer for the 'Union' being called for, which was warmly responded to. Then followed an Ode for the occasion, with beautiful words by Tennyson, the music by Sullivan, the solo being sung by Albani. Bertie read a very long Address, to which I read an Answer. Dear Bertie, who was most kind throughout, then kissed my hand. What thoughts of my darling husband came into mind . . . I curtsied on all occasions when they cheered, which they did tremendously, and proceeded straight up the Hall, going up some steps to the level of the boxes. Here I turned round and curtsied again, before leaving.

We drove to Buckingham Palace, as we had driven from the station, and got there at 1.30. The crowds enormous and most good-humoured and enthusiastic; the heat both inside and out very great. I felt very tired, but much gratified and pleased that all had gone off so well.

BALMORAL, June 20th, 1886

HAVE ENTERED THE 50TH YEAR OF MY REIGN and my Jubilee year ... All my ladies and gentlemen sent me a beautiful large basket of flowers, which touched me very much. Of course the real celebration is only to be next year, when the fifty years are completed. Quantities of people have telegraphed to me.

WINDSOR, July 18th, 1886

WENT TO SEE MY POOR EXCELLENT FOOTMAN LOCKWOOD, who has been ill since the winter and is gradually wasting away. His emaciation is fearful to see. He used to carry me for more than three months, and was a devoted faithful servant. It made me very sad to see him like this.

AIX-LES-BAINS, April 23rd, 1887

THIS WAS THE DAY for our long-planned and wished-for expedition to the Grande Chartreuse. It was a splendid day. The scenery of the Gorge frequently reminded me of the St. Gothard, and is very grand. We passed the distillery of the celebrated and excellent liqueur, called Chartreuse, made by the monks, who alone possess the secret. It is made of herbs and flowers gathered by them in the country round.

BUCKINGHAM PALACE, May 9th, 1887

WENT TO THE THRONE ROOM (wearing my orders), where the Court were assembled, and stood on the steps of the Throne. The Lord Mayor, with about 100 of the Corporation, marched slowly up, and an Address was read by the Recorder, to which I read my Answer ...

May 10th

AFTER LUNCHEON HELD A DRAWING-ROOM, to which besides Beatrice, Alix, Victoria, Lenchen, and her Victoria [*Lenchen's daughter, Princess Helena Victoria of Schleswig-Holstein*] (for the first time in white), Bertie, George C., Christian, and Liko came. It was an interminable Drawing-room. I stayed over an hour and then Alix took my place. I sat down several times, but stood better and was less tired. The Duchess of Athole presented her third daughter, also pretty, and a pretty niece, Miss Violet Mordaunt, who is mad. Lady Blandford came by, I having allowed poor divorced ladies, who have had to divorce their husbands owing to cruelty, desertion, and misbehaviour, but are in no way to blame themselves, to appear at Court.

IN THE TRAIN, June 16th, 1887

VERY HOT INDEED.—Breakfasting out, & remained sitting at the Cottage some little time. Such quantities of letters & telegrams.—At 2, left dear Balmoral, rather dreading

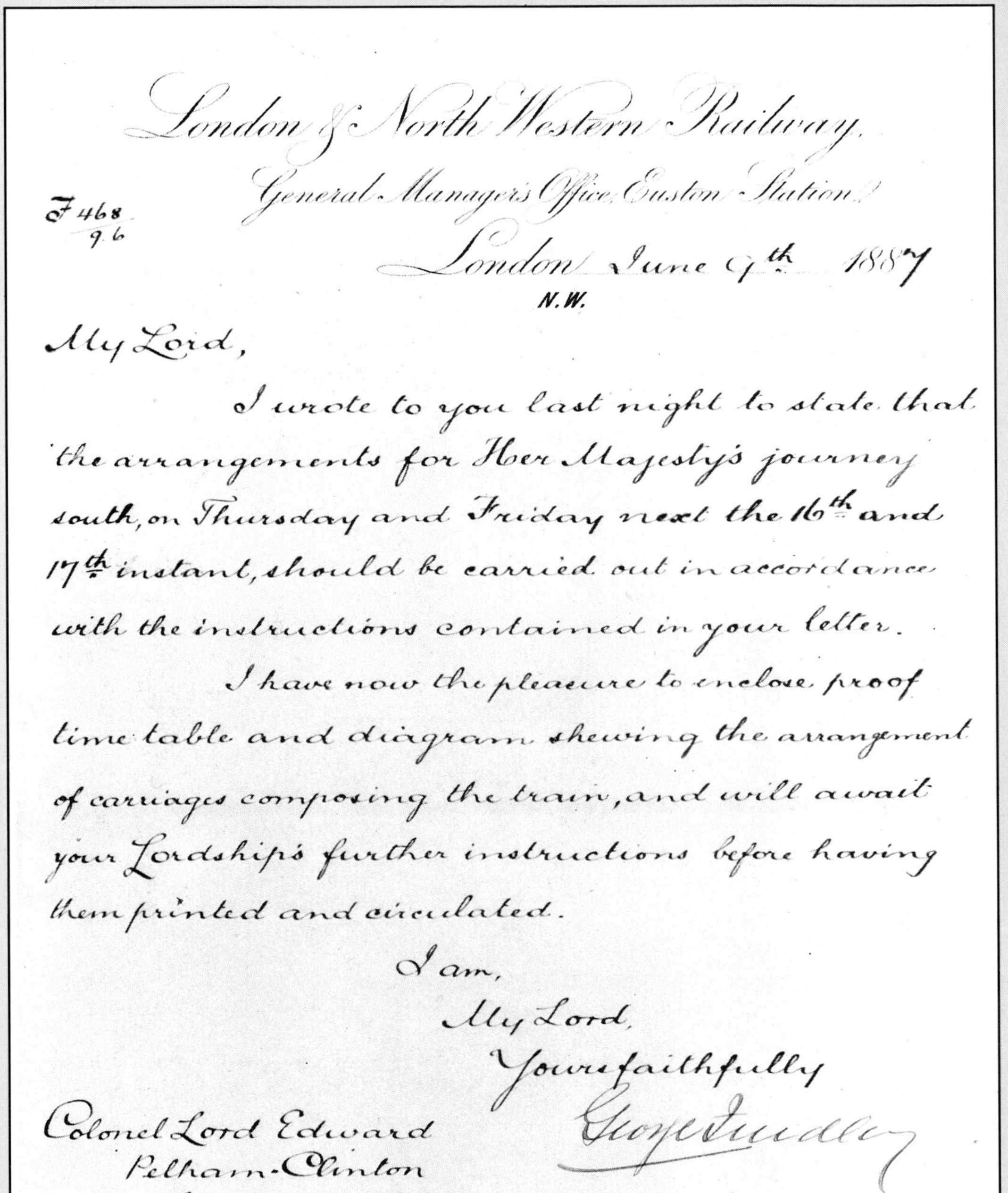

London & North Western Railway.

General Manager's Office, Euston Station,

F 468/96

London June 9th 1887

N.W.

My Lord,

I wrote to you last night to state that the arrangements for Her Majesty's journey south, on Thursday and Friday next the 16th and 17th instant, should be carried out in accordance with the instructions contained in your letter.

I have now the pleasure to enclose proof time table and diagram shewing the arrangement of carriages composing the train, and will await your Lordship's further instructions before having them printed and circulated.

I am,
My Lord,
Yours faithfully
George Findlay

Colonel Lord Edward
Pelham-Clinton
Balmoral Castle

When he was a Groom-in-Waiting, Lord Edward, among other duties, helped to arrange the Queen's railway journeys. This letter from the General Manager of the London and North Western Railway Company refers to her journey from Ballater to Windsor on June 16 and 17, 1887.

all the great fatigue before me. At the station at Ballater, all the schoolchildren were drawn up, holding little flags & nosegays. The heat was awful in the train. We did not get out at Perth, & had our dinner in the train. It got a little cooler later.—

WINDSOR CASTLE, June 17th, 1887

A VERY HOT, UNPLEASANT NIGHT, & quite a haze of heat, when we reached Windsor. Dear Arthur & Louischen were at the station. Such a pleasure to see them again. They drove up to the Castle with me. Many people out & preparations going on, even the statue all wrapped, was already in its place. We all breakfasted together, & then I took leave with much regret, of dear amiable Lily.—Endless boxes & letters awaiting me.—Resting & writing.—Arthur & Louischen have brought back an Indian boy of 10 years old, an orphan, & a Christian, who waited at lunch. He is very quick & attentive & a pretty boy.—Saw Ld. Cranbrook for a moment, & then, had to hold a Council.—Lenchen came to tea, which we took all together at Frogmore, under the well known big ever green oaks. Sat there for some time, talking over all the arrangements, & then we drove by the Rhododendron Drive, which was still out in great beauty.—Just ourselves to dinner.—

ABOVE: *An invitation to the Colonial and Indian Reception and Ball at the Guildhall, London. Representatives of the colonies and of the Indian sub-continent were in London for the Colonial and Indian Exhibition at the Royal Albert Hall.*

RIGHT AND OVERLEAF: *Part of the detailed time-table of the journey showing when the train passed through various stations or where it stopped for refreshments or for the servants and Household to use the lavatory. For some years, only the Queen had a lavatory and the servants and courtiers had literally to go behind bushes. As the design of the trains became more advanced and as old rolling stock was replaced by new, additional lavatories were added. The various railway companies went to great lengths to ensure the safety of the train during its 'progress' through Britain. Inspectors and engineers checked the track; all the engines and rolling stock were inspected and railway officials were instructed to use only 'steady', experienced drivers (ie, not drunkards).*

TIME TABLE

FOR

REGULATING THE PROGRESS OF THE TRAIN

TO CONVEY

HER MAJESTY

FROM

BALLATER TO WINDSOR,

VIA ABERDEEN, CARLISLE, AND BUSHBURY JUNCTION.

On THURSDAY, the 16th,

AND

FRIDAY, the 17th JUNE, 1887.

McCORQUODALE & Co., LIMITED, CARDINGTON STREET, LONDON, N.W.

BALLATER TO WINDSOR—*Continued.*

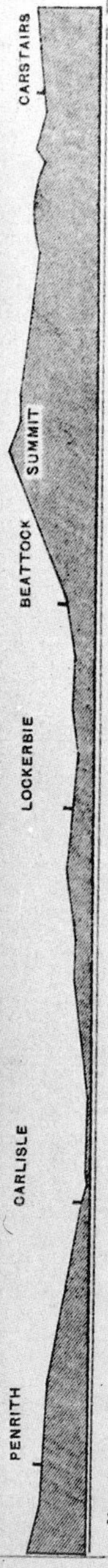

Gradient.	Distance from Ballater.	Name of Station.	Time Table.	Actual Time.
	Miles.	*[16th June, 1887.]*	P.M.	P.M.
	208½	Cleghorn ... ... pass	9 23	
CARSTAIRS	211¼	Carstairs ... ... „		
	216½	Thankerton ... ... „	9 35	
	218	Symington Junction „	9 37	
	221½	Lamington ... ... „	9 43	
	226¾	Abington ... ... „	9 51	
	232	Elvanfoot ... ... „	10 0	
SUMMIT	235	**Beattock Summit** arr.	**10 5**	
		„ dep.	**10 10**	
	239½	Greskine ... ... pass	10 17	
BEATTOCK	245	Beattock ... ... „	10 25	
	250¼	Wamphray ... ... „	10 32	
	253	Dinwoodie ... ... „	10 37	
	256	Nethercleugh ... „	10 41	
LOCKERBIE	259½	Lockerbie ... ... „	10 45	
	262¼	Castlemilk ... ... „	10 50	
	264½	Ecclefechan ... ... „	10 54	
	268	Kirtlebridge ... „	10 59	
	271¾	Kirkpatrick ... ... „	11 5	
	276¼	Gretna ... ... „	11 11	
	278½	Floriston ... ... „	11 15	
	280¾	Rockcliffe ... ... „	11 18	
CARLISLE	284¾	**Carlisle** ... ... arr.	**11 25**	
		(*Refreshments*—20 mins.)		
		Carlisle ... ... dep.	**11 45**	
	289¾	Wreay ... ... pass	11 54	
	292	Southwaite ... ... „	11 58	
		[17th June, 1887.]	A.M.	
	295½	Calthwaite ... ... „	12 4	
	297¾	Plumpton ... ... „	12 8	
PENRITH	302¾	Penrith... ... ... „	12 15	
	303¾	Eamont Junction „	12 17	

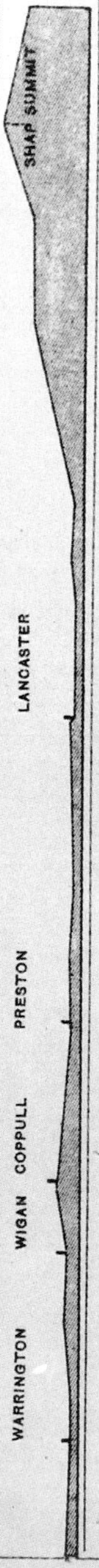

Gradient.	Distance from Ballater.	Name of Station.	Time Table.	Actual Time.
	Miles.	*[17th June, 1887.]*	A.M.	A.M.
	307	Clifton & Lowther pass	12 22	
	314¼	Shap ... ... „	12 35	
SHAP SUMMIT	316¼	Shap Summit ... „	12 39	
	321¾	Tebay ... ... „	12 49	
	326	Low Gill ... ... „	12 56	
	327½	Grayrigg ... ... „	12 59	
	335	**Oxenholme** ... arr.	**1 11**	
		„ . dep.	**1 18**	
	340½	Milnthorpe ... ... pass	1 26	
	343	Burton and Holme „	1 30	
	347¾	Carnforth ... ... „	1 36	
	349½	Bolton-le-Sands ... „	1 39	
	351	Hest Bank ... ... „	1 41	
LANCASTER	354	Lancaster ... ... „	1 45	
	358¼	Galgate... ... ... „	1 51	
	362¼	Scorton... ... ... „	1 57	
	365½	Garstang & Catteral „	2 2	
	367½	Brock ... ... „	2 5	
	370	Barton & Broughton „	2 9	
PRESTON	374¾	Preston... ... ... „	2 17	
	377¼	Farington ... ... „	2 21	
	378¾	Leyland ... ... „	2 24	
COPPULL	384¼	Coppull ... ... „	2 33	
WIGAN	390	**Wigan** ... ... arr.	**2 43**	
		„ ... ... dep.	**2 50**	
	391¼	Springs Branch Jun. pass	2 52	
	396	Golborne Junction „	3 0	
	398¼	Winwick Junction „	3 4	
WARRINGTON	401¾	Warrington... ... „	3 9	
	407¼	Preston Brook ... „	3 19	
	409¾	Weaver Junction „	3 24	

BALLATER TO WINDSOR.

Gradient.	Distance from Ballater.	Name of Station.	Time Table.	Actual Time.
	Miles.	[*16th June, 1887.*]	P.M.	P.M.
BALLATER	...	**Ballater ... ...dep.**	**2 50**	
	4	Cambus O'May ... pass	2 58	
ABOYNE	6½	Dinnet ... ... ,,	3 3	
	11	Aboyne... ... ... ,,	3 15	
	14	Dess ... ... ,,	3 22	
	16½	Lumphanan ... ... ,,	3 28	
	19½	Torphins ... ... ,,	3 35	
	22	Glassel ... ... ,,	3 39	
BANCHORY	26½	Banchory ... ... ,,	3 49	
	32½	Park ... ... ,,	4 1	
	35¾	Culter ... ... ,,	4 7	
	38	Murtle ... ... ,,	4 11	
	39½	Cults ... ... ,,	4 14	
ABERDEEN	43½	**Aberdeen ... ... arr.**	**4 22**	
		,, ...dep.	**4 27**	
	48¼	Cove ... ...pass	4 36	
	52	Portlethen ... ... ,,	4 42	
	54	Newtonhill ... ... ,,	4 46	
	55¼	Muchalls ... ... ,,	4 48	
STONEHAVEN	60	Stonehaven ... ... ,,	4 56	
	65¼	Newmill ... ... ,,	5 6	
	67	Drumlithie ... ... ,,	5 9	
	71	Fordoun ... ... ,,	5 15	
	74¼	Laurencekirk ... ,,	5 20	
	77½	Marykirk ... ... ,,	5 26	
	79½	Craigo ... ... ,,	5 29	
	81	Kinnaber Junc. ... ,,	5 32	
DUBTON JUNC.	83	Dubton Junc. ... ,,	5 34	
	85½	**Bridge of Dun arr.**	**5 39**	
		,, dep.	**5 44**	
	88¾	Farnell Road ... pass	5 50	
	92	Glasterlaw ... ... ,,	5 56	
	94	Guthrie... ... ... ,,	5 59	
	98¾	Clocksbriggs ... ,,	6 6	
FORFAR	101	Forfar ... ... ,,	6 10	

Gradient.	Distance from Ballater.	Name of Station.	Time Table.	Actual Time.
	Miles.	[*16th June, 1887.*]	P.M.	P.M.
	104	Kirriemuir Junc... pass	6 15	
	106¾	Glamis ... ... ,,	6 19	
	109	Eassie ... ... ,,	6 22	
	113	Alyth Junction ... ,,	6 28	
	115¼	Ardler ... ... ,,	6 31	
COUPAR ANGUS	117¾	Coupar-Angus ... ,,	6 34	
	120	Woodside ... ... ,,	6 38	
	126¼	Stanley... ... ... ,,	6 47	
	128¼	Strathord ... ... ,,	6 51	
	129½	Luncarty ... ... ,,	6 53	
	131¾	Almond Valley Jn. ,,	6 57	
PERTH	133½	**Perth ... ... arr.**	**7 2**	
		,, ...dep.	**7 12**	
	135½	Hilton Junction ... pass	7 18	
	137½	Forgandenny ... ,,	7 21	
	140½	Forteviot ... ... ,,	7 25	
	147¼	Auchterarder ... ,,	7 38	
CRIEFF JUNC.	149½	Crieff Junction ... ,,	7 42	
	151¾	Blackford ... ... ,,	7 46	
	155¾	Greenloaning ... ,,	7 52	
	158¾	Kinbuck ... ... ,,	7 57	
	161½	Dunblane ... ... ,,	8 1	
	163½	Bridge of Allan ... ,,	8 4	
STIRLING	166½	Stirling... ... ... ,,	8 9	
	168½	Bannockburn ... ,,	8 12	
	172½	Alloa Junction ... ,,	8 18	
	174½	**Larbert Station arr.**	**8 22**	
		,, dep.	**8 27**	
GREENHILL	178	Greenhill ... ... pass	8 34	
	183¼	Cumbernauld ... ,,	8 42	
	187½	Glenboig ... ... ,,	8 48	
	188	Garnqueen Junc... ,,	8 49	
	188¾	Gartsherrie... ... ,,	8 50	
	190	Coatbridge ... ... ,,	8 52	
	195½	Motherwell ... ... ,,	9 2	
	197	Wishaw ... ... ,,	9 5	
	200	Garriongill ... ... ,,	9 10	
LAW JUNC.	200¾	Law Junction ... ,,	9 11	
	204	Braidwood ... ... ,,	9 16	

VERTICAL SCALE 2000 FEET TO AN INCH. 1000 500 0 1000 2000 Feet

HORIZONTAL SCALE 12 MILES TO AN INCH. 0 3 6 9 12 15 18 21 24 Miles

COPY.] [No. 25711.

THE LONDON GAZETTE.

War Office, June 18, 1887.

By The QUEEN.

A PROCLAMATION

FOR EXTENDING PARDONS TO SOLDIERS WHO MAY HAVE DESERTED FROM OUR LAND FORCES.

VICTORIA, R.

WHEREAS We are desirous to mark the completion of the fiftieth year of Our reign by extending Our Pardon to soldiers who may have deserted from Our Land Forces previously to the issuing of this Our Royal Proclamation, We have thought fit, by and with the advice of our Privy Council, to publish this Our Royal Proclamation, and do hereby accordingly grant Our Most Gracious pardon to all men who having, before the date of this Proclamation, deserted or absented themselves without leave from Our Regular Forces, Militia, or Reserve Forces, or having fraudulently enlisted within the meaning of Section 13 of the Army Act, or having while in the Army Reserve irregularly enlisted in Our Regular Forces or Militia, shall report themselves within two months from the date of this Proclamation, if residing in the United Kingdom, the Channel Islands, or the Isle of Man, or within four months therefrom, if residing elsewhere; and We do hereby declare that such men shall, on so reporting themselves, be released and discharged from all prosecutions, imprisonments, and penalties, other than loss of service, pay, deferred pay, or pension, commenced or incurred by reason of such offences; and We do further declare that all such men who enlisted before the 21st June, 1877, or who have been in a state of desertion or absence without leave for a period exceeding five years, or who may be physically unfit for military service, will not be called upon to rejoin for service, but will be granted protecting certificates on their so reporting themselves.

The men to whom this Our Proclamation applies are not to report themselves in person, but are to do so by letter, giving full particulars by which they can be identified. and if they are suffering from physical disability rendering them unable to rejoin the Service, they are to state the same clearly.

If they belonged to—	They should write to—
The Cavalry now serving at Home ..	To the Officer Commanding the Regiment.
The Cavalry now serving Abroad	To the Officer Commanding Cavalry Depot, Canterbury.
The Royal Artillery	To the Deputy Adjutant General, Royal Artillery, Record Office, Woolwich.
The Royal Engineers	To the Officer in charge of Royal Engineer Records, Chatham.
The Foot Guards	To the Officer commanding Regiment, Whitehall, London.
The Infantry of Line	To the Officer Commanding Regimental District.
The Royal Malta Fencible Artillery ..	To the Officer Commanding the Corps.

A 2

WINDSOR CASTLE, June 19th 1887

A RATHER DISTURBED NIGHT, which is not unnatural, owing to all the excitement & fatigue.—We breakfasted together at Frogmore under the trees, & then went to service in the Mausoleum, performed by the Dean, who preached a very fine sermon.—Dear lovely Ella & Serge, [*Princess Alice's daughter Elizabeth and Grand Duke Serge of Russia*] who arrived at Clarence House a few days ago, came to luncheon, also Affie & Marie.—Saw Ld. Salisbury afterwards. He said the state of excitement & preparation in London was quite marvellous, the only anxiety one felt, was about the enormous number of people, half a million being expected to come into London. Talked of the troubles in Parliament, but of the success of the Govt. Ld. Salisbury heard that Mr. Chamberlain & Ld R. Churchill, wished to rejoin the Govt., but we agreed that the latter, must on no account do so. Mr. Goschen was very staunch & very conservative & Ld. Hartington very loyal & true.—Took tea at Frogmore, & a short drive afterwards.—

GOLDEN JUBILEE
BUCKINGHAM PALACE, June 20th, 1887

THE DAY HAS COME, & I AM ALONE, though surrounded by many dear Children. I am writing after a very fatiguing day, in the Garden at Buckingham Palace, where I used to sit so often in former happy days. 50 years today since I came to the throne. God has mercifully sustained me through many great trials & sorrows.

WINDSOR CASTLE, June 23rd, 1887

AT ½ P. 5, DROVE WITH BEATRICE, Irène & Alicky, [*the Queen's grand-daughters*] little Daisy between them, down through the town, still quite 'en fête', past the S. Western station, & there, all along the road to Datchet were drawn up detachments of Volunteer Fire Brigades, from all over England, Scotland & Wales, all in different uniforms. After having driven down their line, we turned up the avenue in the Home Park, where, on the grass, 6000 children of the neighbourhood, had been regaled with tea, under a big tent, & games had been provided for them. They were all drawn up in line, cheering vociferously. Then drove on to Frogmore to tea. Beatrice left us, to go & receive the 'Fürstlichkeiten,' who were coming.—The King of Saxony, Carlos & Amélie of Portugal, William & Dona [*her grandson William, who in the following year was to become the Kaiser William II, and his wife Dona—Princess Augusta of Schleswig-Holstein*], with their little boy, Henry of Prussia, & the Duc d'Aosta arrived. They, & our party in the house, Lenchen & Christian, Ct. & Cts. San Miguel (with Carlos & Amélie) Cts. Brockdorff (Dona's mistress of the Robes) Gen: von Carlowitz (with the King of Saxony) Gen: von Hahuke (with William) Cavaliere Balbo

LEFT: *One of the results of the Golden Jubilee was this proclamation in the* London Gazette *which pardoned deserters from the army.*

FOLLOWING PAGES: *Seating plans for the Golden Jubilee service held in Westminster Abbey on June 21, 1887.*

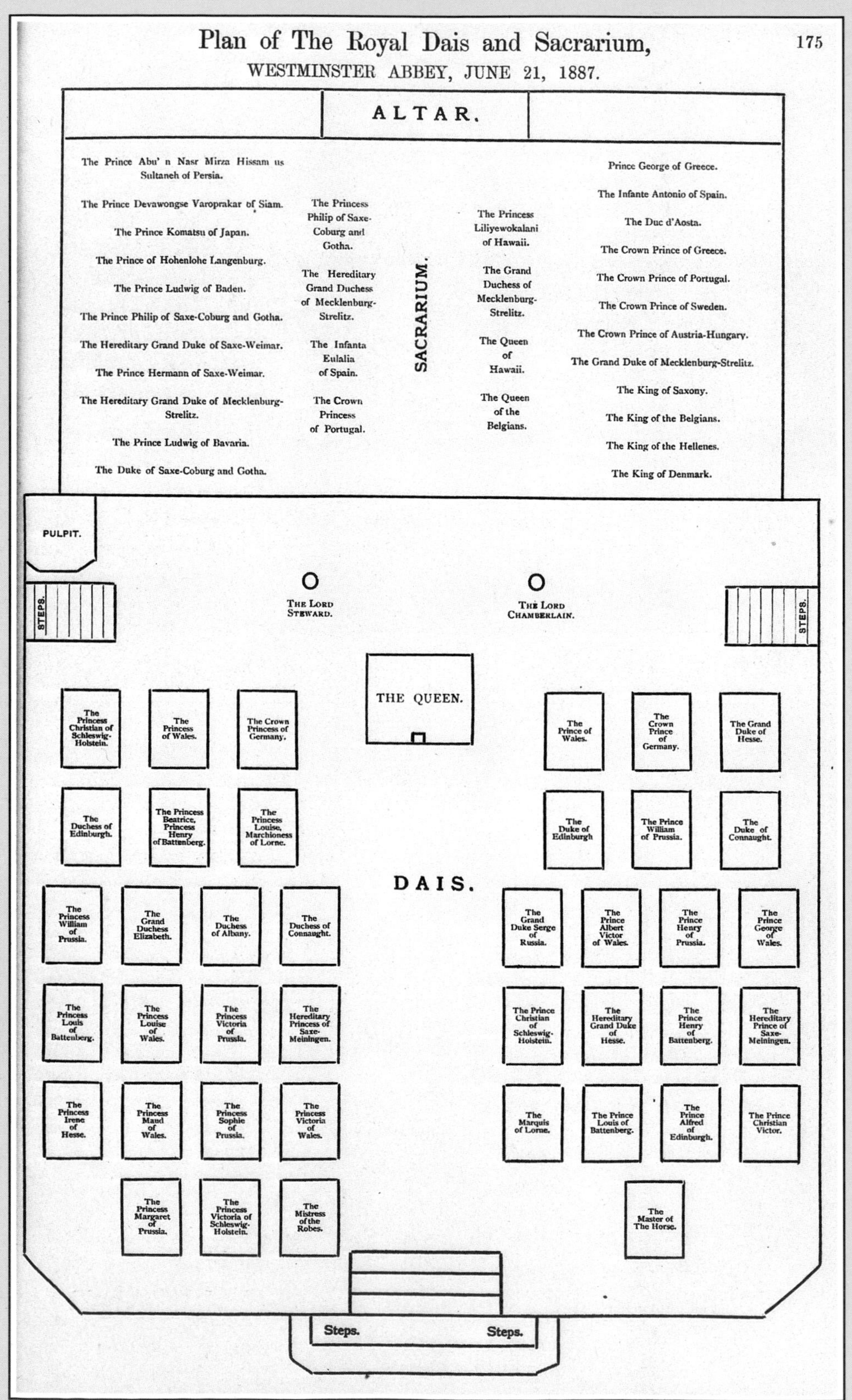

Plan of The Royal Dais and Sacrarium,
175
WESTMINSTER ABBEY, JUNE 21, 1887.
ALTAR.
The Prince Abu' n Nasr Mirza Hissam us Sultaneh of Persia.
The Prince Devawongse Varoprakar of Siam.
The Prince Komatsu of Japan.
The Prince of Hohenlohe Langenburg.
The Prince Ludwig of Baden.
The Prince Philip of Saxe-Coburg and Gotha.
The Hereditary Grand Duke of Saxe-Weimar.
The Prince Hermann of Saxe-Weimar.
The Hereditary Grand Duke of Mecklenburg-Strelitz.
The Prince Ludwig of Bavaria.
The Duke of Saxe-Coburg and Gotha.
The Princess Philip of Saxe-Coburg and Gotha.
The Hereditary Grand Duchess of Mecklenburg-Strelitz.
The Infanta Eulalia of Spain.
The Crown Princess of Portugal.
SACRARIUM.
The Princess Liliyewokalani of Hawaii.
The Grand Duchess of Mecklenburg-Strelitz.
The Queen of Hawaii.
The Queen of the Belgians.
Prince George of Greece.
The Infante Antonio of Spain.
The Duc d'Aosta.
The Crown Prince of Greece.
The Crown Prince of Portugal.
The Crown Prince of Sweden.
The Crown Prince of Austria-Hungary.
The Grand Duke of Mecklenburg-Strelitz.
The King of Saxony.
The King of the Belgians.
The King of the Hellenes.
The King of Denmark.
PULPIT.
STEPS.
The Lord Steward.
The Lord Chamberlain.
STEPS.
THE QUEEN.
The Princess Christian of Schleswig-Holstein.
The Princess of Wales.
The Crown Princess of Germany.
The Prince of Wales.
The Crown Prince of Germany.
The Grand Duke of Hesse.
The Duchess of Edinburgh.
The Princess Beatrice, Princess Henry of Battenberg.
The Princess Louise, Marchioness of Lorne.
The Duke of Edinburgh.
The Prince William of Prussia.
The Duke of Connaught.
DAIS.
The Princess William of Prussia.
The Grand Duchess Elizabeth.
The Duchess of Albany.
The Duchess of Connaught.
The Grand Duke Serge of Russia.
The Prince Albert Victor of Wales.
The Prince Henry of Prussia.
The Prince George of Wales.
The Princess Louis of Battenberg.
The Princess Louise of Wales.
The Princess Victoria of Prussia.
The Hereditary Princess of Saxe-Meiningen.
The Prince Christian of Schleswig-Holstein.
The Hereditary Grand Duke of Hesse.
The Prince Henry of Battenberg.
The Hereditary Prince of Saxe-Meiningen.
The Princess Irene of Hesse.
The Princess Maud of Wales.
The Princess Sophie of Prussia.
The Princess Victoria of Wales.
The Marquis of Lorne.
The Prince Louis of Battenberg.
The Prince Alfred of Edinburgh.
The Prince Christian Victor.
The Princess Margaret of Prussia.
The Princess Victoria of Schleswig-Holstein.
The Mistress of the Robes.
The Master of The Horse.
Steps.
Steps.

HER MAJESTY'S JUBILEE THANKSGIVING SERVICE,

WESTMINSTER ABBEY, 21ST JUNE, 1887.

PLAN OF THE CHOIR.

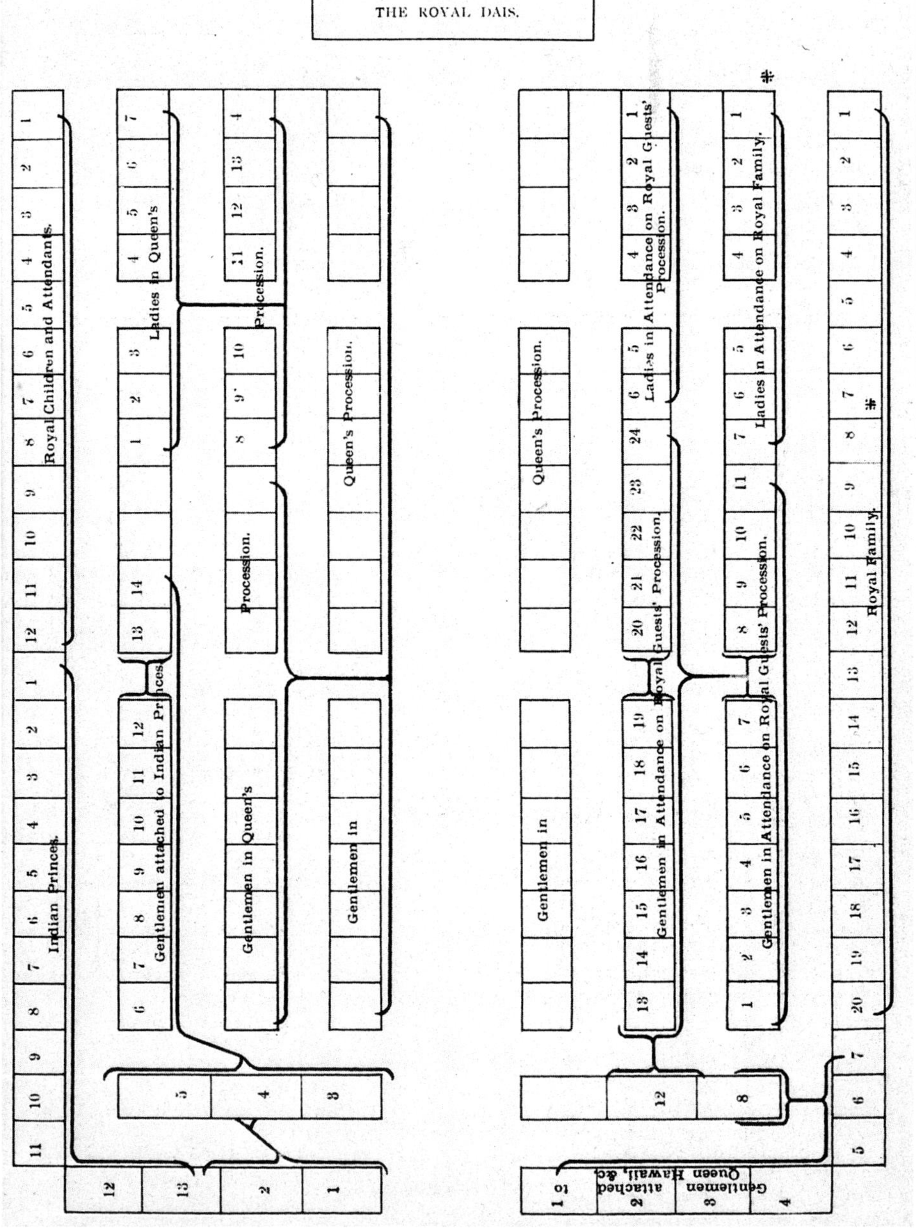

JUBILEE CEREMONY.

Westminster Abbey, 21st June, 1887.

DISTRIBUTION OF SEATS BY PLAN.

Entrance.	Position.	To whom allotted.
PLAN 1.		
North Door	North Transept	House of Commons.
Poets Corner Door	South Transept	House of Lords.
Poets Corner Door	South Transept, Diplomatic Gallery	
S.E. Cloister Door .. .. (Dean's Yard)	South Transept, Reserved Gallery	Lord Lieutenants.
S.E. Cloister Door .. .. (Dean's Yard)	Nave South, Mezzanine	High Sheriffs. Lord Mayor and Corporation of London and City Companies. Lord Provost and Baillies of Edinburgh. Mayors, Provosts. Chambers of Commerce and Agriculture. Metropolitan Board of Works. Representatives of Army, Navy, Reserve Forces, Civil Service, and other Bodies. Burgesses of Westminster.
S.W. Cloister Door	Nave South	
North Clock Tower Door .. (window entrance)	Nave North, Mezzanine	
North Nave Door	Nave North, Mezzanine	
	Nave North	
Deanery Entrance	.. ..	Officiating Clergy.
West Entrance	.. ..	Royal Personages and Processions.
PLAN 2.		
North Door	Transept Gallery, North	House of Commons. Church of Scotland. Various Non-Conformist Bodies.
North East New Door ..	Sacrarium Gallery, North	Dean, for Houses of Convocation and other Church Bodies, and Clergy.
Poets Corner .. .. .. (window entrance)	Sacrarium Gallery, East	Ditto. Ditto.
Poets Corner .. .. .. (window entrance)	Queen's Gallery, South Sacrarium	

Entrance.	Position.	To whom allotted.
PLAN 2—*continued.*		
POETS CORNER .. .. .. (window entrance)	Diplomatic Gallery, Upper	
SOUTH DOOR, ST. FAITH'S CHAPEL (Dean's Yard)	Transept Gallery, South	Law. Peeresses.
SOUTH TRIFORIUM DOOR .. (Dean's Yard, spiral staircase)	Transept South, Household Gallery	Her Majesty's Household.
S.E. CLOISTER DOOR	South Choir Gallery ..	India.
S.E. CLOISTER DOOR	Chorus, South Gallery ..	Singers.
S.E. CLOISTER DOOR	Chorus, North Gallery ..	Do.
S.W. CLOISTER .. .. .. (window entrance)	Nave Gallery, South ..	Army, Navy and Civil Service, &c.
NORTH CLOCK TOWER DOOR .. (window entrance)	West Gallery	General Public.
NORTH WINDOW ENTRANCE ..	Nave Gallery, North ..	Army, Navy and Civil Service, &c.
NORTH SIDE DOOR	North Choir Gallery ..	Foreign Suites. Colonies.
NORTH SIDE DOOR	Press Gallery	Press.
PLAN 3.		
NORTH DOOR	North Transept, Upper Gallery	House of Commons.
NORTH-EAST NEW DOOR ..	Sacrarium, Upper Gallery B	Dean, for Houses of Convocation and other Church Bodies, and Clergy.
POETS CORNER DOOR	Sacrarium, Upper Gallery A	Ditto. Ditto.
SOUTH DOOR, ST. FAITH'S CHAPEL (Dean's Yard)	South Transept, Upper Gallery	Learned and other Societies and General Public.
NORTH CLOCK TOWER DOOR .. (window entrance)	West Gallery, Middle ..	General Public.
PLAN 4.		
NORTH SIDE DOOR	Triforium, North	General Public and various Representative Bodies.
NORTH-EAST NEW DOOR .. (spiral staircase)	Triforium, North-east	
POETS CORNER DOOR .. .. (spiral staircase)	Triforium, South-east	
SOUTH TRIFORIUM DOOR .. (Dean's Yard)	Triforium, South	
NORTH CLOCK TOWER DOOR .. (window entrance)	West Upper Gallery ..	Trades, Working Men, &c.

Harrison and Sons, Printers in Ordinary to Her Majesty, St. Martin's Lane.

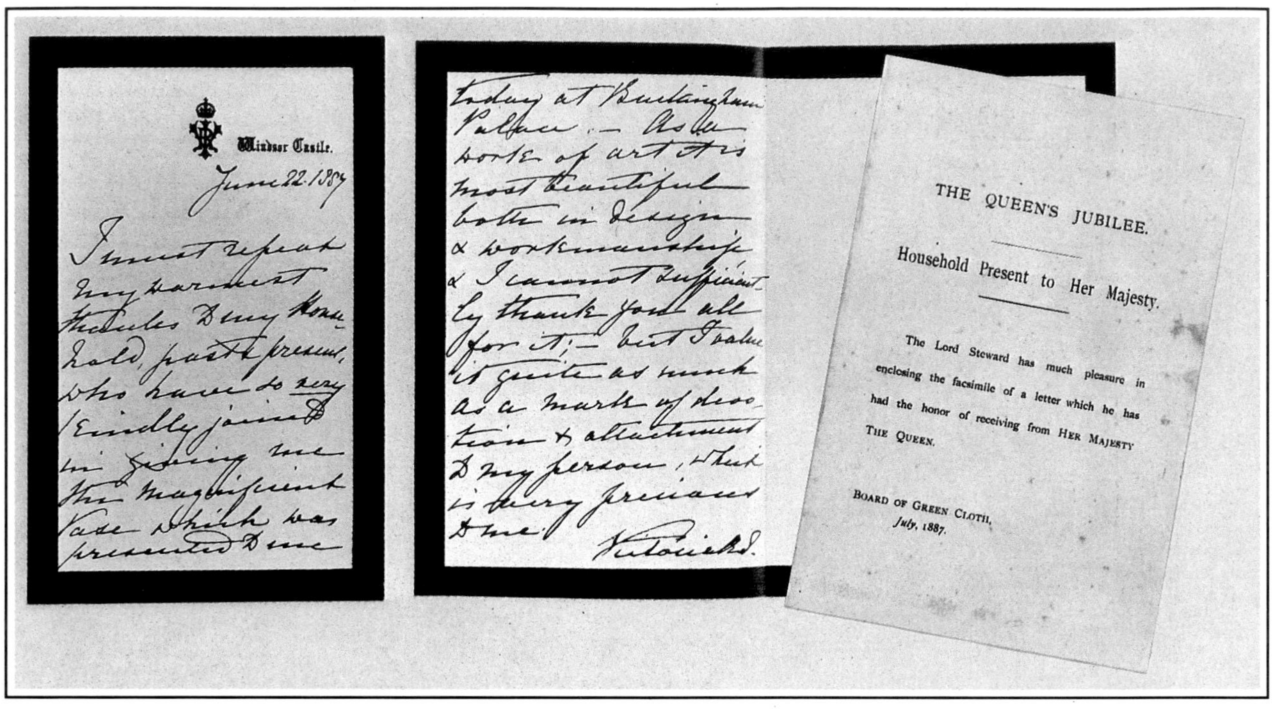
Windsor Castle.
June 22. 1887

I must repeat my warmest thanks to my Household, past & present, who have so very kindly joined in giving me the magnificent Vase which was presented to me today at Buckingham Palace. — As a work of art it is most beautiful both in design & workmanship & I cannot sufficiently thank you all for it; — but I value it quite as much as a mark of devotion & attachment to my person, which is very precious to me.

Victoria R.I.

THE QUEEN'S JUBILEE.

Household Present to Her Majesty.

The Lord Steward has much pleasure in enclosing the facsimile of a letter which he has had the honor of receiving from HER MAJESTY THE QUEEN.

BOARD OF GREEN CLOTH,
July, 1887.

ABOVE: *A letter in Queen Victoria's handwriting, dated June 22, 1887, to her Household, thanking them for the Golden Jubilee present to which they had all subscribed. A facsimile of the letter was presented to members of her Household.*

RIGHT: *A dinner menu for June 23, 1887, during the week the Golden Jubilee was celebrated, showing the splendid choice of food set before the Queen and her guests.*

(with the Duc d'Aosta), the Dss. of Roxburghe, J. Ely, & Ld. Bridport dined. The Band of the Grenadiers played on the terrace outside the window of the Dining Room. The good, amiable King of Saxony was delighted with everything. I sat between him & Carlos. Directly after dinner, we went into the corridor to see a torch light procession of the fire brigade, & other people of Windsor who came with Bands. They were very loyal & cheered very much, but the torches burnt down so quickly, that they had to throw them away. I then, went to my room, being very tired & anxious to get a little rest. The others went to the Drawingroom.—

WINDSOR CASTLE, June 25th, 1887

BREAKFASTING AT FROGMORE with Alicky, and Louise Schleswig Holstein joined us there. Went to the Mausoleum.—Resting, and writing.—Beatrice and Liko returned just before luncheon, with Ella and Serge, who lunched with us. Louis, Irène, and Ernie were to return later.—Afterwards I received a Deputation from the Charterhouse Boys, including Albert of Schleswig Holstein, who presented me with a very handsome silver vase, or Sazza, which I thought very nice of them.—To Frogmore for tea with Ella and

DIEU ET MON DROIT

WINDSOR.

HER MAJESTY'S DINNER,

Thursday, 23rd June, 1887.

Potages.

A la Chiffonade. Au Lièvre à l'Anglaise.

Poissons.

Les Truites bouillies. Les Filets de Merlans frits.

Entrees.

Les Croquettes à la Milanaise.
Les Côtelettes d'Agneau aux Concombres.
Les Pigeons braisés aux Pois.

Releves.

Les Dindoneaux à la Perigueux.
Les Longes de Veau piqués à la Crême. Roast Beef.

Rots.

Les Cailles bardées. Les Poulets.

Entremets.

Les Haricots verts à la Poulette. Les Mayonaises de Poulets
Les Gateaux de Riz à l'Ananas.
Les Biscottes à la Chantilly. Les Crèmes à la d'Orleans.

Side Table.

Cold Fowl. Cold Beef. Tongue.

Alicky. Beatrice and Serge, joined us later, and I drove with them through Windsor and Eton. The decorations have all remained, and looked very pretty.—Had a great dinner in St. George's Hall, at which I sat between the King of Denmark and Willy of Greece. Bertie, and Alix, their 2 Boys, the 2 Greek Boys, Arthur and Louischen, Eulalie and Antonie, Serge and Ella, Lenchen and Christian, Beatrice and Liko, Louis, Irène and Ernie, Ernest of Coburg, Pce. Louis of Bavaria, the Herdy Grand Duke of Weimar, Hermann Weimar, Charlotte and Bernhard and Ernest Meiningen, Hermann Hohenlohe, Ludwig and Victoria Battenberg, Adolphus and Elisabeth of Mecklenburg Strelitz, Ludwig of Baden, all the suites, the Great Officers of State, Ld. Salisbury, Ct. Karolyi, Mide Staat, Ct. Hatzfeld, &c.—dined. More people came after dinner. It was the largest Banquet I almost remember, and looked very handsome indeed. The King of Denmark again proposed my health and Bertie the Sovereigns, and Royal Guests. It was very hot. Went into the Waterloo Gallery to hear performers from the School of Music play, which they did very well. The Ambassadors were profuse in their admiration of everything. The Turkish Envoy speaks German quite fluently, but not French well. The Artillery band played beautifully during dinner.

WINDSOR CASTLE, June 28th, 1887

MY CORONATION DAY, 49 YEARS AGO, & much the same weather as then.—Took leave of dear Leopold & Marie, Mary, Franz, [*TSH the Duke and Duchess of Teck*] & May [*HSH Princess May*

Queen Victoria at breakfast in Nice, 1895, with her daughter, Princess Beatrice (back to camera) and her granddaughter Princess Helena Victoria of Schleswig-Holstein. Her Majesty's Indian servants, Sheikh Ghulam Mustafa and Sheikh Chidda, are in attendance.

of Teck, later Queen Mary wife of King George V] & drove down to Frogmore with Irène and Alicky. Breakfasted under the trees. The Indians always wait now, & do so, so well & quietly.—It was too hot to walk. Sat writing for some time.—Ludwig & Victoria at luncheon. The others had gone to London. I was so tired, I could do very little but doze, & felt still not very well.—Beatrice & Liko drove down to tea with me, to Frogmore, & later was joined by Victoria & Alicky, with whom I drove through Datchet to Ditton Park, where the Dowr. Dss. of Buccleuch had a school break in honour of the Jubilee. Stopped there, the Duchess standing near the carriage, & heard the children sing 'God save the Queen'. A bouquet was given me, & the Duchess presented an old lady of 92, a Lady G. Medham. Drove round part of the grounds, & back again through Datchet, which was very prettily decorated.—Victoria & Alicky, & all the Ladies dined, and we sat out afterwards.

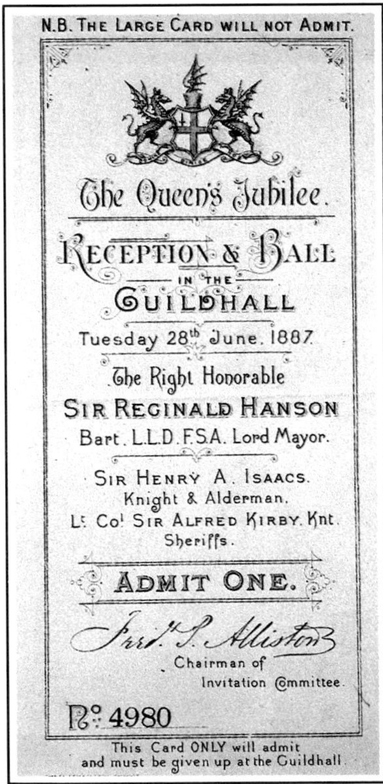

N.B. THE LARGE CARD WILL NOT ADMIT.

The Queen's Jubilee.

RECEPTION & BALL
IN THE
GUILDHALL

Tuesday 28th June. 1887.

The Right Honorable
SIR REGINALD HANSON
Bart. LL.D. F.S.A. Lord Mayor.

SIR HENRY A. ISAACS.
Knight & Alderman.
Lt. Col. SIR ALFRED KIRBY. Knt.
Sheriffs.

ADMIT ONE.

Chairman of
Invitation Committee.

No. 4980

This Card ONLY will admit
and must be given up at the Guildhall.

Both the Golden and Diamond jubilees provoked scenes of tremendous rejoicing. Parties were thrown, receptions held, the gentry danced the night away and vast numbers of official and semi-official functions were arranged throughout Britain. This invitation is for one of the grandest official functions of the Golden Jubilee: a reception and ball held in the Guildhall in the City of London by the Lord Mayor (the Rt Hon. Sir Reginald Hanson) and Corporation on June 28, 1887. It is certain that by the time of the Golden Jubilee in 1887, the nation and Empire genuinely loved their Queen. But by the Diamond Jubilee, feelings were much stronger. She was adored by millions. She had become the greatest monarch the world had ever known as well as the most powerful and almost certainly the richest. It may never be known how wealthy she was, but it is believed in certain quarters that she left about ten million pounds.

OSBORNE, December 31st, 1887

WENT UPSTAIRS AND JANE C. READ TO ME, and I remained quietly writing. After twelve Beatrice and Liko came in and wished me a happy New Year.

It was with great regret that I parted with the old eventful one. The Jubilee time was so richly blessed, not one mishap or disturbance, not one bad day, including the last pretty little ceremony of the unveiling of my statue at Balmoral. Never, never can I forget this brilliant year, so full of the marvellous kindness, loyalty, and devotion of so

The cover of the programme for the ball held by the Volunteer Officers to celebrate the Diamond Jubilee.

many millions, which really I could hardly have expected. I felt sadly the absence of those dear ones, who would so entirely have rejoiced in this eventful time. Then, how thankful I must be for darling Beatrice coming safely through her severe confinement, and now again in the great improvement in dear Fritz's condition! We had been in such terrible anxiety about him in November. May God help me further!

IN THE TRAIN, April 23rd, 1888

PASSED THROUGH PISTOJA, Bologna, Modena, Mantua, and Verona during the night. At Ala we crossed the frontier into Austria, and had already passed Botzen, when I was ready for breakfast. Splendid scenery amongst the Alps and crossing the Brenner.

At half-past one, we reached Innsbruck, the position of which is magificent, surrounded by high mountains. The day had become very fine and hot. At the station, on the platform, stood the Emperor Francis Joseph, in full uniform. We got out at once, and the Emperor led me into a room, where luncheon was prepared. I had not seen him since 1863 at Coburg. We lunched *à quatre* with Beatrice and Liko in a room full of flowers. I unfortunately had a very bad sick headache and could eat next to nothing. The Emperor was most kind, and talked very pleasantly on many subjects . . .

Charlottenburg Castle, Berlin, at night. Once one of the homes of the kings of Prussia, it is now a museum containing many Rembrandts and the bust of Nefertiti.

CHARLOTTENBURG, April 24th, 1888

A FAIR NIGHT, and got up in good time. Very soon after we were up we found we were going quite close round the outskirts of Berlin, and saw soldiers drilling; the country flat beyond belief. The morning was rather grey, but quite warm.

BUCKINGHAM PALACE, February 26th, 1889

IT WAS A VERY FULL AND LONG DRAWING-ROOM. I had a dreadful misadventure. Tirard [*her hairdresser*] had not pinned my cap and veil sufficiently firmly, and when, as I felt the room warm, I asked Louisa Buccleuch to remove the lace scarf I had on my shoulders, happening to turn my head round at the same moment to speak to Lord Lathom, off came the whole thing completely! The ladies rushed to put it on again, but badly of course, and Alice and Lenchen helped, but it was dreadful, though most ludicrous. Young Lady Ewart came by, looking very pretty. Violet Granby [*later Dowager Duchess of Rutland*] very handsome, in a dress of old brocade which they found in a box at Belvoir, and which had been worn by a Marchioness of Granby in 1770, grandmother to the present Duke. Remained over an hour, and then Alix took my place.

BIARRITZ, March 27th, 1889

WE REACHED SAN SEBASTIAN, the position of which is beautiful, just before one, Spanish time—and saw the Queen Regent standing on the platform, surrounded by her Court. There was of course a Guard of Honour. We got out at once, and I embraced the young Queen, kissing her on both cheeks. Then I presented Beatrice and Liko to her. She spoke German to us, with the pleasant Viennese accent. She is an Archduchess, daughter of the late Archduke Frederick and the Archduchess Elisabeth, Marie of Belgium's elder sister. Her grandfather was the celebrated Archduke Charles, whose wife was a Princess of Nassau, and she is second cousin to Helen, also second cousin to Lily, on her mother's side. The Queen has a very charming face and manner, brown eyes, a good nose, and a slight graceful figure.

WINDSOR CASTLE, July 17th, 1889

LOUISE OF S.-H. CAME TO LUNCHEON, and stayed with us to hear Albani and the two de Reszkes sing. We went to the Red Drawing-room. The two brothers have most glorious voices and sing in the most perfect manner. Jean, the elder, a tenor, reminded me more of Mario than anyone I have yet heard, and Edouard has a splendid deep bass voice, which comes out so fully and powerfully. The duet from *Lohengrin*, which is quite a long scene, was beyond anything beautiful, so dramatic, and Albani almost acted it. She was in great force. The music lasted till four, and I could have listened to it much longer. It was indeed a treat.

OSBORNE, August 2nd, 1889

ALL ON THE *QUI VIVE* for William's [*Kaiser Wilhelm II, Emperor of Germany and her grandson*] arrival, which had been expected at five. The Guard of Honour with the band was drawn up and waited and waited. At length, at near half-past seven, he appeared . . .

August 5th

ALL THE PRINCES AND PRINCESSES went with William at twelve to a Naval review, and the Duchess of Athole lunched with me. From the window we could see a good deal. I decided to go out in the *Alberta* [*a royal yacht*] and see the German ships, which were all anchored close to Osborne Bay, so at five embarked with the Duchess of Athole, Harriet P., Sir J. McNeill, and Major Bigge. Went round and through the German ships, who all played 'God Save the Queen' in turn as we passed them. Home at seven.

The Kaiser, grandson of Queen Victoria, c. *1880.*

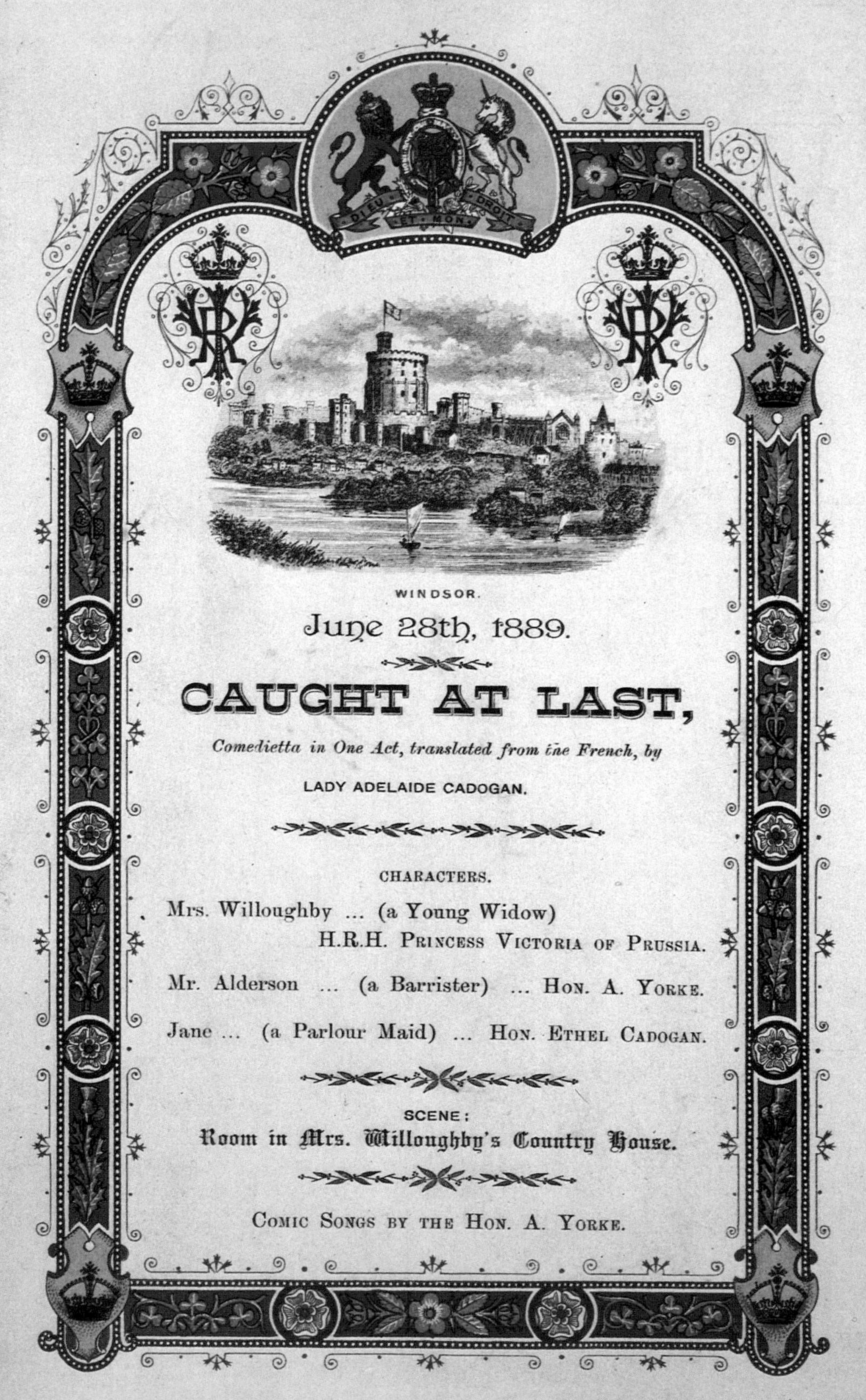

DIEU ET MON DROIT

WINDSOR.

June 28th, 1889.

CAUGHT AT LAST,

Comedietta in One Act, translated from the French, by

LADY ADELAIDE CADOGAN.

CHARACTERS.

Mrs. Willoughby ... (a Young Widow) H.R.H. PRINCESS VICTORIA OF PRUSSIA.

Mr. Alderson ... (a Barrister) ... HON. A. YORKE.

Jane ... (a Parlour Maid) ... HON. ETHEL CADOGAN.

SCENE:

Room in Mrs. Willoughby's Country House.

COMIC SONGS BY THE HON. A. YORKE.

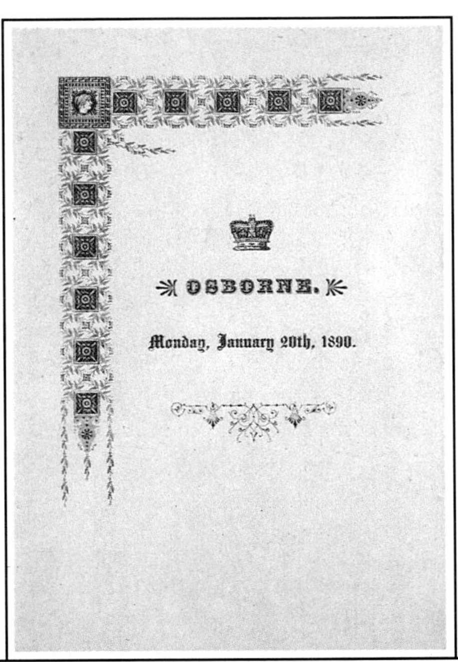

OSBORNE.

Monday, January 20th, 1890.

TABLEAUX VIVANTS,

MONDAY, JANUARY 20, 1890.

I.

ESTHER.

Queen Vashti - - H.R.H. the DUCHESS OF ALBANY.
Queen Esther - - - - - - Miss MCNEILL.
King Ahasuerus - - - - - - Mr. MUTHER.
Ladies - - - - - The Hon. ADELINE LOFTUS. Miss COWELL.
Attendants - - MUNSHI HAFIZ ABDUL KARIM. SAIYAD AHMAD HUSAIN. MIRZA YUSUF BEG.

II.

FOTHERINGAY.

Mary, Queen of Scots - H.R.H. Princess LOUISE, Marchioness of LORNE.
The Duchess of Argyll H.R.H. Princess BEATRICE, Princess HENRY OF BATTENBERG.
Mary Beaton - - H.R.H. the Duchess of ALBANY.
Mary Seaton - - Countess FEODORE GLEICHEN.
Sister Veronica - - - Miss ALBERTA PONSONBY.
Secretary - - - - - - Lt.-Colonel A. COLLINS.
Queen's Confessor - - - - Mr. VICTOR BIDDULPH.

III.

THE ÷ SURRENDER ÷ OF ÷ CALAIS.

Queen Philippa - - - - H.R.H. Princess LOUISE, Marchioness of LORNE.
Edward III. - - - - Gen. Sir HENRY PONSONBY.
The Earl of Derby - - - The Marquis of LORNE.
The Earl of Shrewsbury - Major the Hon. H. LEGGE.
Lord Cobham - - - - - - - Mr. A. COWELL.
Sir Walter Manny - - - - Mr. JOHN PONSONBY.
Eustache de St. Pierre - - - - - Mr. MUTHER.
Jehan d'Aire - - - - - - - - - Dr. REID.
Jacques de Wissant - - - - - - Major BIGGE.
Dominican Friar - - - - Mr. VICTOR BIDDULPH.

IV.

A BEDOUIN ENCAMPMENT.

H.R.H. Princess BEATRICE, Princess HENRY OF BATTENBERG.
Miss MCNEILL. Hon. ADELINE LOFTUS.
Major the Hon. H. LEGGE. Mr. ARTHUR PONSONBY.
MUNSHI HAFIZ ABDUL KARIM.
SAIYAD AHMAD HUSAIN. MIRZA YUSUF BEG.

V.

TWELFTH ✱ NIGHT.

REVELS.

The Queen of the Revels H.R.H. Princess BEATRICE, Princess HENRY OF BATTENBERG.
The King of Misrule - - The Marquis of LORNE.

REVELLERS.

H.R.H. Princess LOUISE, Marchioness of LORNE.
Countess FEODORE GLEICHEN. Miss ALBERTA PONSONBY.
Miss COWELL. Mr. ARTHUR PONSONBY. Major BIGGE.
Mr. VICTOR BIDDULPH. Major-General Sir JOHN MCNEILL.
Jester - - - Mr. A. COWELL.

STAGE MANAGERS:
Honble. Lady PONSONBY, Mr. MUTHER.

Wigs by Mr. CLARKSON.
Costumes by Messrs. SIMMONS.

ABOVE: *Another of the many entertainments presented specially for the Queen was held at Osborne on January 20, 1890, when* tableaux vivants *delighted the audience, principally because so many members of the Royal Family took part. Not only her relations, Household and friends, but even the Munshi, Hafiz Abdul Karim, and her two other Indian servants were involved. It seems unlikely that so many titled and royal personages had ever joined together before to present such an entertainment.*

LEFT: *This entertainment,* Caught at Last, *presented by her granddaughter, Princess Victoria of Prussia, and members of her Household, led as usual by the Hon. Sir Alick Yorke, used a menu card as its programme. It was to Sir Alick Yorke that the Queen declared, 'We are not amused.'*

OSBORNE, January 20th, 1890

At length the day had arrived when the long expected, arranged & postponed Tableaux, were to take place.—Fine & mild with rather a high wind.—Out with Ethel C.—Resting & writing—Received letters & details about the death of the poor Duke of Aosta, which were very sad reading.—Drove from 4 to 5 with Feo & Harriet P.—The Children were very funny at tea, but had a regular fight.—All the performers dined at 7, and I at ½ p. 8, with Ly. Waterpark, Harriet P., Ethel C., Miss Maxwell, Ernie Hohenlohe (come for 3 nights), the Bishop of Ripon, & Sir J. McNeill. Little Alice & Charlie [*Princess Alice and Prince Charles, daughter and son of the Queen's son, Prince Leopold. Princess Alice was eventually to become Princess Alice, Countess of Athlone.*] came after dinner. At ½ p. 9, all went over to the Council Room, where the stage & seats were arranged as 2 years ago. The invitations to the guests were divided between the 4 days of the Performances. A portion of the

After the death of Prince Leopold, Duke of Albany, his widow, the former Princess Helena of Waldeck-Pyrmont, and their children Princess Alice of Albany (late countess of Athlone) and Prince Charles of Albany (born four months after his father's death), spent a great deal of time with the Queen.

excellent string Band of the Marines, played appropriate pieces, during & between the Tableaux. The latter were 5 in number. *Esther*, in which took part Helen, Ina Mc Neill, Adeline Loftus, Alice Cowell, Mrs. Muther, Abdul, & my 2 Indian servants Ahmed Husain, & Gusuf Beg,—*Fotheringay*, in which took part, Louise, as Mary Queen of Scots, Beatrice, Helen, Feo Gleichen, Betty Ponsonby, Col: Collins & Victor Biddulph,—*The Surrender of Calais*, in which took part, Louise as Queen Philippa, Sir H. Ponsonby as Edward III, Lorne, Major Legge, Bertie Cowell, Johnnee Ponsonby, Major Bigge, Mr. Muther, Victor Biddulph, & Dr. Reid,—*A Bedouin Encampment* in which took part, Beatrice, Ina Mc Neill, Adeline Loftus, Major Legge, Arthur Ponsonby, Abdul, Ahmed Husain, & Yusuf Beg,—*Twelfth Night*, in which took part, Beatrice, as Queen of the Revels & Lorne as the King of Misrule, Louise, Feo Gleichen, Betty Ponsonby, Major Bigge, Sir J. McNeill Victor Biddulph & Bertie Cowell.—

The curtain was as usual dropped twice to allow of one's having 3 views. The Tableaux were really lovely & so well arranged. Abdul had helped to arrange the oriental draperies for the ladies. The Esther tableau was taken from a painting of Horace Veruet. Fotheringay represented the moment, when poor Mary Queen of Scots, took leave of her ladies. Louise looked lovely as the Queen standing on the steps looking up, & Beatrice as her half sister the Dss. of Argyle, leaning against her. Louise changed the position a little each time, but very appropriately. In the 2nd. scene, she no longer stood on the steps, but gave her hand to 'Maitland' her Secretary (Col: Collins), who knelt & kissed it. Louise's expression was beautiful & sad beyond measure. Beatrice also looked sweet, with hands upraised, & looking up as in prayer. Mozart's 'Ave Verum' was played during this scene. Then, came the 'Surrender of Calais' a really gorgeous scene, Sir H[*enry*]. Ponsonby looking so well, in real armour, & so like the representations of Edward III. Louise looked beautiful as Queen Philippa, & Major Legge particularly well, as the Earl of Shrewsbury. All the men were in armour, which came from Windsor.

OSBORNE, February 10th, 1890

THE 50TH ANNIVERSARY OF MY WEDDING, and I am already 29 years a widow. Still, the reflection of those twenty-two years of great happiness remains. Had many kind telegrams. Dear Beatrice brought me in at breakfast a sweet little gold basket with lovely orange flowers and myrtles and a large prayer book, given me by all my children. Tennyson wrote the following beautiful lines for it:

Remembering him who waits thee far away,
And with the mother taught us first to pray,
Accept on this your golden bridal day
This book of prayer.

The Household presented me with a lovely red enamel of my wedding picture, framed in white leather, with a spray of gold orange blossoms on the top. It gave me great pleasure. I also received endless lovely nosegays, and was quite overcome at so much kindness.

[*It was a paradox that the Queen had so much enjoyed her own marriage, referred to it constantly and was delighted when her relations married, but she did not like to see her courtiers marry and in some cases, strongly opposed their marriage. One of the reasons she gave was that married men were more likely to tell their wives their secrets in bed!*]

DARMSTADT, April 25th, 1890

AFTER TEA, LOUIS AND LIKO went to the station to meet William, who arrived at seven. He came up to see me at once, and was very kind and friendly. There was a large dinner in uniform, downstairs in the dining-room. Sat between Louis and William. The latter was very cheerful and gay.

April 26th

AT A QUARTER TO ELEVEN we started for a review of the troops of the Darmstadt garrison. At the door I met Dona, whom I had not seen since she was Empress, and who had just arrived from Berlin. Drove with her in a phaeton with four horses. We were received with royal honours.

WINDSOR CASTLE, June 27th, 1890

AFTER LUNCHEON STARTED FOR LONDON, and from Paddington station drove in a closed carriage to Kensal Green Cemetery. There were crowds out, we could not understand why, and thought something must be going [*on*], but it turned out it was only to see me. Got out and walked a short way along a path, where the vault is in which dear Janie Ely rests. Placed our wreaths there. Unfortunately, there were such crowds that the privacy of my visit was quite spoilt; still, I felt glad so many bore witness to this act of regard and love paid to my beloved friend.

BALMORAL, October 11th, 1890

AFTER DINNER, THE OTHER LADIES AND GENTLEMEN JOINED US in the Drawing-room, and we pushed the furniture back and had a nice little impromptu dance, Curtis's band being so *entraînant*. We had a quadrille, in which I danced with Eddy!! It did quite well, then followed some waltzes and polkas.

Principal Events

1891–1901

1891: The Queen launched the battleship *Royal Sovereign* and the first-class cruiser *Royal Arthur* at Portsmouth (February 26).
The Earl of Granville died, aged seventy-five (March 31).
Free elementary education introduced.
German Emperor and Empress visited England (July 4–13).
The Prince of Naples visited England (July 22–August).
Thomas Hardy's *Tess of the D'Urbervilles* published.
Tchaikovsky's *Nutcracker* ballet suite first performed.

1892: Duke of Clarence and Avondale died at Sandringham (January 14); military funeral at Windsor (January 20).
William Gladstone Prime Minister (August 18).
Death of Alfred, Lord Tennyson, Poet Laureate aged eighty-three (October 6); interred Westminster Abbey (October 12).
Toulouse-Lautrec's painting *At the Moulin Rouge* first exhibited.

1893: Opening of Parliament; the Queen's speech introduced the Second Irish Home Rule Bill (January 31) which was rejected by the Lords.
Independent Labour Party formed.
Visit to the Queen by her daughter the Empress Frederick (February 1–April 4).
The Imperial Institute inaugurated by the Queen (May 10).
Marriage of the Duke of York and Princess May of Teck (later Queen Mary) at St James's Palace (July 6).

The Duke and Duchess of York with Queen Victoria at Osborne House during their honeymoon in 1893.

1894: Empress Frederick visited Osborne (February 2–March 9).
William Gladstone resigned; succeeded by the Earl of Rosebery (March 3 for one year and 21 days).
Death duties first introduced.
Manchester ship canal inaugurated by the Queen (May 21).
Debussy's *L'Après-midi d'un Faune* first performed.
Birth of Prince Edward Albert Christian George Andrew Patrick David of York—later King Edward VIII; subsequently the Duke of Windsor (June 23).

1895: Death of Lord Randolph Churchill (January 24).
Resignation of Rosebery administration (June 21).
Marquis of Salisbury Prime Minister again (June 25).
Visit of the German Emperor (her grandson 'Kaiser Bill') to the Queen at Osborne (August 5).
King of the Belgians and Princess Clementine visited the Queen (December 3–9).
The National Trust founded.
Professor Röntgen discovered X-rays.
Sigmund Freud's first work on psychoanalysis—on hysteria—published.
Guglielmo Marconi pioneered the use of wireless telegraphy.

Sigmund Freud, the father of psychoanalysis.

1896: Death of Alfred Nobel, founder of Nobel Prizes (first awarded 1901).
Death of Prince Henry of Battenburg (January 20).
American aeronautical pioneer, Samuel Langley introduced his 'flying machine' (a steam-driven *model* aircraft).
A. E. Housman's collection *A Shropshire Lad* published.
Queen Victoria became the longest reigning monarch in British history (September 23).

1897: Queen Victoria's Diamond Jubilee (June 20).
Klondike Gold Rush.

Tate Gallery, London, opened (presented to nation by Sir Henry Tate).
Grand Naval review at Spithead (June 26).
George Bernard Shaw's *Candida* first performed.

1898: Death of former Prime Minister William Ewart Gladstone (May 19).
Kitchener defeated Dervishes at Omdurman.
Marie and Pierre Curie discovered radium.
H. G. Wells' *War of the Worlds* published.
'Lewis Carroll' died – pseudonym of Charles Lutwidge Dodgson (January 14).

1899: A message from Queen Victoria received by Parliament in gratitude to Lord Kitchener and officers for services in the Sudan (June 5).
Board of Education established.
Elgar's *Enigma Variations* first performed.
South African War began following Transvaal Crisis (July 28).
German Emperor and Empress visited the Queen at Windsor (November 20–25).

Sir Edward Elgar, who became Master of the King's Musick to George V.

Oscar Wilde photographed in 1894. A year later he was sentenced to two years' imprisonment with hard labour for homosexual practices.

1900: Death of the Duke of Teck, aged sixty-two (January 21).
Relief of Ladysmith and Mafeking (May 17).
Joseph Conrad's *Lord Jim* published.
Elgar's oratorio *The Dream of Gerontius* first performed.
The Queen visited London to 'see her people' (March 7–10); visited Ireland (April 2–27).
Assassination attempt on Prince of Wales at Brussels (April 4).
Prince Alfred (Duke of Edinburgh), Duke of Saxe–Coburg and Gotha, died aged fifty-five (July 30).
Sir Arthur Sullivan died aged fifty-eight (November 22).
The Queen sent messages of gratitude to her soldiers in South Africa (December 19).
Death of Oscar Wilde (November 30).

1901: Death of Queen Victoria at Osborne 6.30pm (January 22).

OSBORNE, January 1st, 1891

. . . MAY HE PRESERVE ME YET FOR SOME YEARS!

WINDSOR CASTLE, March 6, 1891

VERY BRIGHT & WINDY.—Saw Sir H. Ponsonby after breakfast.—Out with Vicky & went down to the Slopes. On coming home, I got out at the state entrance & went to look at the stage put up in the Waterloo Gallery for a theatrical performance. There was a very handsome curtain. The orchestra was almost concealed by plants & flowers which Jones had arranged beautifully. A platform had been placed on which the seats were raised one behind the other, reaching up almost to the Gallery, so that there were no steps, but a slightly inclined plain from St. George's Hall. It really was very pretty.—In the afternoon drove with Vicky & Beatrice, to Ascot & back by Winkfield.—A family dinner at 8, which included Affie & Marie, come for 2 nights, Louise & Lorne, & Arthur & Louischen. Lenchen, Christian & their girls, joined us afterwards. At 9, we went over to the Waterloo Gallery, where all the seats were filled by the Ladies & Gentlemen of the Household. All the Princes & Princesses sat with me in the front row. The 'Gondoliers', the last of Sir A. Sullivan's comic operas was performed by D'Oyly Carte's company of the Savoy Theatre, & lasted about 2 hours & ½. The music, which I know & am very fond of, is quite charming throughout & was well acted & sung. The opening scene with the Contadine singing & binding flowers, with a lovely view of Venice & the deep blue sea & sky, was really extraordinarily pretty. The dancing which often comes in was very graceful & pretty. The dialogue is written by Gilbert & very amusing. The Grand Inquisitor (Mr. W. H. Denny) was excellent & most absurd, also Mr. Rutland Barrington, who is very fat, as one of the Gondolieri. Miss Jessie Bond is a clever little actress & sings nicely. The dresses are very gay & smart, & the whole ensemble brilliant & well put on the stage, which for an extemporised one was wonderful. I really enjoyed the performance very much. Afterwards I spoke to Mr. [*Richard*] D'Oyly Carte, & complimented him. We then went to the Drawingroom into which all the company came, but I only stayed a short while. Everybody was much pleased.

WINDSOR CASTLE, March 17th, 1891

WE ALL WENT OVER TO THE WATERLOO GALLERY to see a performance of the play 'A Pair of Spectacles', which was very good. It is a very pretty play, adapted from the French. Mr. Hare acts admirably and so does Mr. Groves; in fact, all did very well. The piece, which was in two acts, was followed by a short one-act one, called 'A Quiet Rubber'. Mr. Hare was again wonderfully good. We again went to the drawing-room, where I received the company. Mr. Hare is a very small, spare gentleman-like man, and is a gentleman, as so many (actors) are nowadays.

WINDSOR CASTLE, July 2nd, 1891

WENT TO THE GREEN DRAWING-ROOM and heard Mr. Paderewski play on the piano. He does so quite marvellously, such power and such tender feeling. I really think he is quite equal to Rubenstein. He is young, about 28, very pale, with a sort of aureole of red hair standing out.

WINDSOR CASTLE, July 11th, 1891

HEARD EVERYTHING HAD GONE OFF ADMIRABLY at the lunch in the City where William [*the German Emperor—her grandson*] and Dona had an enthusiastic reception. The Lord Mayor made a touching allusion to my beloved Albert and to dear Vicky and Fritz, dwelling on William's being *my* grandson, which is the reason for their receiving him so well.

OSBORNE, July 24th, 1891

AT HALF-PAST SEVEN THE PRINCE OF NAPLES, only child of the King of Italy, arrived, Arthur and Louischen accompanying him. I received him in the hall, and took him into the drawing-room. where, after a few minutes, he presented his three gentlemen. Colonel Slade, Military attache to my Embassy at Rome, came along with Count Tornielli, the Italian Ambassador. The young Prince, who is in his twenty-third year, has a fine head and gentle expression, but he is dreadfully short. He is wonderfully well-informed, intelligent and amiable. Arthur then took him to his rooms, and I received Count and Countess Hohenau, who came with Arthur. They are great friends, as well as relations, of Louischen's, and were with her and Arthur in India two years ago.

Had a big dinner. The table looked very handsome with all fine decorations of flowers, most tastefully arranged by the gardener. Several of my Jubilee presents had been sent down, including the splendid silver rose bowl from the Rothschilds. The Prince led me in and I sat between him and Arthur. The excellent Marine band played during and after dinner, and we went out on the terrace. I proposed the health of the King and Queen of Italy and the Prince mine. I talked to as many as I could after dinner. The Prince of Naples took leave, as he has to go back to London quite early tomorrow morning.

BALMORAL, September 4th, 1891

JUST BEFORE LUNCHEON I received in the drawing-room the Kunevar Harnam Singh and his wife, both in Indian dress, somewhat modified. Hers was very becoming. She said she heard I spoke Hindustani, and addressed a few words to me, I saying some to her, with which she was delighted. She remarked that if only the English ladies in India would follow my example it would do much good. They have seven children, of which three sons are being educated in Edinburgh. They were Hindus but became Christians, thereby losing their position and rights in India. They came over in '87 to my Jubilee.

Dined earlier on account of the performance of Sullivan's operetta, the 'Mikado'. At half-past nine we went down to the ballroom. There were many neighbours invited and some of the servants and tenants. The stage had been a little widened. The orchestra, as well as the whole company, came. The music is gay, but to my thinking inferior to the 'Gondoliers', and though there are many witty remarks and amusing topical allusions, the story is rather silly. The operetta was well put on the stage, and forty people took

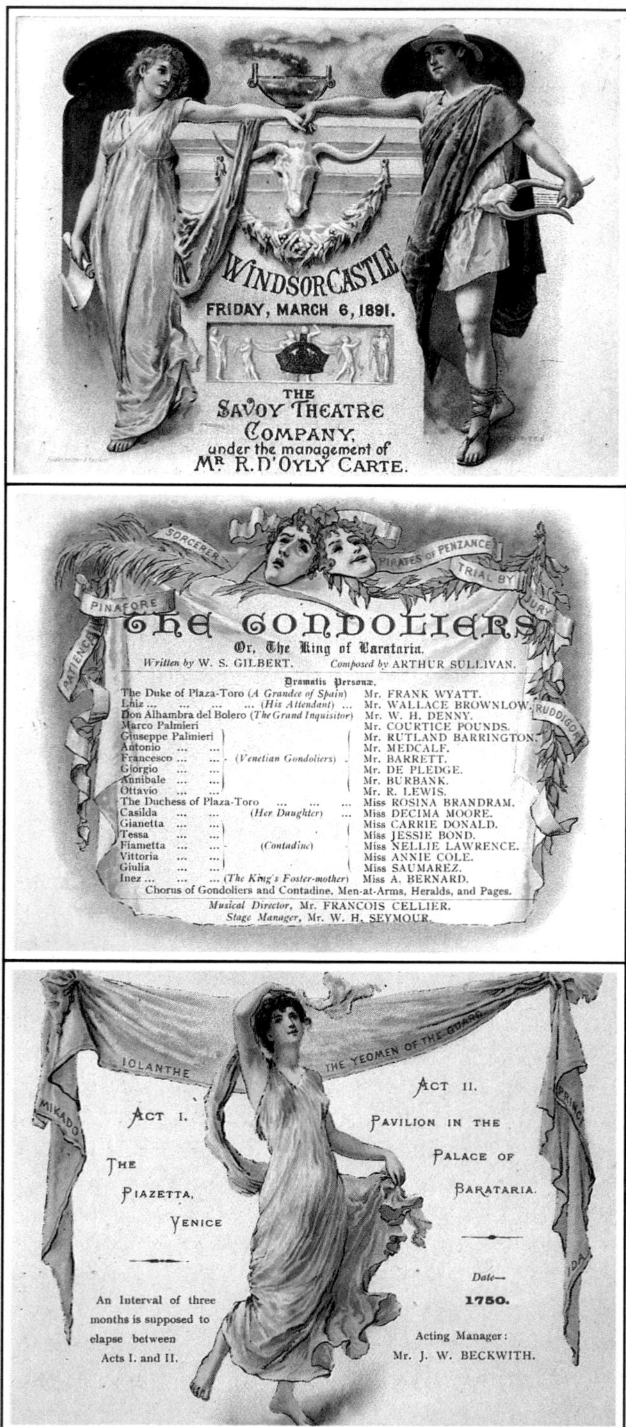

THE GONDOLIERS
Or, The King of Barataria.
Written by W. S. GILBERT. *Composed by* ARTHUR SULLIVAN.

Dramatis Personæ.

The Duke of Plaza-Toro	*(A Grandee of Spain)*	Mr. FRANK WYATT.
Luiz	*(His Attendant)* ...	Mr. WALLACE BROWNLOW.
Don Alhambra del Bolero	*(The Grand Inquisitor)*	Mr. W. H. DENNY.
Marco Palmieri	*(Venetian Gondoliers)*	Mr. COURTICE POUNDS.
Giuseppe Palmieri		Mr. RUTLAND BARRINGTON.
Antonio		Mr. MEDCALF.
Francesco		Mr. BARRETT.
Giorgio		Mr. DE PLEDGE.
Annibale		Mr. BURBANK.
Ottavio		Mr. R. LEWIS.
The Duchess of Plaza-Toro		Miss ROSINA BRANDRAM.
Casilda	*(Her Daughter)* ...	Miss DECIMA MOORE.
Gianetta	*(Contadine)*	Miss CARRIE DONALD.
Tessa		Miss JESSIE BOND.
Fiametta		Miss NELLIE LAWRENCE.
Vittoria		Miss ANNIE COLE.
Giulia		Miss SAUMAREZ.
Inez	*(The King's Foster-mother)*	Miss A. BERNARD.

Chorus of Gondoliers and Contadine, Men-at-Arms, Heralds, and Pages.

Musical Director, Mr. FRANCOIS CELLIER.
Stage Manager, Mr. W. H. SEYMOUR.

ACT I.
THE PIAZZETTA, VENICE

An Interval of three months is supposed to elapse between Acts I. and II.

ACT II.
PAVILION IN THE PALACE OF BARATARIA.

Date— 1750.

Acting Manager: Mr. J. W. BECKWITH.

One of the Queen's favourite Savoy Operas was The Gondoliers *which was presented at Windsor Castle by the Savoy Theatre company under the management of Richard D'Oyly Carte on March 6, 1891. There was an especially pretty programme and the Queen records in her Journal how much she enjoyed it all.*

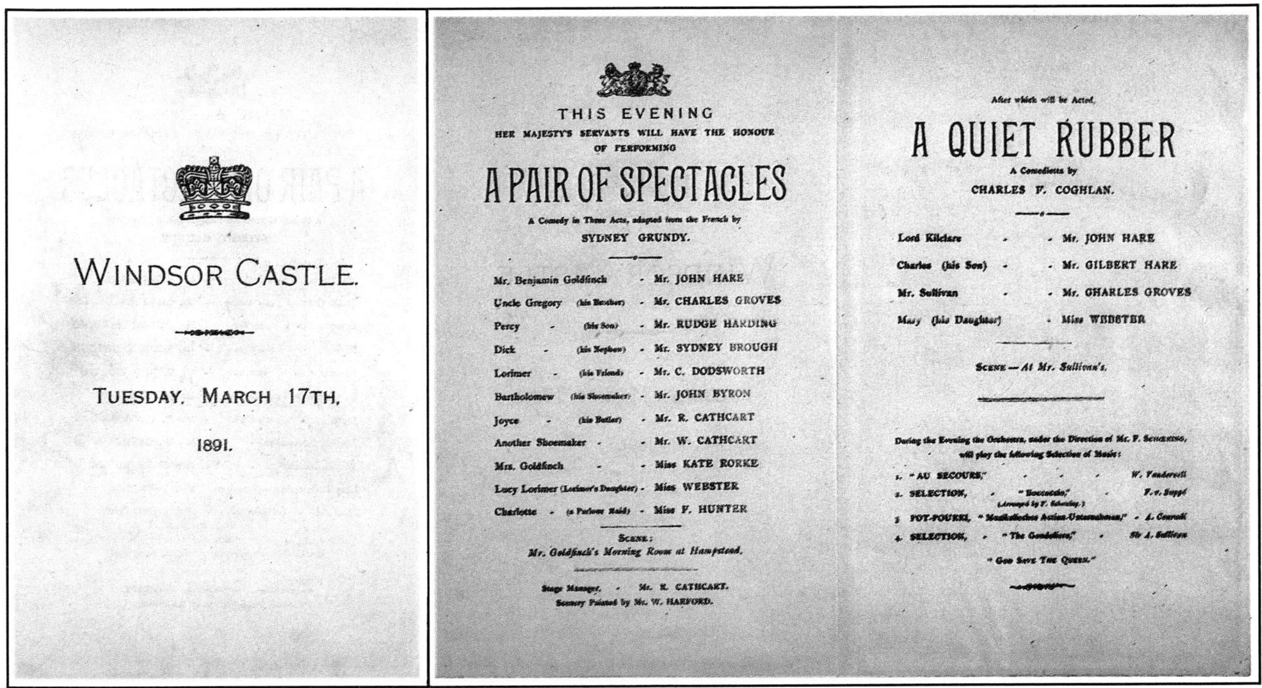

WINDSOR CASTLE.

TUESDAY. MARCH 17TH.

1891.

THIS EVENING
HER MAJESTY'S SERVANTS WILL HAVE THE HONOUR
OF PERFORMING

A PAIR OF SPECTACLES

A Comedy in Three Acts, adapted from the French by
SYDNEY GRUNDY.

Mr. Benjamin Goldfinch		Mr. JOHN HARE
Uncle Gregory	(his Brother)	Mr. CHARLES GROVES
Percy	(his Son)	Mr. RUDGE HARDING
Dick	(his Nephew)	Mr. SYDNEY BROUGH
Lorimer	(his Friend)	Mr. C. DODSWORTH
Bartholomew	(his Shoemaker)	Mr. JOHN BYRON
Joyce	(his Butler)	Mr. R. CATHCART
Another Shoemaker		Mr. W. CATHCART
Mrs. Goldfinch		Miss KATE RORKE
Lucy Lorimer	(Lorimer's Daughter)	Miss WEBSTER
Charlotte	(a Parlour Maid)	Miss F. HUNTER

SCENE:
Mr. Goldfinch's Morning Room at Hampstead.

Stage Manager, - Mr. R. CATHCART.
Scenery Painted by Mr. W. HARFORD.

After which will be Acted,

A QUIET RUBBER

A Comedietta by
CHARLES F. COGHLAN.

Lord Kilclare	Mr. JOHN HARE
Charles (his Son)	Mr. GILBERT HARE
Mr. Sullivan	Mr. CHARLES GROVES
Mary (his Daughter)	Miss WEBSTER

SCENE—*At Mr. Sullivan's.*

During the Evening the Orchestra, under the Direction of Mr. F. [illegible],
will play the following Selection of Music:

1. "AU SECOURS," - - - *W. Vanderell*
2. SELECTION, - "Boccaccio," - *F. v. Suppé*
(Arranged by F. [illegible].)
3. POT-POURRI, "Musikalisches Actien-Unternehmen," - *A. Conradi*
4. SELECTION, - "The Gondoliers," - *Sir A. Sullivan*

"GOD SAVE THE QUEEN."

A programme for a performance of two plays at Windsor.
The Queen recorded that 'Mr. Hare acts admirably'.

part in it. The Japanese dresses were very correct. The choruses were very good; the women good-looking.

WINDSOR CASTLE, November 26th, 1891

AT FOUR, WE ALL WENT TO THE WATERLOO GALLERY, Lenchen, Christian, Thora, Louise, [*Their Highnesses Princesses Thora and Marie Louise were the daughters of Prince and Princess Christian*] Lorne, Beatrice, Liko, Victoria, Maude, [*her granddaughters—children of the Prince and Princess of Wales*] Alge Teck, and little Drino and Ena, [*her grandchildren, son and daughter of Princess Beatrice. Princess Ena was to become Queen of Spain.*] where the opera of 'Cavalleria Rusticana', by a young Italian composer, of the name of [*Pietro*] Mascagni, was performed. I had not heard an Italian opera for thirty-one years. The story was most pathetic and touching beyond words. The whole performance was a great success and I loved the music, which is so melodious, and characteristically Italian.

WINDSOR CASTLE, November 27th, 1891

A LITTLE AFTER SIX we went down into the drawing-room and had a great treat in hearing Sarasate play on the violin, accompanied by a Madame Bertha Marx, a French lady, who plays also quite beautifully, with wonderful execution and a lovely touch. I never heard finer execution or more feeling than Sarasate has. His Spanish dances were quite new to me, and charming. He is very pleasing and modest, and has a very singular melancholy countenance.

WINDSOR CASTLE, December 5th, 1891

... HEARD ON RETURNING THAT EDDY WAS THERE and wished to see me. I suspected something at once. He came in and said, 'I have some good news to tell you; I am engaged to May Teck.' This had taken place at a ball at Luton, the de Falbes' place. I was quite delighted. God bless them both! [*Eddy, Prince Albert Victor, was the eldest son of the Prince and Princess of Wales. He died less than a month later and his brother Prince George—later* HM *King George V—subsequently courted and married Princess May of Teck.*]

OSBORNE, January 9th, 1892

HAD A LETTER FROM MARY TECK from Sandringham, whither they had all gone for Eddy's birthday, in which she says that he was not well, and unable to come down to dinner. It seemed to be a bad cold.

OSBORNE, January 10th, 1892

WAS STARTLED AND RATHER TROUBLED BY A TELEGRAM from Bertie, saying dear Eddy had a 'very sharp attack of influenza and had now developed some pneumonia in left lung, the night restless, but strength well maintained.'

OSBORNE, January 13th, 1892

WHILST I WAS DRESSING, BEATRICE ASKED TO SEE ME, and brought a bad telegram from Dr. Broadbent to Dr. Reid to the following effect: 'Condition very dangerous.' How terrible! Felt I ought to fly to Sandringham.

OSBORNE, January 14th, 1892

A NEVER-TO-BE-FORGOTTEN DAY! Whilst I was dressing, Lenchen came in, bringing the following heartrending telegram from poor dear Bertie: 'Our darling Eddy has been taken from us. We are broken-hearted.' Words are far too poor to express one's feelings of grief, horror and distress! Poor, poor parents; poor May to have her whole bright future to be merely a dream! Poor me, in my old age, to see this young promising life cut short! I, who loved him so dearly, and to whom he was so devoted! God help us! This is an awful blow to the country too!

OSBORNE, January 21st, 1892

THE NEWSPAPERS FULL OF TOUCHING ACCOUNTS. Special services almost everywhere.

Prince Albert Victor, Duke of Clarence and Avondale, eldest son of the Prince and Princess of Wales. He was second in line to the throne and his death from pneumonia, less than a month after his engagement to Princess May of Teck had been announced, left his parents and the Queen broken-hearted.

London a wonderful sight, every possible house, shop, and theatre voluntarily closed, and everyone in mourning. The account of the departure from Sandringham is, perhaps, the most heartrending of all. Poor Bertie walked the whole way to the private station with Fife and Franz, followed by his gentlemen. George [*Prince George who was recovering from typhoid*] went in the carriage with Alix and the girls, Louise, Mary, and May all followed in carriages, going in the same train with the loved remains. Beatrice returned at half-past one and told me much. Philip Coburg had come down with her and Liko, and was at luncheon. He was very kind and sympathising.

OSBORNE, January 28th, 1892

I WROTE A LETTER, as I have done several times before, to be published in the papers, which it was today, and there are several very kind articles about it. The one in The Times was particularly fine. My letter seems to have been much liked and appreciated.

OSBORNE, August 25th, 1892

AFTER BREAKFAST TOOK LEAVE of my dear good old Emilie Dittweiler, who has been my dresser for 33 years. She knew my happy as well as sad days, and was with me through all my sorrows. I shall miss her sadly. She was a devoted, loyal, and trustworthy servant.

BALMORAL, November 9th, 1892

... HAVE BEEN SUFFERING A GOOD DEAL lately from rheumatism in my legs, which makes them very stiff, and I am not able to walk much, which is very tiresome.

WINDSOR CASTLE, April 30th, 1893

RECEIVED A TELEGRAM FROM GEORGIE from Sheen House to say he was engaged to May Teck, and asked for my consent. I answered that I gladly did so ... arranged that the news should be put in tomorrow's papers. I have so much wished for this engagement, that it gives me the greatest satisfaction.

WINDSOR CASTLE, July 1st, 1893

JUST BEFORE TWO, THE YOUNG CESAREWITCH ARRIVED, and I received him at the top of the staircase. All were in uniform to do him honour, and to show him every possible civility. He is charming and wonderfully like Georgie. He always speaks English, and almost without a fault, having had an English tutor, a Mr. Heath, who is still with him. He is very simple and unaffected. After luncheon M. de Staal came into the corridor, and 'Nicky', as he is always called, presented his three gentlemen. Then went into the Audience room, where I invested Nicky with the Garter, after which he took leave.

OSBORNE, August 26th, 1894

MY LEG HAS BEEN SO PAINFUL the last two or three days that I can hardly put my foot down, so that I have had to put off my departure for Balmoral.

BALMORAL, August 29th, 1894

DID NOT GET OUT AT PERTH FOR BREAKFAST on account of my leg, and had it brought in to me. Before leaving Dr. Reid asked to speak to Beatrice, and I fancied there must be something wrong. She came in almost directly to say something very sad had happened.

Poor good Sir John Cowell [*Master of the Household and Lord Edward Pelham-Clinton's predecessor*] had died in his sleep early this morning! It is too awful, as we had seen him at the door yesterday afternoon when we left Osborne, and he was quite well. Everyone was thunderstruck by the news, and we feel so much for his poor wife, as they were so devoted to each other and never apart.

WINDSOR CASTLE, November 16th, 1894

A BEAUTIFUL DAY, but the river has risen 8 inches. Out with Ethel C. and went to the Kennels, where I looked at all the dogs. After luncheon drove with Louise and Beatrice to

The christening in 1894 of the Queen's great-grandson, Prince Edward of York, brought together four generations of British monarchs, the Queen herself, her son – the future Edward VII, her grandson – the future George V, and the infant Prince – the future Edward VIII.

look at the floods, which are awful. There is much suffering amongst the poor, the water coming into all their houses. We are doing all we can for them.

OSBORNE, December 31st, 1894

WE HAD RATHER AN EARLIER TEA on account of dining early for the tableaux. Jane C., Ina McNeill, the Ponsonbys and Maggie, Sir J. McNeill, and Colonel Carrington, and Dr. Reid dined with me. At nine went down to the Durbar room, Helen sitting near me for the first four tableaux. All were very successful. Albert Mensdorff looked wonderfully like the picture of Charles I, and Beatrice personified Henrietta Maria extremely well. After the performance was over, we went into the drawing-room for me to receive the company, and all the performers passed by. Went upstairs directly afterwards.

Thus ended the last day of the year. I am very grateful for God's preservation of all I hold most dear; but '94 has brought many sad events and the loss of many friends and members in my Household, whom I sincerely regret, and several of my good servants. May God preserve me and mine in the next year!

MEMORANDUM BY QUEEN VICTORIA

OSBORNE, January 15th, 1895

It is important, now that poor Sir Henry Ponsonby's illness must last some time, that his two offices [*Private Secretary and Keeper of the Privy Purse*] should, though at present only temporarily, be divided as they always were before; and that the duties should be defined to a great extent, though not without a certain elasticity, each acting with the other, and, in the temporary absence of one, the other acting for him.

I wish that Sir Fleetwood [*Edwards*] should undertake the duties of Keeper of the Privy Purse, which would compromise all concerning expense, alterations of buildings at the Palaces, especially at Osborne and Balmoral, and other personal estates, as well as the arrangement of these estates, all charities, applications for help, etc. Colonel Bigge, on the other hand, would be the Private Secretary. On him would devolve the communications with the Ministers, the Horse Guards, the different offices, and with people in general.

This is as it used to be till Sir T. Biddulph died; General Grey and then Sir H. Ponsonby succeeded him, having been the Private Secretaries. Sir Fleetwood and Colonel Bigge may on consultation find further suggestions to make for which I should be grateful.

I wish to add that I trust they will act cordially and fully with Lord Edward Clinton, as Master of the Household, as his judgement is excellent, and he has much experience. They will take care not to let Mr. Muther [*the Librarian at Windsor Castle*] feel that he is under them, though he belongs to the Privy Purse Department, as they know his touchiness and that he requires careful handling . . .

All communications with Lord Chamberlain and his department to go through the Privy Purse. All with the Lord Steward through the Master of the Household. All those with the Master of the Horse, except those of expense and the appointment of Pages of Honour, to go through the Private Secretary, as he is an Equerry.

V.R.I.

WINDSOR CASTLE, March 11th, 1895

SAW LORD ROSEBERY who, though better, is still very weak, as he cannot sleep at all. Talked of many things, foreign and home politics, of the retirement of the Speaker, who will be a great loss, of his successor, which is a great difficulty.

After tea saw Lord Salisbury, who had come for a night, and who has also been ill with influenza, but is quite well again. Lady Salisbury was still very unwell, but he hoped to get her abroad soon.

WINDSOR CASTLE, May 3rd, 1895

SHORTLY BEFORE TWO, WENT DOWNSTAIRS to receive the Queen Regent of the Netherlands and her daughter, the young Queen Wilhelmina. Beatrice had been to meet them at the station, and Helen [*Duchess of Albany*] came with them. The young Queen, who will be fifteen in August, has her hair still hanging down. She is very slight and graceful, has fine features, and seems to be very intelligent and a charming child. She speaks English extremely well, and has very pretty manners. Drove at 4.30 with the Queen Regent, who is very amiable and sympathetique, so clever and sensible. [*There is a story that, during this meeting with Queen Wilhelmina, Queen Victoria put her arm round her and said: 'As we are both Queens together, we may say whatever we like!'*]

In December, 1895, Prince Henry of Battenberg, Princess Beatrice's husband, joined the Ashanti expedition. The news came on January 22, 1896, that he had died.

OSBORNE, January 22nd, 1896

A TERRIBLE BLOW HAS FALLEN ON US ALL, especially on my poor darling Beatrice. Our dearly loved Liko has been taken from us! Can I write it? He was so much better, and we were anxiously awaiting the news of his arrival at Madeira. What will become of my poor child! All she said in a trembling voice, apparently quite stunned, was, 'The life is gone out of me.' She went back to her room with Louischen, who, as well as dear Arthur, has been most tender to her.

The Queen attends the funeral of her son-in-law, Prince Henry of Battenberg (Liko), husband of her youngest child, Princess Beatrice.

OSBORNE, February 5th, 1896

THIS WAS A TERRIBLE DAY, but one never to be forgotten! It dawned very dull & dark & unfortunately unlike yesterday, remained dull & dreary, & there was once or twice a

Osborne.

30th January, 1896.

The Funeral of the late Colonel His Royal Highness Prince Henry of Battenberg will take place on Wednesday next, the 5th February.

Those wearing Military and Naval Uniforms only will walk in the procession from Trinity Pier. Other Guests will go straight to Whippingham Church by 12.30, p.m.

Vehicles will be provided at Cowes for Guests who arrive by the special train leaving Waterloo at 9.5, a.m.

Only eleven years after his marriage to Princess Beatrice, Prince Henry of Battenberg died. The ceremonial for the funeral was as detailed as ever, and the Queen wrote about it at great length in her Journal.

Ceremonial

OBSERVED

On the Reception and on the Interment of The Remains of His Royal Highness The Prince Henry Maurice of Battenberg, K.G., Husband of Her Royal Highness The Princess Henry of Battenberg, Princess Beatrice of Great Britain and Ireland, Son-in-Law of Her Majesty The Queen, who died on active Service, whilst returning from the Ashanti Expedition, on board Her Majesty's Ship "Blonde," on January 20th, 1896.

The Remains of His Royal Highness having been transferred to Her Majesty's Ship "Blenheim," on the arrival of the "Blonde," at Madeira, the "Blenheim" sailed for England on the 30th January in charge of Colonel Lord William Cecil, Equerry to His Royal Highness, and Mr. H. L. Hertslet, of The Lord Chamberlain's Department, who had been specially sent out there for the purpose.

On the arrival of Her Majesty's Ship "Blenheim" at Portsmouth on Tuesday, the 4th of February, Her Royal Highness The Princess Henry of Battenberg, accompanied by Her Royal Highness The Princess Christian of Schleswig-Holstein, His Royal Highness The Duke of Connaught and Strathearne, K.G., and Their Serene Highnesses The Prince Louis and The Prince Francis Joseph of Battenberg, crossed to Portsmouth in the Royal Yacht "Alberta," and attended a short service on board the "Blenheim."

little drizzle.—Slept fairly well, but awoke dreading what was before us.—Edward Weimar, Franz Teck & Dolly & Ernest Leiningen had all come yesterday but the 2 last named were on board the Yacht. The others as well as Helen, Tara & Christle [*Prince Christian of Schleswig-Holstein, son of the Queen's daughter, Princess Helena*] are at Osborne Cottage. Alix & the 2 dear girls breakfasted with. Then dear Beatrice came in. She had gone down to the *Alberta* at 9, with Arthur, Louis, Franzjos [*Prince Francis Joseph of Battenberg*], the 2 eldest children & Lenchen. She was calm, but the deepest grief depicted in her poor young face.—Shortly after 12 drove down to Trinity Pier with darling Beatrice, Ena & little Leopold, in a landau & pair. There were great crowds along the road, which was lined with troops. To attempt properly to describe the whole of the sad proceedings & ceremony, is more than I can do, so I will confine myself to a few particulars, impressions & feelings, & have asked Sir A. Bigge to write an account, the copy of which I annex. At the Pier on either side of the pontoon, stood all the Princes, except the actual Chief Mourners, & we remained on one side, the gun carriage on the other. We had to wait but a short time, when the Blue-Jackets of the 'Victoria & Albert' appeared, bearing their precious burden, followed by Louis, Franzjos & dear little Drino, looking so small and touching. Most easily was the coffin placed on the gun carriage, drawn by 6 horses, & we began slowly to move. There were so many Princes, Representatives & Deputations, such as from the Guardes du Corps, & Liko's Bulgarian Regt. that we could not follow as close as we should have wished.

Wednesday, February 5th, 1896
[*Sir A. Bigge's account*]

> Soon after 12 the wharf at Trinity Pier presented a striking scene, for thither had assembled all the Royal Princes, Representatives & those Naval & Military friends & officials invited to the Funeral . . . Within a few minutes of 2 o'clock the gun carriage had reached the Lych gate of Whippingham Church & the massed Bands in an adjoining field, played the Chorale 'Jesus meine Zwersicht'. Beyond them 300 Riflemen of the Princess's Regt. who later fired the volley as a salute to their Chief. The music of brass and reed gives way to that of Choristers. Already the sweet refined voices of the St. George's Choir are chanting the opening sentences as we watch this last stage in the lone journey of the weary traveller, who starting amidst African forest & swamp & surf, traversing thousands of ocean miles is now borne by the flower of British soldiery back to that same country church from which, not alone, but as a happy wedded man, he had started on the first stage of his English life.—

OSBORNE, February 14th, 1896

WROTE A LETTER TO BE PUBLISHED in the papers, thanking my people for their kind sympathy with Beatrice and me in our great sorrow.

RIGHT: *The dinner menu for the day of the funeral of the Queen's son-in-law, Prince Henry of Battenberg.*

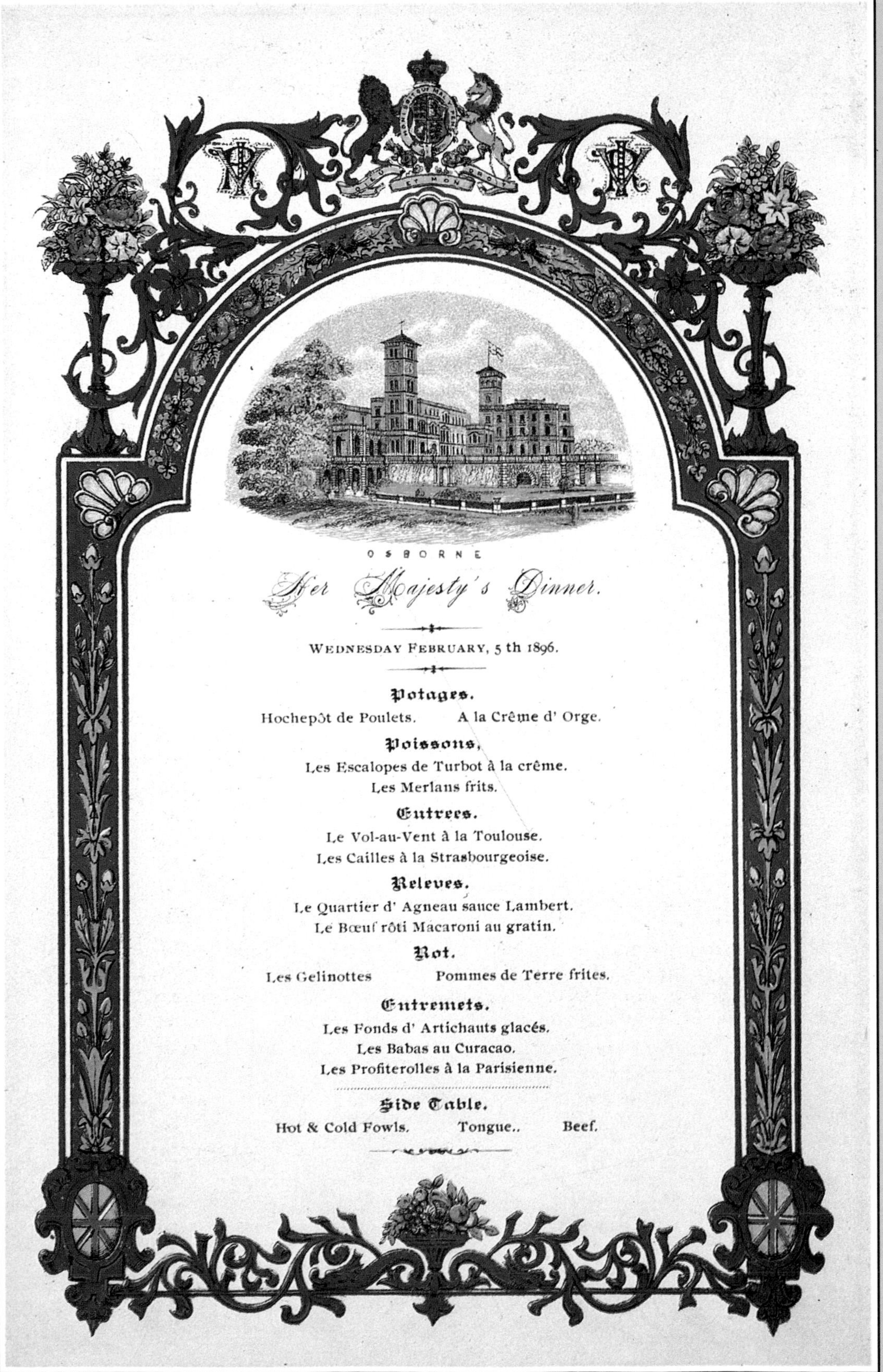

OSBORNE

Her Majesty's Dinner.

WEDNESDAY FEBRUARY, 5 th 1896.

Potages.

Hochepôt de Poulets. A la Crême d' Orge.

Poissons,

Les Escalopes de Turbot à la crême.

Les Merlans frits.

Entrees.

Le Vol-au-Vent à la Toulouse.

Les Cailles à la Strasbourgeoise.

Releves.

Le Quartier d' Agneau sauce Lambert.

Le Bœuf rôti Macaroni au gratin.

Rot.

Les Gelinottes Pommes de Terre frites.

Entremets.

Les Fonds d' Artichauts glacés.

Les Babas au Curacao.

Les Profiterolles à la Parisienne.

Side Table.

Hot & Cold Fowls. Tongue.. Beef.

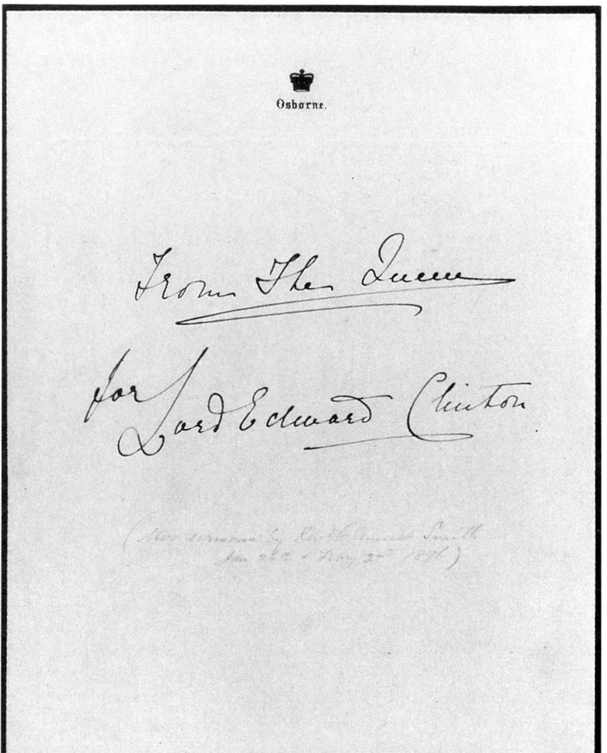

Osborne.

From The Queen
for Lord Edward Clinton

LEFT: *The Queen loved sermons and asked clergymen to send her copies of those she had particularly enjoyed. In turn, she sent them to her close friends whom she thought would also enjoy them. These two, by the Rev. Clement Smith, preached on January 26 and February 2, 1896, were sent by the Queen to Lord Edward Pelham-Clinton. The inscription is in the Queen's own handwriting.*

RIGHT: *Two pages from Lord Edward's 'Court Kalendar': his official diary for 1896. The entries show not only the Queen's movements, but the arrivals and departures of her guests and the dates of her third and fourth Drawing Rooms.*

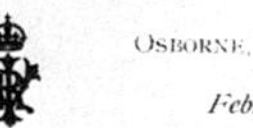

OSBORNE,

February 14th, 1896.

I have, alas! once more to thank my loyal subjects for their warm sympathy in a fresh grievous affliction which has befallen me and my Beloved Daughter, Princess Beatrice, Princess Henry of Battenberg.

This new sorrow is overwhelming, and to me is a double one, for I lose a dearly loved and helpful Son, whose presence was like a bright sunbeam in my Home, and my dear Daughter loses a noble devoted Husband to whom she was united by the closest affection.

To witness the blighted happiness of the Daughter who has never left me, and has comforted and helped me, is hard to bear. But the feeling of universal sympathy so touchingly shown by all classes of my subjects has deeply moved my Child and myself, and has helped and soothed us greatly. I wish from my heart to thank my People for this, as well as for the appreciation manifested of the dear and gallant Prince who laid down his life in the service of his adopted Country.

My beloved Child is an example to all, in her courage, resignation, and submission to the will of God.

VICTORIA, R.I.

LEFT: *A letter to her people from the Queen thanking them for their 'warm sympathy' on the death of Prince Henry of Battenberg.*

1896.

MAY.		MORNING.	EVENING.
Friday	1	The Queen arrives at Windsor from Cimiez at 8.15 P.M.	
Saturday	2	Bishop of Winchester arrives at	
Sunday	3	Bishop of Winchester.	
Monday	4	The Prince of Wales & the Duke & Dss of Connaught arrive & remain 1 night.	
Tuesday	5	Viscount Wolseley to receive Gold Stick after lunch. Sir Reginald Gipps for 1. night. & Count de Pontavice	
Wednesday	6	Royal Academy opens to the Public. Princess Louise & Marquis of Lorne to lunch.	
Thursday	7	3rd Drawing Room	
Friday	8	Mr Charles [illegible] Minister for Switzerland to be received. Hon: Wm Barrington to kiss hands as Minister to Buenos Ayres	
Saturday	9	Rt Hon: G and Mrs Goschen for one night. Rt Hon: A Balfour for one night	
Sunday	10	Professor [illegible] H. E. Ryle D.D. (of Cambridge)	
Monday	11	~~Rt Hon G & Mrs Goschen & Rt Hon A Balfour for 1 night~~ Princesses of Connaught arrive at 4.20. Surg: Major General Taylor for one night	
Tuesday	12	Comte de Ficalho Grand Maître of King of Portugal ~~to be received at 3 P.M.~~ Rt Hon: Sir H Drummond Wolff to be received at 3 o'c Council at 3. o'clock	
Wednesday	13		
Thursday	14	Ascension Day (a Collar Day) ~~Sir H. Drummond Wolff to be received at 3 P.M.~~ Duke of Cambridge dine & sleep. Duchess of Albany Postponed to 20 The Queen will receive address from the Convocation of [illegible] Investiture of Order of Knighthood at 3 P.M.	
Friday	15	Dean of Windsor & Mrs Eliot to dine.	
Saturday	16		

1896.

MAY.		MORNING.	EVENING.
Sunday	17	Dean of Windsor.	
Monday	18	4th Drawing Room. Duke & Duchess of Fife & Mr & Mrs Chamberlain for one night. Queen presents photos to the Bearers of Prince H. of Battenberg	
Tuesday	19		
Wednesday	20	Queen's Birthday Kept. Queen will receive an Address from Convocation of Canterbury	
Thursday	21	The Earl & Countess of Pembroke for 1 night. Mr Genl Sir Francis Scott for 1 night. Sir H. E. Maxwell for 1 night. The Princess of Wales arrives 11 a.m. & leaves 12.58	
Friday	22	~~[illegible]~~ [illegible] Duke & Duchess of York, [illegible] Lady Salisbury, Major General [illegible]. Bishop of Ripon for 2 nights.	
Saturday	23	Duchess of Albany & Suite arrive at — for three nights	
Sunday	24	Whit Sunday (a Collar Day) The Queen's Birthday (a Collar Day) Bishop of Ripon preaches.	
Monday	25	Whit Monday (a Collar Day) The Princess Helena (Princess Christian of Schleswig-Holstein) born (1846)	
Tuesday	26	Whit Tuesday (a Collar Day) The Duchess of York born (1867) The Queen leaves Windsor for Balmoral at 8.25 P.M.	
Wednesday	27		
Thursday	28		
Friday	29	The Restoration of the Royal Family (a Collar Day)	
Saturday	30		
Sunday	31	Trinity Sunday (a Collar Day)	

BALMORAL, June 20th, 1896

FIFTY-NINE YEARS SINCE I CAME TO THE THRONE! What a long time to bear so heavy a burden! God has guided me in the midst of terrible trials, sorrows, and anxieties, and has wonderfully protected me. I have lived to see my dear country and vast Empire prosper and expand, and be wonderfully loyal! Received many kind telegrams.

WINDSOR CASTLE & BUCKINGHAM PALACE
July 22, 1896

A COOLER DAY. NOT VERY BRIGHT.—Lenchen & Thora breakfasted with me in the garden, under the trees close to the house, where it was very pleasant.—Sat out for a short while and then went in to dress, going downstairs at ½ p. 12, to the Bow Room, where all the family were assembled. I wore a black satin dress with embroideries & jet, a lace veil of old

Buckingham Palace, London, in spring.

point, & diamond diadem & ornaments. After a few minutes, I was rolled through the Hall, Dining room &c, to the vestibule of the Chapel, Christle and little Arthur going with me, & Louisa Buccleuch, Louisa A., Harriet Phipps, & the Ld. Chamberlain in attendance. There I got out of my chair & was met by the Great Officers of State, & all my Household. A procession was formed & I went into the Chapel assisted by Christle, & was conducted to my seat. The Chapel was very prettily decorated with wreaths of red & white roses twined round the pillars. Above the altar was a large cross of white roses, & palms & white flowers on either side. All the Princes & Princesses bowed to me as they came in preceded by Heralds, &c. Dear Alix, looking so young & lovely in a pale grey dress and many diamonds came in last with her brother Freddy. She sat on my left, & Freddy & Louise of Denmark on my right. Next came the Bridegroom, in Danish naval uniform, supported by his brothers Christian & Harald, & very soon after followed the dear Bride, led by Bertie & supported by Georgie. She had 8 Bridesmaids: Victoria, Ingeborg & Thyra of Denmark, Thora, Daisy & Patsy [*Princesses Margaret and Patricia of Connaught*], Alice [*Princess Alice of Albany, later Countess of Athlone*], & little Alix Duff. Dear Maud [*Princess Maud of Wales, daughter of the Prince & Princess of Wales*] looked very pretty in her white satin dress, with a very long train bordered with orange blossoms, on her head, her mother's wedding veil, & a wreath of orange, blossoms. The Archbishop of Canterbury performed the ceremony, assisted by the Bishops of London & Winchester, other Clergy being also present. The Archbishop delivered a short & good address. After the Benediction, Maud came forward to her Parents & then to me & I kissed both her & the Bridegroom. The Processions reformed in reverse order, & passed to the sounds of Mendelssohn's Wedding March, as in coming, through the covered Gallery which had been arranged on the Terrace. I returned privately as I came & rejoined all the family in the 44 Room [*the 1844 Room*], where the Register was signed. When this was over I went upstairs to my room, & lunched quietly with Harriet P., whilst the wedding breakfast was going on below. My thoughts were dwelling sadly on my darling Beatrice who will be spending tomorrow the first sad lonely anniversary of her wedding day, & the contrast of her shattered happy married life, with the one begun today most piteous.—After luncheon Maud & Charles came to wish me goodbye & I saw them from the window drive away up Constitution Hill. I then took leave of Freddy & Louise of Denmark & their nice daughters. They were full of kind expressions & she said she would do all she could for Maud.—Had some tea & at ¼ p. 6 left with Thora, returning to Windsor. The evening was fine & the crowds were most enthusiastic, which was very gratifying.—Louisa Buccleuch, Louisa A., Sir J. McNeill & Fritz Ponsonby dined with us.

OSBORNE, August 4th, 1896

TEA OUT, AND DROVE WITH SOPHIE AND ISMAY S. to Trinity Pier, where we embarked on board the 'Alberta'. The Empress [*Eugénie*] joined us, and my ladies and gentlemen were also on board. We steamed up to Spithead and through the really splendid Fleet. We went quite close to the large ships, amongst which was the 'Blenheim'. We turned and passed through the Torpedo boats.

OSBORNE, August 25th, 1896

SAW LORD SALISBURY and spoke of the sudden death of the Sultan of Zanzibar, which we

The Queen's granddaughter, Princess Maud of Wales, and her husband Prince Charles of Denmark (the future King Haakon VII of Norway) with the bridesmaids after their wedding on July 22, 1896.

feared was not a natural one. It will no doubt cause difficulties in the succession. There are two rivals, one of whom it is thought we ought to support.

WINDSOR CASTLE, November 23rd, 1896

After tea went to the red drawing-room, where so-called 'animated pictures' were shown off, including the group taken in September at Balmoral. It is a very wonderful process, representing people, their movements and actions, as if they were alive.

CIMIEZ, April 19th, 1897

Sixteen years since my kind friend Lord Beaconsfield died.

CIMIEZ, April 22nd, 1897

At half-past six the celebrated and famous actress Sarah Bernhardt, who has been acting at Nice and is staying in this hotel, performed a little piece for me in the drawing-

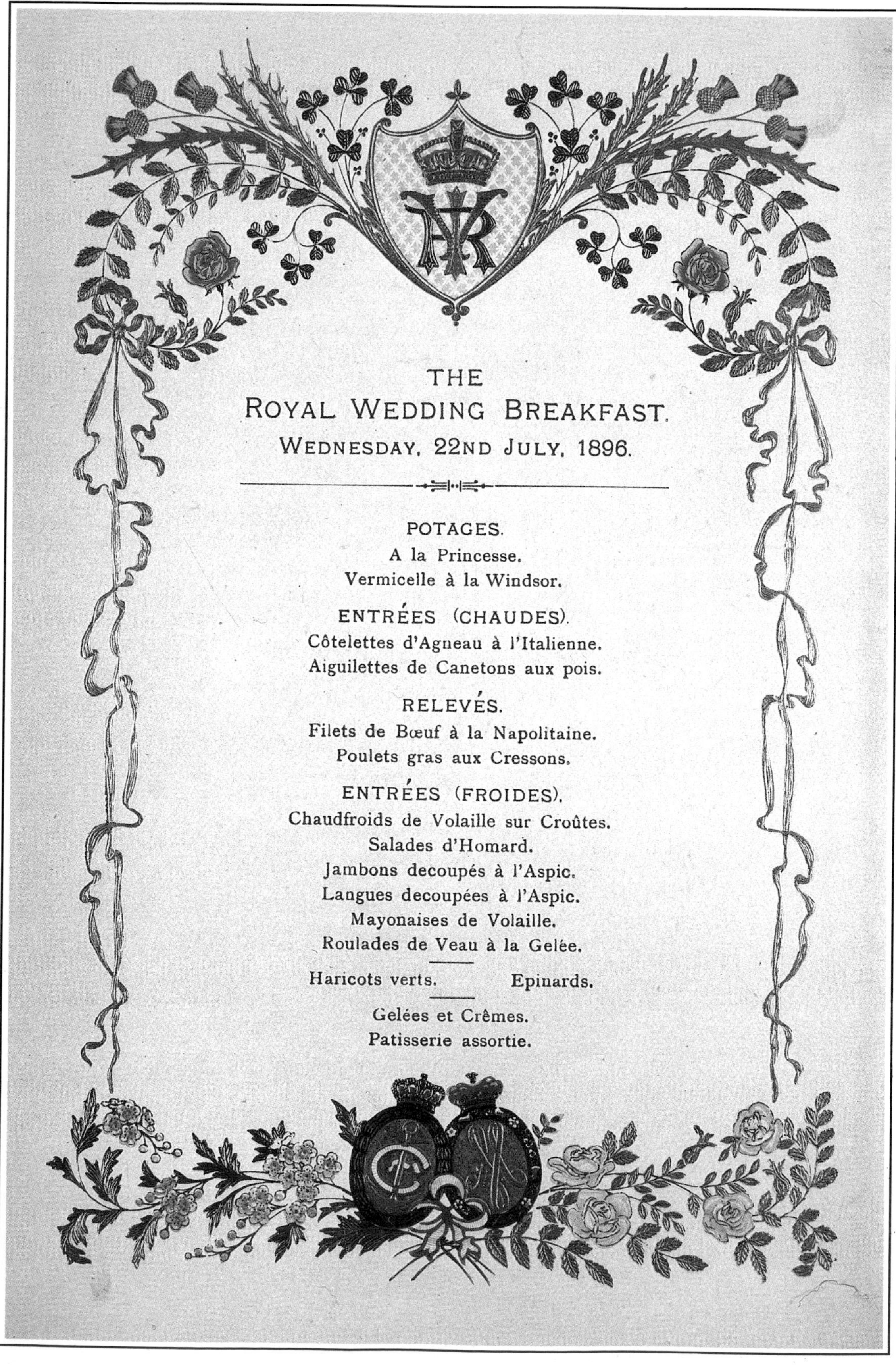

THE
ROYAL WEDDING BREAKFAST.
WEDNESDAY, 22ND JULY, 1896.

POTAGES.
A la Princesse.
Vermicelle à la Windsor.

ENTRÉES (CHAUDES).
Côtelettes d'Agneau à l'Italienne.
Aiguilettes de Canetons aux pois.

RELEVÉS.
Filets de Bœuf à la Napolitaine.
Poulets gras aux Cressons.

ENTRÉES (FROIDES).
Chaudfroids de Volaille sur Croûtes.
Salades d'Homard.
Jambons decoupés à l'Aspic.
Langues decoupées à l'Aspic.
Mayonaises de Volaille.
Roulades de Veau à la Gelée.

Haricots verts. Epinards.

Gelées et Crêmes.
Patisserie assortie.

ABOVE: *The arrival of Czar Nicholas II of Russia and his wife, Queen Victoria's granddaughter Alix of Hesse, at Balmoral, September 23, 1896. From a painting by Orlando Norie.*

LEFT: *The design on the menu card for the wedding breakfast includes the couple's monogram at the bottom joined by a love knot in red and white, the Danish national colours.*

A photograph of the famous French actress, Sarah Bernhardt. In the foreground is a glass flower which belonged to her, now in the possession of the Garrick Club.

A still from the 'animated pictures' referred to by the Queen on November 23, 1896. Czar Nicholas II stands behind the Queen, who is in her pony carriage. Next to the Queen are her granddaughters, the Duchess of Fife (Princess Louise of Wales) and the Czarina (Princess Alix of Hesse); her daughter-in-law the Duchess of Connaught (Princess Louise of Prussia) and the Duchess's daughter, Princess Margaret of Connaught. Princess Patricia of Connaught is in the foreground.

room at her own request. The play was called 'Jean Marie', by Adrien Fleuriet, quite short, only lasting half-an-hour. It is extremely touching, and Sarah Bernhardt's acting was quite marvellous, so pathetic and full of feeling. She appeared much affected herself, tears rolling down her cheeks.

BALMORAL, May 24th, 1897

A FINE MORNING Dear Beatrice came in to me early, as usual on this day. My poor old birthday again came round, and it seems sadder each year, though I have such cause for thankfulness, and to be as well as I am, but fresh sorrow and trials still come upon me. My great lameness, etc., makes me feel how age is creeping on. Seventy-eight is a good age, but I pray yet to be spared a little longer for the sake of my country, and dear ones.

DIAMOND JUBILEE
WINDSOR CASTLE, June 20th, 1897

THIS EVENTFUL DAY, 1897, has opened, and I pray God to help and protect me as He has hitherto done during these sixty long eventful years! I feel sad at the new losses I have sustained, expecially the last one of our beloved Liko! God will surely help me on! How well I remember this day sixty years ago, when I was called from my bed by dear Mama to receive the news of my accession! . . . At eleven I, with all my family, went to St. George's Chapel, where a short touching service took place.

QUEEN'S HALL, W.

THANKSGIVING DAY

Sunday Afternoon, June 20th, at 3.

COMMEMORATION CONCERT

IN CELEBRATION OF

HER MAJESTY'S DIAMOND JUBILEE.

MADAME FANNY MOODY. MISS CLARA SAMUELL.
MR. BEN DAVIES. MR. FFRANGCON-DAVIES.

THE QUEEN'S HALL ORCHESTRA OF 103 PERFORMERS.

Principal Violin - - - MR. ARTHUR W. PAYNE.
Organist and Accompanist - MR. H. W. RICHARDS.

QUEEN'S HALL CHORAL SOCIETY.

Choir Boys from the London Training School for Choristers.

Conductor - - Mr. Alberto Randegger.

PRICE SIXPENCE.

The programme for the Diamond Jubilee Concert in the Queen's Hall, London, on June 20, 1897.

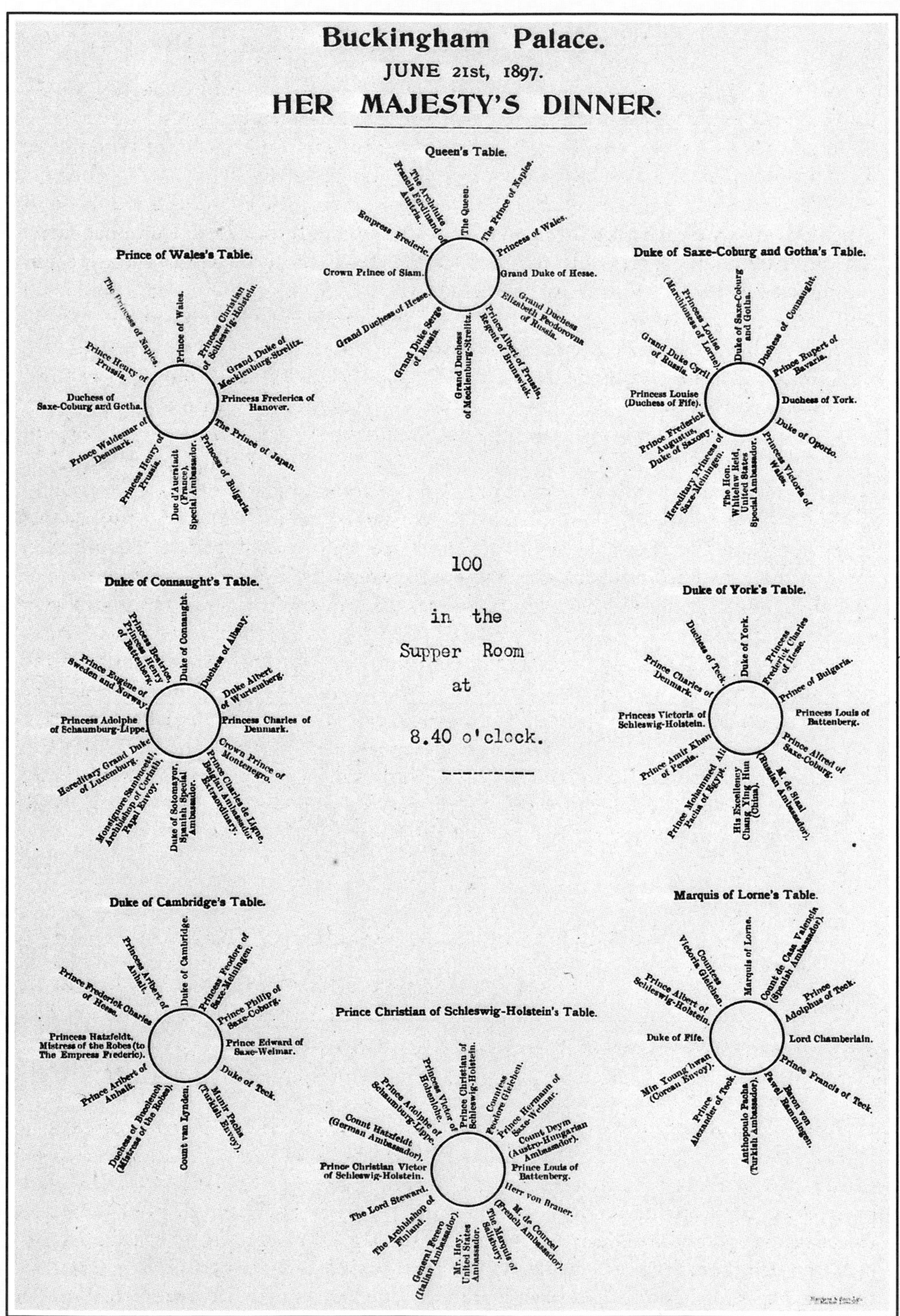

The seating plan for the magnificent dinner held at Buckingham Palace on Diamond Jubilee Day, June 21, 1897. The ill-fated Archduke Francis Ferdinand of Austria, whose assassination in Sarajevo on June 28, 1914, sparked off the First World War, sat on the Queen's right.

BUCKINGHAM PALACE, June 21st, 1897

THE 10th ANNIVERSARY OF THE CELEBRATIONS of my fifty years Jubilee. Breakfasted with my three daughters at the Cottage at Frogmore. A fine warm morning.

At quarter to twelve we drove to the station to start for London. The town was very prettily decorated, and there were great crowds, who cheered very much. . . . Then we proceeded at a slow trot, with a Sovereign's escort of the 1st Life Guards. Passed through dense crowds, who gave me a most enthusiastic reception. It was like a triumphal entry. . . . On entering the park, through the Marble Arch, the crowd was even greater, carriages were drawn up amongst the people on foot, even on the pretty little lodges well-dressed people were perched. Hyde Park Corner and Constitution Hill were densly crowded. All vied with one another to give me a heartfelt, loyal, and affectionate welcome. I was deeply touched and gratified. The day had become very fine and very hot.

Reached the Palace shortly after 1 . . . I was taken round in my wheeled chair to the Bow Room, where all my family awaited me, including Marie Coburg, whom I had not yet seen. Seated in my chair, as I cannot stand long, I received all the foreign Princes in succession, beginning with the Archduke Franz Ferdinand [*the heir to the Austrian throne: murdered at Sarajevo, on June 28th, 1914*]. Dressed for dinner. I wore a dress of which the whole front was embroidered in gold, which had been specially worked in India, diamonds in my cap, and a diamond necklace, etc. The dinner was in the Supper-room at little tables of twelve each. All the family, foreign royalties, special Ambassadors and Envoys were invited. I sat between the Archduke Franz Ferdinand and the Prince of Naples. After dinner went into Ball-room, where my private band played and the following were presented to me: the Colonial Premiers with their wives, the Special Envoys, the three Indian Princes, and all the officers of the two Indian escorts, who, as usual, held out their swords to be touched by me, and the different foreign suites. The Ball-room was very full and dreadfully hot, and the light very inefficient. It was only a little after eleven when I got back to my room, feeling very tired. There was a deal of noise in the streets, and we were told that many were sleeping out in the parks.

BUCKINGHAM PALACE, June 22nd, 1897

A NEVER-TO-BE-FORGOTTEN-DAY. No one ever, I believe, has met with such an ovation as was given to me, passing through those six miles of streets, including Constitution Hill. The crowds were quite indescribable, and their enthusiasm truly marvellous and deeply touching. The cheering was quite deafening, and every face seemed to be filled with real joy. I was much moved and gratified.

The night had been very hot, and I was rather restless. There was such a noise going on the whole time, but it did not keep me from getting some sleep. Dull early and close. Breakfasted with Vicky, Lenchen and Beatrice in the Chinese luncheon room. The head of the procession, including the Colonial troops, had unfortunately already passed the Palace before I got to breakfast, but there were still a great many, chiefly British, passing by. I watched them for a little while. At a quarter-past eleven, the others being seated in their carriages long before, and having preceded me a short distance, I started from the State entrance in an open State landau, drawn by eight creams. Dear Alix looked very pretty in lilac, and Lenchen sat opposite me. I felt a good deal agitated, and had been so all these days, for fear anything might be forgotten or go wrong. Bertie and George C.

LIST OF PRECEDENCE

APPROVED BY THE QUEEN

June, 1897

Her Majesty The Queen and Her Imperial Majesty The Empress Frederic.
Her Royal Highness The Crown Princess of Italy.
Her Royal Highness The Princess of Wales.
Her Royal Highness The Grand Duchess of Mecklenburg-Strelitz.
Her Royal Highness The Grand Duchess of Hesse.
Her Royal Highness The Princess Christian of Schleswig-Holstein.
Her Royal Highness The Princess Louise, Marchioness of Lorne.
Her Royal Highness The Princess Beatrice, Princess Henry of Battenberg.
Her Royal and Imperial Highness The Duchess of Saxe-Coburg and Gotha (Duchess of Edinburgh).
Her Imperial Highness The Grand Duchess Serge of Russia.
Her Royal Highness The Princess Henry of Prussia.
Her Royal Highness The Duchess of Connaught and Strathearn.
Her Royal Highness The Duchess of Albany.
Her Royal Highness The Princess Frederica of Hanover.
Her Royal Highness The Princess of Bulgaria.
Her Royal Highness The Princess Louise, Duchess of Fife.
Her Royal Highness The Princess Victoria of Wales.
Her Royal Highness The Princess Charles of Denmark.
Her Royal Highness The Duchess of York.
Her Royal Highness The Duchess of Teck.
Her Royal Highness The Hereditary Princess of Saxe-Meiningen.
Her Royal Highness The Princess Adolph of Schaumburg-Lippe.
Her Royal Highness The Princess Frederic Charles of Hesse.
Her Grand Ducal Highness The Princess Louis of Battenberg.
Her Highness The Princess Victoria of Schleswig-Holstein.
Her Highness The Princess Aribert of Anhalt.
Her Serene Highness The Princess Feodore of Saxe-Meiningen.

His Imperial and Royal Highness The Archduke Francis Ferdinand of Austria.
His Royal Highness The Crown Prince of Italy.
His Royal Highness The Prince of Wales.
His Royal Highness The Grand Duke of Hesse.
His Royal Highness The Grand Duke of Mecklenburg-Strelitz.
His Royal Highness The Crown Prince of Siam.
His Royal Highness The Prince Henry of Prussia.
His Imperial Highness The Grand Duke Serge of Russia.
His Royal Highness The Prince Albert of Prussia.
His Royal Highness The Duke of Saxe-Coburg and Gotha (Duke of Edinburgh).
His Royal Highness The Prince Waldemar of Denmark.
His Imperial Highness The Prince of Japan.
His Royal Highness The Prince Eugène of Sweden.
His Imperial Highness The Grand Duke Cyril of Russia.
His Royal Highness The Prince Rupert of Bavaria.
His Royal Highness The Prince Frederick Augustus of Saxony.
His Royal Highness The Duke of Oporto.
His Royal Highness The Duke of Connaught and Strathearn.
His Royal Highness The Duke Albert of Wurtemberg.
His Royal Highness The Hereditary Grand Duke of Luxemburg.
His Royal Highness The Duke of York.

His Royal Highness The Duke of Cambridge.
His Royal Highness The Prince Charles of Denmark.
His Royal Highness The Hereditary Prince of Saxe-Coburg and Gotha.
His Imperial Highness The Prince Amir Khan of Persia.
His Highness The Crown Prince of Montenegro.
His Royal Highness The Prince of Bulgaria.
His Royal Highness The Prince Philip of Coburg.
His Royal Highness The Prince Christian of Schleswig-Holstein.
His Highness The Prince Frederic Charles of Hesse.
His Highness The Prince Hermann of Saxe-Weimar.
His Highness The Prince Edward of Saxe-Weimar.
His Highness The Prince Mohammed Ali Pacha.
His Highness The Prince Aribert of Anhalt.
His Serene Highness Prince Adolph of Schaumburg-Lippe.
His Highness The Duke of Teck.
His Highness The Prince Christian Victor of Schleswig-Holstein.
His Highness The Prince Albert of Schleswig-Holstein.
His Serene Highness The Prince Louis of Battenberg.
His Serene Highness The Prince Adolphus of Teck.
His Serene Highness The Prince Francis of Teck.
His Serene Highness The Prince Alexander of Teck.
The Marquis of Lorne.
The Duke of Fife.
The Baron Pawel Rammingen.

Precedence varies from time to time, the only person whose precedence is invariable being the sovereign. The precedence of all others within the kingdom lies within the sovereign's prerogative. These tables of precedence were approved by the Queen for the Diamond Jubilee celebrations in 1897.

HRH the Duke of Cambridge. His daughter, Mary, married the Duke of Teck and their daughter, Princess May of Teck, married the Queen's grandson, the Duke of York.

Col.
Lord E. Pelham Clinton,
K.C.B.

Her Majesty's Diamond Jubilee.

The Queen's Procession will leave Buckingham Palace

on Tuesday, 22nd June, 1897, at 11.15 o'clock.

The attendance of the Master of the Household

is required at 10 o'clock.

S. Ponsonby Fane

FULL DRESS COAT, WITH TROUSERS.

(For Instructions, see other side.)

Shortly before the Queen's grand procession from Buckingham Palace, through London to St Paul's Cathedral, Lord Edward Pelham-Clinton, as Master of the Household, had to make sure that all was in readiness and bid farewell to the Queen at the Grand Entrance to the Palace. He then had to be back in his place at the Grand Entrance after the procession to receive Her Majesty on her return to the Palace. Protocol decreed that he actually had to be summoned to attend.

[*George Cambridge—the 2nd Duke of Cambridge (1819–1904)—Commander-in-Chief of the British Army 1856–95. His daughter, Princess Mary, married the Duke of Teck and was the mother of Princess May of Teck, later Queen Mary wife of George V.*] rode one on each side of the carriage . . . Before leaving I touched an electric button, by which I started a message which was telegraphed throughout the whole Empire. It was the following:
'From my heart I thank my beloved people, May God Bless them!' At this time the sun burst out, Vicky was in the carriage nearest me, not being able to go in mine, as her rank as Empress prevented her sitting with her back to the horses, for I had to sit alone. Her carriage was drawn by four blacks, richly caparisoned in red. We went up Constitution Hill and Piccadilly, and there were seats right along the former, where my own servants and personal attendants and members of the other Royal Households, the Chelsea Pensioners, and the children of the Duke of York's and Greenwich schools had seats. St. James's Street was beautifully decorated with festoons of flowers across the road and many loyal inscriptions. Trafalgar Square was very striking, and outside the National Gallery stands were erected for the House of Lords. The denseness of the crowds was immense, but the order maintained wonderful. The streets in the Strand are now quite wide, but one misses Temple Bar. Here the Lord Mayor received me and presented the sword, which I touched. He then immediately mounted his horse in his robes, and galloped past bare-headed, carrying the sword, preceding my carriage, accompanied by his Sheriffs. As we neared St. Paul's the procession was often stopped, and the crowds broke out into singing God Save the Queen. In one house were assembled the survivors of the Charge of Balaclava.

In front of the Cathedral the scene was most impressive. All the Colonial troops, on

81, ECCLESTON SQUARE. S.W.
June 22nd/97
Please Pass the Bearer –
Mrs. Farnham to my room
in Buckingham Palace.
Edward Pelham-Clinton –
Master of the Household

Jubilee Day, 1897, and a note from Lord Edward Pelham-Clinton to his niece, Mrs Catherine Farnham of Quorn, instructing the staff at Buckingham Palace to admit her to his room, no doubt to enable her to get an inside view of the Jubilee procession as it left and as it returned to the Palace.

foot, were drawn up round the square. My carriage, surrounded by all the Royal Princes, was drawn up close to the steps, where the Clergy were assembled, the Bishops in rich copes, with their croziers, the Archbishop of Canterbury and the Bishop of London each holding a very fine one. A Te Deum was sung, specially composed by Dr. Martin [*organist at St Paul's Cathedral*]; the Lord's Prayer, most beautifully chanted, a special Jubilee prayer, and the benediction concluded the short service, preceded by the singing of the Old 100th, in which everyone joined. God Save the Queen was also sung. I then spoke to the Archbishop and Bishop of London. As I drove off, the former gave out, 'Three cheers for the Queen'.

I stopped in front of the Mansion House, where the Lady Mayoress presented me with a beautiful silver basket full of orchids. Here I took leave of the Lord Mayor . . .

. . . Got home at a quarter to two. Had a quiet luncheon with Vicky, Beatrice and her three children. Troops continually passing by. Then rested and later had tea with Lenchen in the garden. There was a large dinner in the Supper-room.

. . . Felt very tired but tried to speak to most of the Princes and Princesses; the suites also came in, but no one else. I wore a black and silver dress with my Jubilee necklace and the beautiful brooch given me by my Household. In the morning I wore a dress of black silk, trimmed with panels of grey satin veiled with black net and steel embroideries, and some black lace, my lovely diamond chain, given me by my younger children, round my neck. My bonnet was trimmed with creamy white flowers, and white aigrette and some black lace. I left the Ball-room at eleven. There were illuminations, which we did not see, but could hear a great deal of singing and cheering. Gave souvenirs to my children and grandchildren.

A. J. Gow's painting of Queen Victoria arriving at St Paul's Cathedral for the Diamond Jubilee Thanksgiving Service.

WINDSOR CASTLE, June 23rd, 1897

At 3.30 I went to the ball-room [*in Buckingham Palace*], where the heat was dreadful, and received Addresses from the House of Lords and House of Commons . . . This over, the Chairmen of the County Councils came by, one by one, followed by 400 Mayors and Provosts. The whole lasted about an hour. It being so hot and dark in the room, I felt quite sleepy. Left Buckingham Palace at half-past five, driving with Vicky, Beatrice and Arthur. I inspected the Yeomen of the Guard, who were drawn up in the garden on the lawn facing the water. They were under the command of Lord Waldegrave. Then we drove on quite slowly, escorted by a Sovereign's escort of the 2nd Life Guards and by the Indian escort of my army. The crowd was almost more dense along Constitution Hill than yesterday. The stands on the left were filled by 10,000 schoolchildren from the elementary schools of London.

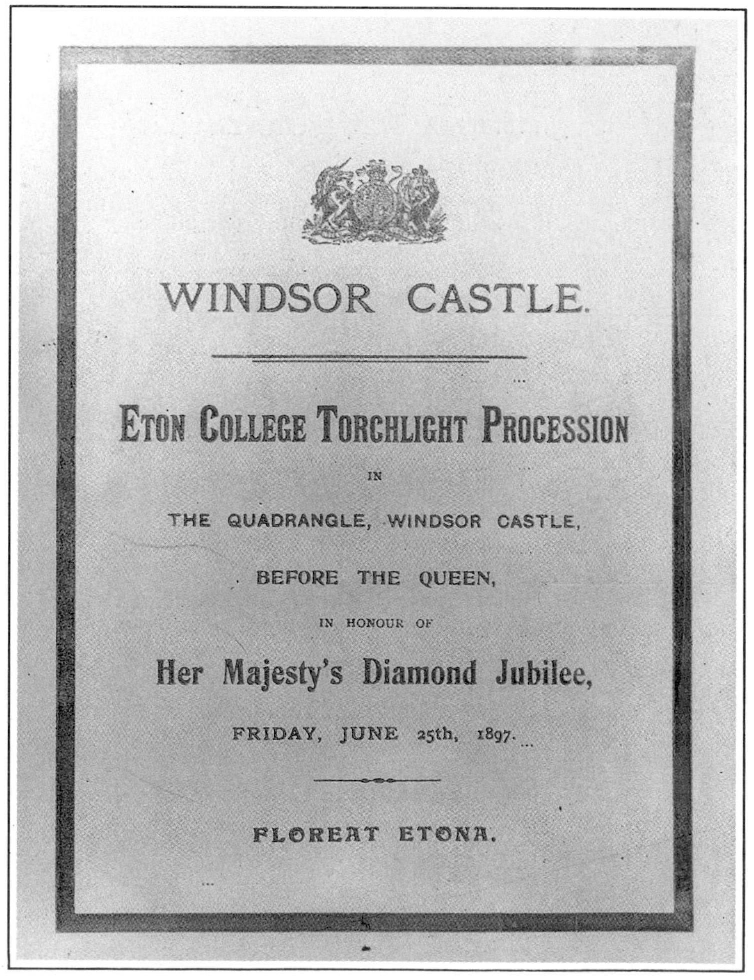

WINDSOR CASTLE.

ETON COLLEGE TORCHLIGHT PROCESSION

IN

THE QUADRANGLE, WINDSOR CASTLE,

BEFORE THE QUEEN,

IN HONOUR OF

Her Majesty's Diamond Jubilee,

FRIDAY, JUNE 25th, 1897.

FLOREAT ETONA.

Among the thousands of events held to celebrate the Diamond Jubilee was a torchlight procession in the Quadrangle of Windsor Castle. The procession, which was formed by boys from Eton College, took place on June 25, 1897 and was watched by the Queen. The programme is printed in Eton blue.

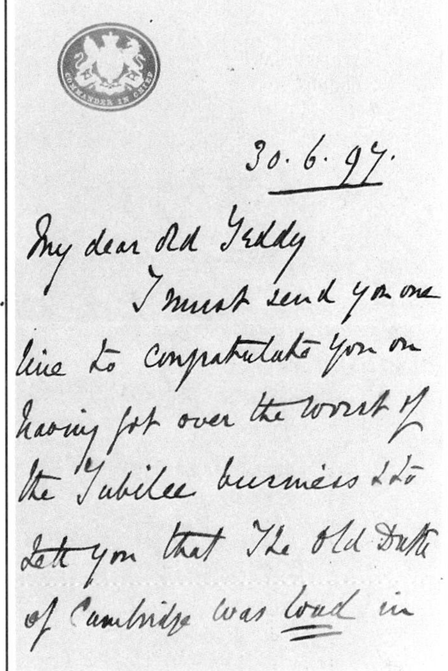

30. 6. 97.

My dear Old Teddy

I must send you one line to congratulate you on having got over the worst of the Jubilee business & to tell you that The Old Duke of Cambridge was loud in

praises of the way you had done Everything; he said he never saw anything better done or to compare, at our Court, with the way you had managed Everything – I told him I

wd. tell you & he said "do! from me"!!

Yrs. as ever

Rowdy

TOP LEFT: *Field-Marshal Lord Wolseley, who succeeded the Duke of Cambridge as Commander-in-Chief.*

ABOVE: *'My dear old Teddy,' wrote Field-Marshal Lord Wolseley to Lord Edward, stating that* HRH *the Duke of Cambridge had praised the part Lord Edward had taken in the Jubilee celebrations.*

A painting by C. Dixon of the Diamond Jubilee Naval Review at Spithead.

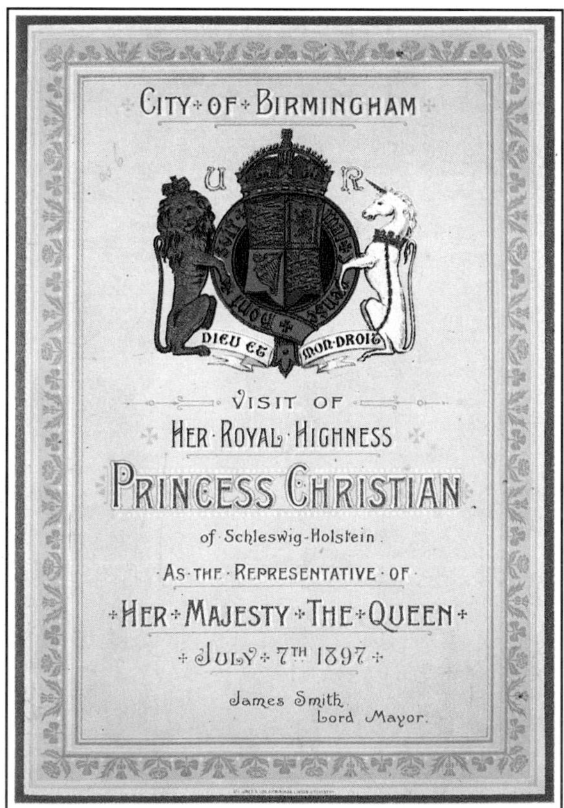

The Queen's daughter, Princess Helena (Princess Christian of Schleswig-Holstein), represented her mother on a visit to Birmingham on July 7, 1897.

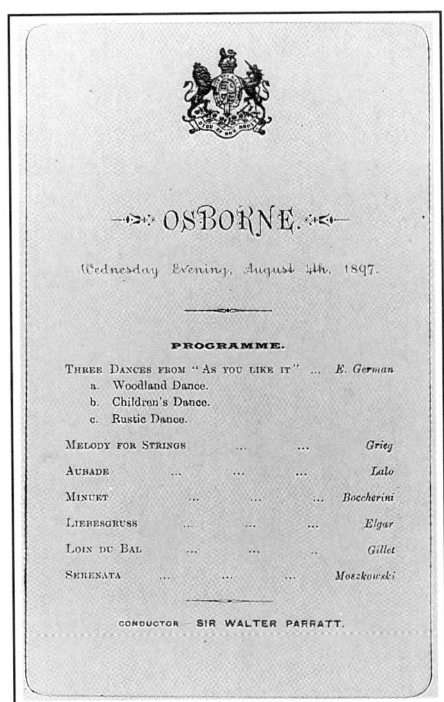

OSBORNE.

Wednesday Evening, August 4th, 1897.

PROGRAMME.

Three Dances from "As you like it" ... *E. German*
 a. Woodland Dance.
 b. Children's Dance.
 c. Rustic Dance.

Melody for Strings ... ... *Grieg*

Aubade ... ... *Lalo*

Minuet ... ... *Boccherini*

Liebesgruss ... ... *Elgar*

Loin du Bal ... . *Gillet*

Serenata ... ... *Moszkowski*

CONDUCTOR – SIR WALTER PARRATT.

OSBORNE.

Thursday Evening, August 5th, 1897.

PROGRAMME.

Overture ... "Le Philtre" ... *Auber*

Elegie (Serenade) ... ... *Tschaikowsky*

Country Dance ... ... *F. H. Cowen*

Orientale ... ... *Glazounow*

Gavotte (Armide) ... ... *Gluck*

Serenade (for Oboe and Strings) ... *Taubert.*

Contretänze ... ... *Beethoven.*

CONDUCTOR – SIR WALTER PARRATT.

OSBORNE.

Friday Evening, August 6th, 1897.

PROGRAMME.

Overture ... "Il Barbiere di Seville" *Rossini*

Septuor (Adagio and Allegro con brio) ... *Beethoven*

Simple Aveu ... ... *F. Thomé*

Gavotte ... ... *Arensky*

Canzonetta ... ... *Mendelssohn*

Dances ... ... *E. German*
 a—Woodland Dance
 b—Children's Dance
 c—Rustic Dance

CONDUCTOR – SIR WALTER PARRATT.

Programmes from Osborne House for August 4, 5, and 6, 1897, when the orchestra played during and after dinner. On these occasions they were conducted by Sir Walter Parratt, the Huddersfield-born Master of the Queen's Musick.

Sir Walter Parratt, Master of the Queen's Musick, was also the Queen's organist and was Organist and Master of the Choristers at St George's Chapel, Windsor Castle. In his day, Sir Walter was considered to be the finest organist in the world and he combined his heavy royal duties with a professorship at the Royal College of Music and from 1908 to 1918 with his position as Professor of Music at Oxford.

WINDSOR CASTLE, July 2nd, 1897

At five drove with Beatrice and Irene [*Princess Henry of Prussia*] through the Slopes to the field on the left of the Lime Avenue, where all the Colonial troops were drawn up in line, under the command of Lord Roberts, and all were on foot. I was received with a royal salute, and then I drove slowly down the line, Lord Roberts and Lord Methuen walking near the carriage and naming each contingent as we came up to them and we stopped at each.

OSBORNE, August 5th, 1897

... My band played again afterwards very prettily.

August 6, 1897

... The band played in the Drawingroom.

OSBORNE, January 27th, 1898

Heard when we were at breakfast from Mr. Forbes that dear old Mrs. Symon at the shop in the village at Balmoral had passed away. Though she had recovered so well while we were there and greeted us as kindly as ever, she caught a chill a few days ago and was carried off by bronchitis. We had found her and her good amusing husband in the village when we first came to Balmoral in 1848, and we built them their new house and shop. She was quite an institution; and everyone, high and low, used to go and see her.

CIMIEZ, April 25th, 1898

Drove down to the promenade des Anglais a little before eleven, with Beatrice, Marie E., and Drino to see a parade of the troops of the garrison.

WINDSOR CASTLE, May 19th, 1898

Heard at breakfast time that poor Mr. Gladstone, who has been hopelessly ill for some time and had suffered severely, had passed away quite peacefully this morning at five. He was very clever and full of ideas for the bettering and advancement of the country, always most loyal to me personally, and ready to do anything for the Royal Family; but alas! I am sure involuntarily, he did at times a good deal of harm. [*In fact, the Queen loathed Gladstone. She made him stand during his audiences with her when he was in his eighties and once she asked no one in particular: 'Does Mr. Gladstone think this is a public tent?' after he had entered her private tent at the reception after the marriage of the future King George V and Queen Mary in 1893!*]

The Lord Chamberlain is
commanded by The Queen to invite

Mrs Farnham

to a Ball on Monday the
23rd of May 1898, at 10-30 o'Clock.

Buckingham Palace. Full Dress

In consequence of the death of
The Right Hon W. E. Gladstone
The Queen's State Ball
which was to have taken place on
Monday next 23rd inst has been postponed

Lord Chamberlain's Office,
20th May 1898.

Her Majesty's Invitation issued
for the State Ball on the 23rd inst.
which was postponed will be available
for Tuesday evening the 7th June.

Lord Chamberlain's Office.
24th May 1898.

The State Ball arranged for May 23, 1898, had to be cancelled because of the death of Mr Gladstone.

The Lord Chamberlain is commanded by The Queen to invite

Mrs Farnham

to an Evening Party on Monday the 20th of June. 1898 at 10-30 o'Clock.

Buckingham Palace. *Full Dress.*

Music.

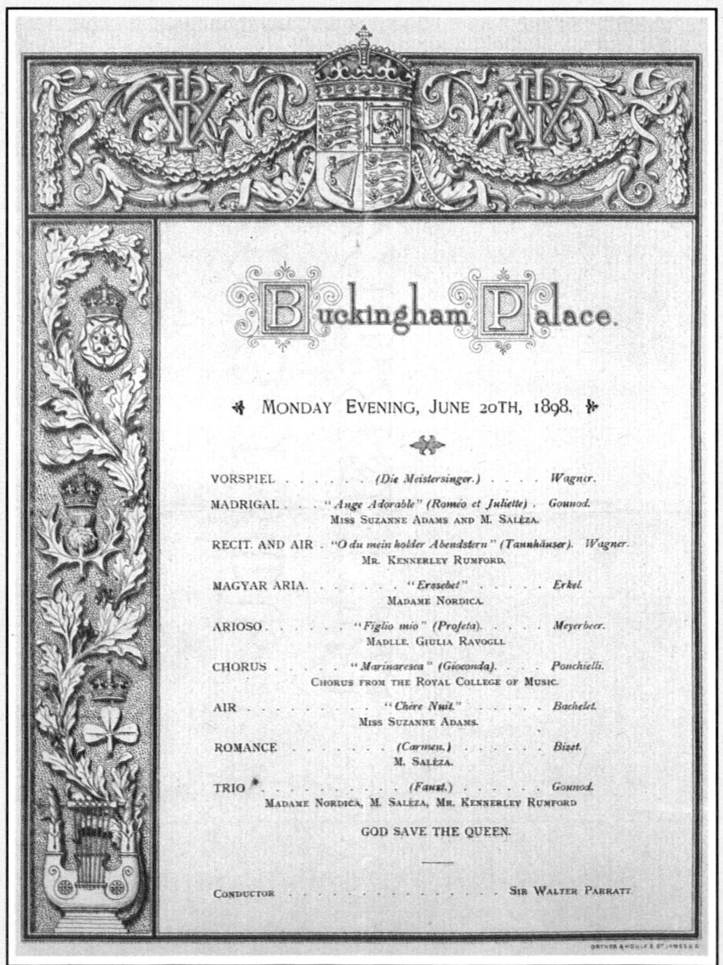

Buckingham Palace.

MONDAY EVENING, JUNE 20TH, 1898.

VORSPIEL . . . . (*Die Meistersinger.*) . . . . *Wagner.*

MADRIGAL . . . "*Ange Adorable*" (*Roméo et Juliette*) . *Gounod.*
MISS SUZANNE ADAMS AND M. SALÈZA.

RECIT. AND AIR . "*O du mein holder Abendstern*" (*Tannhäuser*). *Wagner.*
MR. KENNERLEY RUMFORD.

MAGYAR ARIA. . . . . "*Erzsebet*" . . . . . . *Erkel.*
MADAME NORDICA.

ARIOSO . . . . "*Figlio mio*" (*Profeta*). . . . . *Meyerbeer.*
MADLLE. GIULIA RAVOGLI.

CHORUS . . . . . "*Marinaresca*" (*Gioconda*). . . . *Ponchielli.*
CHORUS FROM THE ROYAL COLLEGE OF MUSIC.

AIR . . . . "*Chère Nuit.*" . . . . . . *Bachelet.*
MISS SUZANNE ADAMS.

ROMANCE . . . . (*Carmen.*) . . . . *Bizet.*
M. SALÈZA.

TRIO * . . . . (*Faust.*) . . . . *Gounod.*
MADAME NORDICA, M. SALÈZA, MR. KENNERLEY RUMFORD

GOD SAVE THE QUEEN.

CONDUCTOR . . . . SIR WALTER PARRATT.

Mrs Farnham's invitation to an evening party at Buckingham Palace, and the programme of music that entertained the guests.

The magnificent Waterloo Chamber at Windsor Castle arranged as a theatre. On this occasion, June 27, 1898, members of the Royal Opera Company were to present Romeo et Juliet.

WINDSOR CASTLE, June 27th, 1898

PUNCTUALLY AT NINE we went over to the Waterloo Gallery, where a performance of Gounod's 'Romeo and Juliet' was given. The music is heavenly, especially that of the two last acts, but I can scarcely say which I admire most, this or 'Faust'. It is impossible to speak too highly of Madame Eames' performance as Juliet. Her voice is beautifully clear and she sings with much feeling. We had a great disappointment in Jean de Reszke being unable to sing, having been taken ill at the last moment, and a M. Saléza, a new tenor, who has a good voice, but sings rather too loud, took his part as Romeo.

BALMORAL CASTLE, September 12th, 1898

THE MURDER OF OUR VICE-CONSUL and the killing and wounding of our officers and men in Crete demand reparation on the part of the Sultan. We cannot let this pass quietly. It is enough to provoke a war. We really cannot wait for the other powers in what concerns us.

CONCERT

GIVEN BY COMMAND BEFORE

HER MAJESTY THE QUEEN

AT

WINDSOR CASTLE

ON

THURSDAY, 24TH NOVEMBER, 1898,

BY

MR. ROBERT NEWMAN'S

QUEEN'S HALL ORCHESTRA,

CONDUCTED BY MR. HENRY J. WOOD.

LEFT: *The Queen particularly enjoyed this concert given at Windsor Castle by Robert Newman's Queen's Hall Orchestra on November 24, 1898. The conductor was the young Henry Wood, who was to achieve fame as the founder-conductor of the Promenade concerts.*

BELOW: *After the concert, the Queen presented Henry Wood with a conductor's baton. This is his letter of thanks addressed to the Lord Chamberlain, but now in Lord Edward Pelham-Clinton's collection.*

1, LANGHAM PLACE, W.

November 25th 1898

To the Lord Chamberlain

Sir

Will you kindly convey to Her Majesty my most grateful thanks for the handsome Conductor's bâton which she has so graciously presented to me

I remain

Sir

Yours Faithfully

Henry J. Wood

BALMORAL, September 29th, 1898

BEATRICE CAME IN TO ME to bring the news of the poor Queen of Denmark's death, which Alix had telegraphed to me in the following words:

'Our beloved Mother passed away at six this morning. No words can describe our sorrow.' I am so much grieved, for I know what a blow it will be to the poor King and all their children, who were so devoted to her.

WINDSOR CASTLE, November 24th, 1898

... AFTERWARDS WE WENT TO THE WATERLOO GALLERY, where we heard the splendid unrivalled orchestra from the Queen's Hall, numbering 106 performers. The Good Friday music from Wagner's 'Parsifal', with which they began, I thought most impressive and beautiful, Saint-Saëns' 'Rouet d'Omphale' was quite charming, and the Adagio out of Tchaikoffski's Symphonie Pathétique, was most touching and wonderfully beautiful. Mr. Wood [*later Sir Henry Wood who founded the Promenade Concerts*] conducted quite admirably, and the orchestra was quite perfect in every little detail. It was a real treat to hear it.

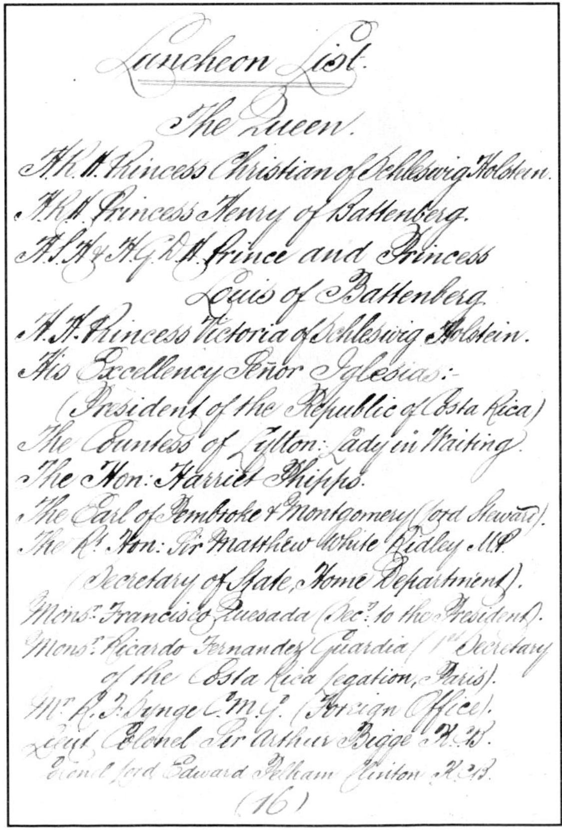

Luncheon List.
The Queen.
H.R.H. Princess Christian of Schleswig Holstein.
H.R.H. Princess Henry of Battenberg.
H.S.H. & H.G.D.H. Prince and Princess
Louis of Battenberg.
H.H. Princess Victoria of Schleswig Holstein.
His Excellency Señor Iglesias:-
(President of the Republic of Costa Rica)
The Countess of Lytton: Lady in Waiting.
The Hon: Harriet Phipps.
The Earl of Pembroke & Montgomery (Lord Steward).
The Rt. Hon: Sir Matthew White Ridley M.P.
(Secretary of State, Home Department).
Monsr. Francisco Quesada (Secy. to the President).
Monsr. Ricardo Fernandez Guardia (1st Secretary
of the Costa Rica Legation, Paris).
Mr. R. F. Synge C.M.G. (Foreign Office).
Lieut. Colonel Sir Arthur Bigge K.C.B.
Colonel Lord Edward Pelham Clinton K.C.B.
(16)

The Queen's guests for luncheon on January 17, 1899.

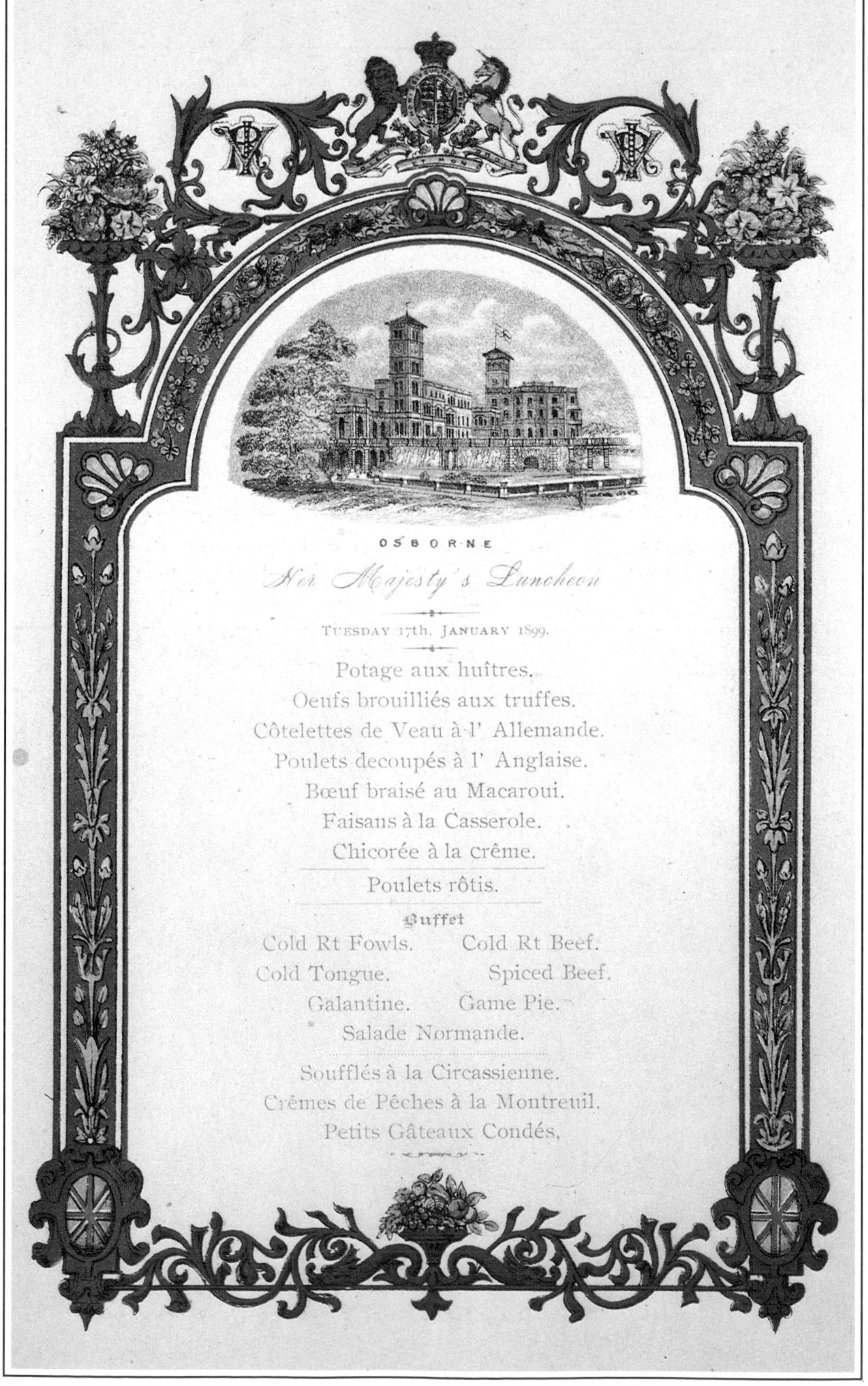
OSBORNE

Her Majesty's Luncheon

TUESDAY 17th. JANUARY 1899.

Potage aux huîtres.
Oeufs brouilliés aux truffes.
Côtelettes de Veau à l' Allemande.
Poulets decoupés à l' Anglaise.
Bœuf braisé au Macaroui.
Faisans à la Casserole.
Chicorée à la crême.

Poulets rôtis.

Buffet

Cold Rt Fowls. Cold Rt Beef.
Cold Tongue. Spiced Beef.
Galantine. Game Pie.
Salade Normande.

Soufflés à la Circassienne.
Crêmes de Pêches à la Montreuil.
Petits Gâteaux Condés,

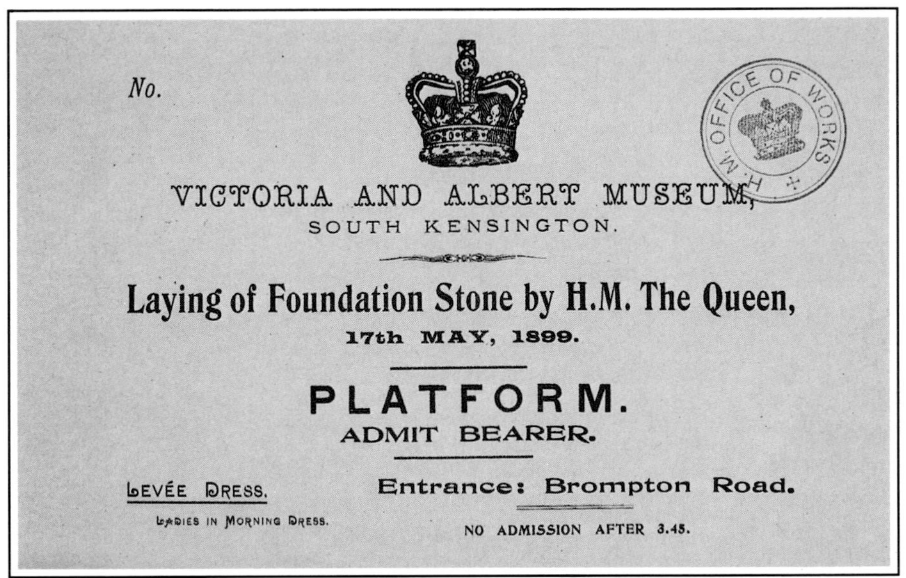
No.

H.M. OFFICE OF WORKS

VICTORIA AND ALBERT MUSEUM,
SOUTH KENSINGTON.

Laying of Foundation Stone by H.M. The Queen,
17th MAY, 1899.

PLATFORM.
ADMIT BEARER.

LEVÉE DRESS.
LADIES IN MORNING DRESS.

Entrance: Brompton Road.
NO ADMISSION AFTER 3.45.

The magnificent Victoria and Albert Museum is at the southern end of the amazing complex of colleges, galleries and museums, originally envisaged by the Prince Consort. The Queen laid the foundation stone on May 17, 1899.

A. Streeton's painting of the building of the West Front of the Victoria and Albert Museum, London.

LEFT: *A menu card from Osborne House for January 17, 1899, showing a varied, splendid luncheon menu.*

OSBORNE, January 27th, 1899

WILLIAM'S [*the Kaiser*] 40th BIRTHDAY. I wish he were more prudent and less impulsive at such an age!

WINDSOR CASTLE, May 17th, 1899

... AT ½ P. 4 STARTED IN THE OPEN LANDAU & 4, the postillions in Ascot Livery, with Lenchen, Beatrice and Arthur, the rest of the family following, as well as the suite. I had a Sovereign's Escort. Went up Constitution Hill, down Knightsbridge and Brompton Road to South Kensington, to the site of the new Victoria and Albert Museum. Immense and enthusiastic crowds everywhere, reminding me of the Jubilee. On arriving I entered a Pavilion, which was very handsome and full of people. Bertie and the rest of the family were on the Dais as well as Ministers, Ambassadors and many notables. Two verses of 'God save the Queen' were sung, as also an Ode, words by the Poet Laureate, and music by McKenzie. Before the latter, the Duke of Devonshire, as Ld. President, read an address. I handed my answer and said 'It gives me great pleasure to lay the foundation stone of this fine Museum which is to bear the name of my dear Husband and myself.' I then laid the stone, Bertie helping me to spread the mortar &c., and struck the stone 3 times with a

TELEPHONE No. 35311.
THE ELECTROPHONE LIMITED.
TELEGRAPHIC ADDRESS: "ELECTROPHONE, LONDON."

PELICAN HOUSE,
34 & 35, GERRARD STREET,
LONDON, W. May 25th. 1899.

Dear Lord Edward Pelham-Clinton.

Very many thanks to you for all your many kindnesses yesterday.

I am at Windsor tonight to pilot the Opera Romeo & Juliet by Electrophone to the Castle which can be heard on the two Tables, both in the Oak Dining Room and also in the Corridor.

It is my pleasure to enclose Programme of the Caste.

Believe me to be.

Very appreciatively yours.

H. S. J. Booth

It is hard to realize that years before the BBC was established, the Queen and her guests heard a transmission of the opera Romeo et Juliet *by 'Electrophone' in May, 1899.*

RIGHT: *The Queen's eightieth birthday on May 24, 1899, was celebrated throughout the world. Her Household held a special dinner party where she was toasted by Lord Edward Pelham-Clinton. Its menu was no less magnificent than the Queen's.*

The Queen's 80th Birth-day.

WINDSOR.

THE HOUSEHOLD DINNER,

Wednesday, 24th May, 1899.

Potages.

Consommé d'Orge à la Princesse. Lohengrin.

Poissons.

Whitebait. Filets de Truite à la Reine.

Entrees.

Zéphirs de Volaille à la Renaissance.
Ris de Veau à la Grande Duchesse.

Releve.

Selle de Mouton rôtie.
Timbale de Chouxfleurs à la Stanley.

Rot.

Cailles.

Entremets.

Asperges, Sauce Mousseline.
Parfaits Glacés à la Victoria.

Releves.

Soufflés à la Sax Weimar.
Œufs de Pluviers en Aspic.

2, BRYANSTON SQUARE.
W.

July 8 1899

Dear Lord Edward

May I send you a special little word of thanks for your kindness & courtesy to our delegates yesterday. I was dreadfully worried about the specified number having been exceeded but you were all so kind about it, & as to the provisions they were more than ample even for the increased demands.

I am sure that such a reception cannot fail to do real good, for the news of it will be carried to many lands. You cannot imagine what a happy & enthusiastic party came back to London.

A letter from the Countess of Aberdeen to Lord Edward Pelham-Clinton thanking him for his help during a Congress of Women which she had arranged, which was honoured by the presence of the Queen.

mallet, after which Bertie in a loud voice said he was commanded by me to declare the stone well and truly laid. A bouquet was presented by one of the students of the Royal College of Music. The ceremony concluded with the Archbishop of Canterbury offering up a prayer and giving the blessing. I drove off amidst a flourish of trumpets, 'God save the Queen' and loud cheers. Went straight to Paddington station where there were also immense crowds. Got back to Windsor shortly before 6.—Only the Ladies to dinner.

WINDSOR CASTLE, July 7th & 8th, 1899

... before which I saw in the Quadrangle, headed by Lady Aberdeen, about 180 of the women of all nations, from India and from the Colonies, who have been having a Congress in London.—Drove after tea with Ismay S. and Fanny D.—A ladies dinner, including Horatia Stafford, who has come for a few days. Sat out in the Quadrangle, it was a beautiful night.

WINDSOR CASTLE, November 21st, 1899

DARLING VICKY'S BIRTHDAY ... There was a banquet [*in honour of the visit of the Emperor and Empress of Germany*] in St. George's Hall, which looked very handsome. We sat down 144. Bertie gave out the healths of William and Dona, which was followed by mine, proposed by William, after which followed dear Vicky's, proposed by Bertie. We went into the Reception-room, and I spoke to a number of guests, including the Ambassadors, the Duke and Duchess of Devonshire, Lord and Lady Landsdowne, Lord Wolseley, Lord Roberts, etc. The late news of dear Marie Leiningen were as bad as possible. It was all very painful for me.

OSBORNE, January 1st, 1900

I BEGIN TODAY A NEW YEAR AND A NEW CENTURY, full of anxiety and fear of what may be before us! May all near and dear ones be protected, above all, darling Vicky, who is far from well! I cannot help feeling thankful that, after all, dear Arthur has not gone out to this terrible war. [*The Boer War. The Boers were Dutch farmers who were much involved in opposing Britain's attempts to occupy the Transvaal during 1877–81. The Boers, led by General Smuts, opposed Britain again during the South African War (Boer War) from 1899–1902.*] I hope and pray dear Christle may be spared and many a tried and devoted friend. I pray that God may spare me yet a short while to my children, friends and dear country, leaving me all my faculties and to a certain extent my eyesight! May He bless our arms and give our men strength to fulfil their arduous task!

OSBORNE, January 22nd, 1900

SAW MR. CHAMBERLAIN. Of course we talked of the war and the Colonies in general. He thinks and hopes that the back of the war will be broken if we can relieve Ladysmith. He will not believe that the numbers of the Boers are as great as is said, and thinks they must be exaggerated, in which I differ with him. He repeated that he had done everything in

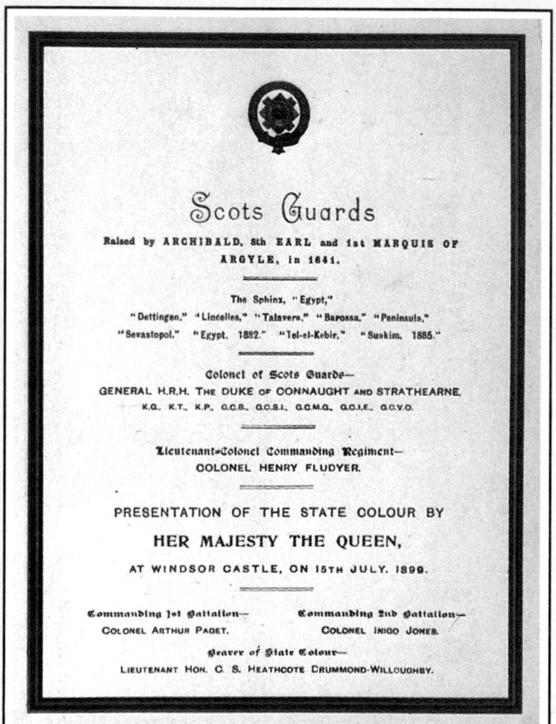

Scots Guards

Raised by ARCHIBALD, 8th EARL and 1st MARQUIS OF ARGYLE, in 1641.

The Sphinx, "Egypt,"
"Dettingen," "Lincelles," "Talavera," "Barossa," "Peninsula,"
"Sevastopol," "Egypt, 1882." "Tel-el-Kebir," "Suakim, 1885."

Colonel of Scots Guards—
GENERAL H.R.H. THE DUKE OF CONNAUGHT AND STRATHEARNE,
K.G., K.T., K.P., G.C.B., G.C.S.I., G.C.M.G., G.C.I.E., G.C.V.O.

Lieutenant-Colonel Commanding Regiment—
COLONEL HENRY FLUDYER.

PRESENTATION OF THE STATE COLOUR BY

HER MAJESTY THE QUEEN,

AT WINDSOR CASTLE, ON 15TH JULY, 1899.

Commanding 1st Battalion—
COLONEL ARTHUR PAGET.

Commanding 2nd Battalion—
COLONEL INIGO JONES.

Bearer of State Colour—
LIEUTENANT HON. C. S. HEATHCOTE DRUMMOND-WILLOUGHBY.

LEFT: *The Scots Guards were delighted when the Queen agreed to present their State Colour, which she did from her carriage.*

RIGHT: *Although Windsor Castle could usually accommodate all the Queen's guests, those who attended them, and also the many servants, there were times when even the Castle was too small. The complete list, only part of which is illustrated, of the Queen's guests in honour of the visit of her grandson and granddaughter-in-law, the German Emperor and Empress, between November 20 and 25, 1899, was enormous and many had to be accommodated in hotels in Windsor. For example, the Emperor and Empress's personal suite numbered fifteen, and the Prince and Princess of Wales had seven servants between them.*

BELOW: *Queen Victoria presenting the State Colour to the Scots Guards at Windsor, July 15, 1899, from the painting by A. Forestier.*

18th NOVEMBER.

Corrected A.B.

being printed without alterations

WINDSOR CASTLE.

List of Her Majesty's Visitors,

WHO WILL ARRIVE AND DEPART BETWEEN THE

20th and 25th NOVEMBER, 1899.

Royal Visitors:—		
THEIR IMPERIAL MAJESTIES THE GERMAN EMPEROR AND EMPRESS	State Apartments	1st Dresser, Fraulein von Beaulieu ......449, West Front 2 Garderobefrau ......436, North Front 1 Kammerdiener ......442, North Front 1 Kammer Lakaien ...434, North Front 2 Damen Lakaien......436, North Front 2 Garderobedieners ...Lobby 457, Star Buildings, F. & E. 1 Kammerdiener ......466, Clock Tower 2 Liebjager ....Lobby 455, Star Buildings, C. & D. 1 Garderobier ....Lobby 455, Star Buildings, G. 2 Liebgendarms ......Lobby 457, Star Buildings, A. & C.
THEIR ROYAL HIGHNESSES THE PRINCE AND PRINCESS OF WALES	255, 256, 257, & 259, Edward 3rd's Tower (First Floor)	2 Dressers..............67 and 68, Edward 3rd's Tower 1 Valet ....71, Edward 3rd's Tower 1 Page ....23, Edward 3rd's Tower Sergeant Footman ..25, Edward 3rd's Tower 2 Footmen ....Box Lobby 29, Edward 3rd's Tower, A. & B.
T. R. H. THE DUKE AND DUCHESS OF CONNAUGHT AND PRINCESS MARGARET	240, 242, 243, and 244, Lancaster Tower, Tapestry Room (First Floor)	1 Dresser ....169, Lancaster Tower 1 Valet ....159, Lancaster Tower 2 Footmen ....Box Lobby 21, Lancaster Tower
T. R. H. THE DUKE AND DUCHESS OF YORK	233, 235, 236, 238, York Tower (First Floor)	1 Dresser ....147, York Tower 1 Valet..................157, York Tower 1 Footman ....Box Lobby 17, York Tower
H. R. H. THE DUKE OF CAMBRIDGE, K.G. (TUESDAY)	323 and 324, Augusta Tower (Baron Stockmar's Rooms)	1 Valet ....610, Victoria Tower
H. R. H. PRINCESS VICTORIA OF WALES	248 & 250, Lancaster Tower, Blue Room (First Floor)	1 Dresser ....171, Lancaster Tower 1 Footman ....Box Lobby 29, Edward 3rd's Tower, C.
T. R. H. THE PRINCES AUGUSTUS WILLIAM AND OSCAR	Audience Chamber, State Apartments	2 Footmen ....Boxes, Star Buildings, 457, B. & D.
H. R. H. PRINCESS LOUISE (MARCHIONESS OF LORNE) AND THE MARQUIS OF LORNE, K.T.	303, 304, and 305, Victoria Tower (Ground Floor)	1 Dresser ....612, Victoria Tower 1 Footman ....609, Victoria Tower
H. R. H. PRINCESS HENRY OF BATTENBERG	219, 227, 228, and 229, Augusta Tower (First Floor)	1 Dresser ....132, Victoria Tower 1 Valet..................48, Clarence Tower 1 Footman ....York Tower Lobby
H. R. H. PRINCE ALBERT OF SCHLESWIG-HOLSTEIN	231, Augusta Tower (First Floor)	1 Valet ....13, Clarence Tower
The Queen's Household in Waiting.		
THE DOWAGER LADY SOUTHAMPTON	152, York Tower (Second Floor)	1 Maid ....155, York Tower
THE HON. MRS. ALARIC GRANT	307, Victoria Tower (Ground Floor)	1 Maid ....312, Victoria Tower
THE HON. FRANCES DRUMMOND (MAID OF HONOUR)	153 and 164, Lancaster Tower	1 Maid ....171, Lancaster Tower
THE HON. BERTHA LAMBART (MAID OF HONOUR)	163 and 162, Lancaster Tower	1 Maid ....169, Lancaster Tower
LORD HARRIS, G.C.S.I., G.C.I.E., (LORD IN WAITING)	544, Ground Floor	1 Valet ....Lobby 412, A.
CAPTAIN WALTER CAMPBELL, M.V.O., GROOM IN WAITING (MONDAY)	430, North Front	1 Valet ....Lobby 412, B.
THE HON. ALEXANDER YORK, M.V.O., GROOM IN WAITING (FROM TUESDAY)	430, North Front	1 Valet ....Lobby 412, B.
COLONEL THE HON. W. CARINGTON, C.B., (EQUERRY-IN-WAITING)	437, North Front	1 Valet ....Lobby 412, C.
CAPTAIN F. E. G. PONSONBY, M.V.O., (EQUERRY-IN-WAITING)	331, York Tower (Sir William Jenner's Room)	1 Valet ....638, York Tower

STATE BANQUET IN ST. GEORGE'S HALL,
TUESDAY, NOVEMBER 21ST, 1899.
(144)

The Lord Steward.

Sir James Reid, Bart.
Colonel Lord Edward Pelham Clinton
Mr. Holmes
Captain F. Ponsonby
Lt. Colonel Right Hon. Sir Fleetwood Edwards
Colonel Egerton
Lieut. Colonel Smith Cuninghame
Mr. Gruneluis
Lieut. General Sir Frederick Marshall
Lieut. General Kelly Kenny
Marquis of Ormonde
Field Marshal Right Hon. Lord Roberts
Captain von Dresky
Admiral of the Fleet Sir Frederick Richards
Right Hon. Sir Henry Fowler
Capt. Lieut. Count Platen zu Hallermund.
Right Hon. G. J. Goschen
Lieut. Colonel von Pritzelwitz
Right Hon. Sir Mathew White Ridley
Earl of Coventry
Lady Edwards
Earl of Kimberley
Miss Minnie Cochrane
Earl Cadogan
Lady Sophia Macnamara
Viscount Cross
Lady Suffield
Archbishop of Canterbury
Marchioness of Lansdowne
H. E. the French Ambassador
Duchess of Buccleuch
H. E. the Austro-Hungarian Ambassador
Princess Victoria of Wales
Duke of York
The Princess Louise (Marchioness of Lorne)
The Prince of Wales
The Empress of Germany
The Prince Christian of Schleswig-Holstein
Princess Henry of Battenberg
H. E. the Turkish Ambassador
Princess Aribert of Anhalt
H. E. the United States Ambassador
Fraulein von Gersdorf
Prince Adolphus of Teck
Duchess of Devonshire
H. E. Count zu Eulenburg
Countess of Pembroke and Montgomery
Duke of Portland
Lady Mary Lygon
Rear Admiral Baron von Senden Bibran
Baroness von und zu Egloffstein.
Kammerherr von dem Knesebeck
Mrs. F. Ponsonby
Lord Harris
Lady Biddulph
Lord George Hamilton
Right Hon. Sir H. Campbell Bannerman
Hon. Sir Spencer Ponsonby Fane
Count Hermann Hatzfeldt
Admiral of the Fleet Sir Edmund Commerell
Captain Kraft
The Dean of Windsor
General Sir Evelyn Wood
Lord Churchill
Baron Mirbach
Captain Grumme, A.D.C.
Captain May, R.N., A.D.C.
Captain Cooper
Lord William Cecil
Sir Charles Cust, Bart.
Colonel Hon. W. Carington

Hon. A. Yorke
Mr. Muther
Lieut. Colonel Sir Arthur Bigge
Lieut. Colonel C. N. Miles
Lieut. Colonel A. Collins
Colonel V. Hatton
Rear Admiral FitzGeorge
Major General Grant
General Sir Dighton Probyn
Lieut. General Sir C. M. Clarke, Bart.
Captain Count Baudessin
Field Marshal Right Hon. Viscount Wolseley
Admiral Sir M. Culme Seymour, Bart.
Doctor Ilberg
Right Hon. Sir Michael Hicks-Beach
Lieut. Colonel von Rauch
Right Hon. J. Chamberlain
Hon. Mrs. Eliot
Lord Tweedmouth
Hon. Mrs. W. Carington
Major General von Scholl
Hon. Bertha Lambart
Marquis of Lansdowne
Hon. Mrs. Egerton
Duke of Devonshire
Countess Stollberg
Marquis of Lorne
Duchess of Portland
H. E. the Spanish Ambassador
Princess Victoria of Schleswig-Holstein
Prince Aribert of Anhalt
Duchess of Connaught
Duke of Cambridge
The Princess of Wales
THE EMPEROR
THE QUEEN
Duke of Connaught
Princess Christian of Schleswig-Holstein
H. E. the Russian Ambassador
Duchess of York
H. E. the Italian Ambassador
Mrs. Choate
Prince Albert of Schleswig-Holstein
Dowager Lady Southampton
Count von Bülow
Dowager Lady Ampthill
The Lord Chancellor
Countess Cadogan
H. E. General von Plessen.
Hon. Mrs. Grant
Earl of Rosebery
Hon. Frances Drummond
Earl of Clarendon
Lady William Cecil
The Speaker
Lady Bigge
Legationsrath Klehmet
Baroness Schrœder
Right Hon. H. H. Asquith
Count Puckler
Captain Rampold
Vice-Admiral Lord Walter Kerr
Earl of Lonsdale
Baron Eckhardstein.
Baron Schrœder
Lieutenant Colonel Grierson
Major General Sir John McNeill
Count Bredow
Hon. Sir William Colville
Colonel Hon. C. Eliot
Hon. S. Greville

The Lord Chamberlain

One hundred and forty-four people sat down to the State Banquet in St George's Hall, Windsor Castle, with the Queen and the Emperor in the centre.

the world to prevent the war, but that as it had come, for come it must have in the future, it was better that it should have been now, before the numbers of the enemy were still greater.

BUCKINGHAM PALACE, March 8th, 1900

GOT SOME GOOD NEWS FROM LORD ROBERTS, who had completely routed the Boers, having turned their flank. They had a very strong position, which would have caused us much loss had we been obliged to make a frontal attack. No end of letters and telegrams of all kinds coming in, some such kind ones.

VICEREGAL LODGE, DUBLIN, April 4th, 1900

WE LANDED AT THE VICTORIA WHARF at half-past eleven, being received by Lord and Lady Cadogan, Arthur, Louischen and their children, also by Lord Dufferin, and Lord Meath. We three wore bunches of real shamrocks, and my bonnet and parasol were embroidered with silver shamrocks ... At Leeson bridge an archway was erected, a fascimile of the entrance of Biggotrath Castle, and according to the ancient custom the gates were closed till the procession approached, when Athlone Pursuiviant-at-Arms advanced saying, 'I demand to be admitted to the presence of the Lord Mayor.' At the same moment the bugler on the top of the arch blew a blast. Athlone passed in, and the gates were reclosed. Bowing to the Lord Mayor he said: 'My Lord Mayor of Dublin, I seek admission to the City of Dublin for her Most Gracious Majesty the Queen'; the Lord Mayor replying, 'On behalf of the City I tender to Her Majesty the most hearty welcome to this ancient city, and on her arrival the gate shall be thrown open on the instant.' This was done, and I passed in, my carriage stopping opposite the Lord Mayor, who with the aldermen, councillors, and officials received me and presented the old city keys, twelve in number, and 600 years old; the city sword was offered by the Lord Mayor [*Mr. Devereux Pile*]. A loyal address was then read and presented to me in a beautiful gold casket. I answered, 'I thank you for your loyal address and this hearty reception. I am very glad to find myself again in Ireland.' I handed him the written answer. [*Queen Victoria's first visit to Ireland was in August, 1849. She was accompanied by the Prince Consort and all their children. She did not like Ireland, or the Irish, but she realized that it was a journey that 'duty' compelled her to make. It was also a sad fact that it had been twenty-eight years since a British monarch had visited the country. The royal party were warmly welcomed in Cork and there is an amusing story that in Kingstown, a woman shouted: 'Oh! Queen dear! Make one of them Prince Patrick, and all Ireland will die for you.' The Queen must have remembered this when she created the Prince of Wales, Earl of Dublin. The Prince Consort, writing to Baron Stockmar said: 'Our Irish visit has gone off well beyond all expectations.' But the Queen neglected Ireland and in all the sixty-three years and seven months of her reign, she only spent five weeks in Ireland, but almost seven years in her beloved Scotland.*]

VICEREGAL LODGE, April 7th, 1900

DROVE WITH LENCHEN AND BEATRICE, the ladies in a second carriage, to the public part of

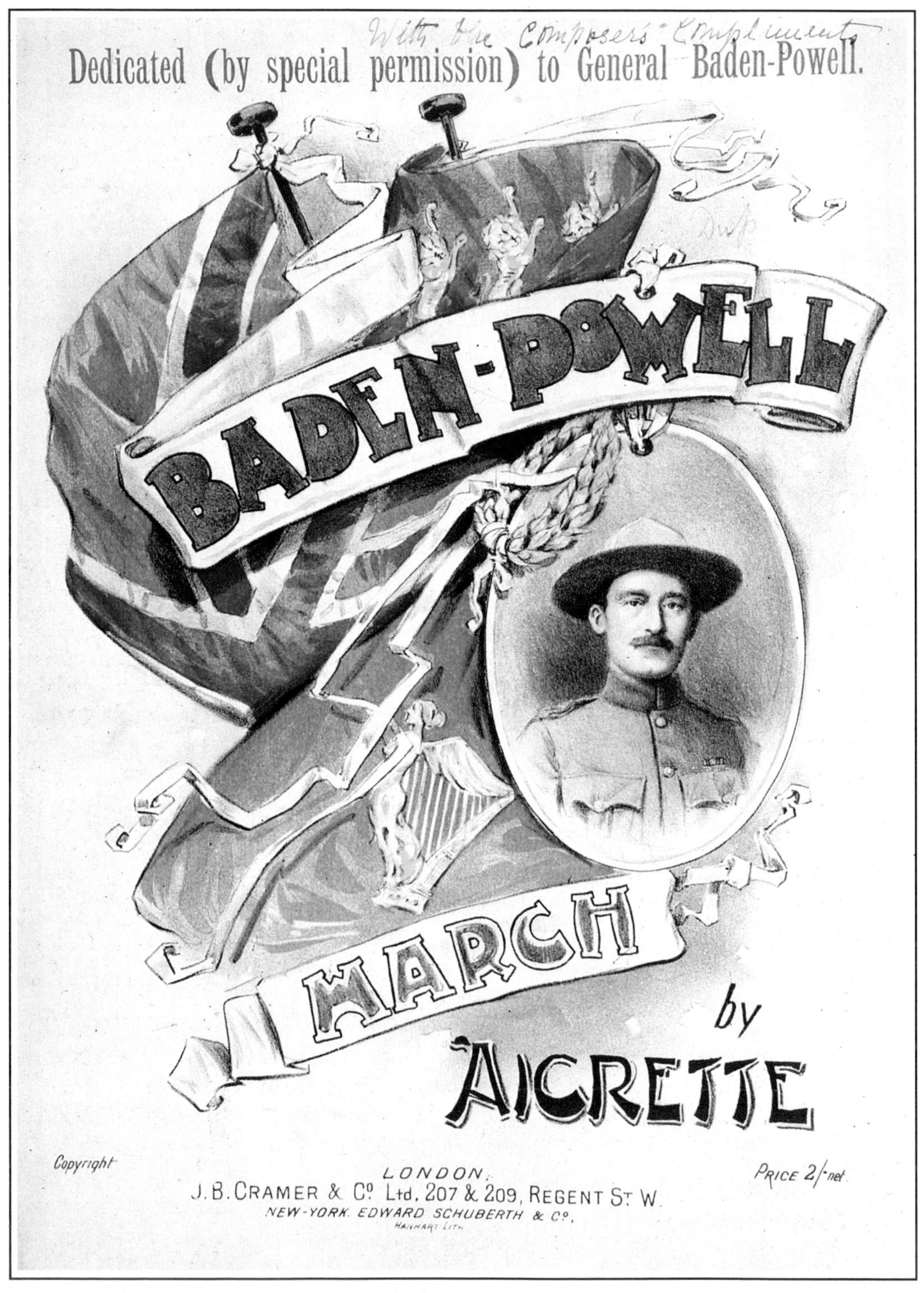

Like Kitchener and Roberts, General Baden-Powell, who founded the Boy Scout movement in 1908, had a march dedicated to him. During the Boer War his force was besieged in Mafeking from October, 1899, to May, 1900.

The relief of Mafeking in 1900, drawn by R. Caton-Woodville.

Phoenix Park, where 52,000 school-children from all parts of Ireland were assembled with their masters and mistresses. It was a wonderful sight, and the noise of the children cheering was quite overpowering.

WINDSOR CASTLE, May 19th, 1900

FINE DAY. Went with Beatrice to the kennels. The following telegram was received from Major-General Baden-Powell [*later Lord Baden-Powell, founder of the Boy Scouts*], dated 17th May: 'Happy to report Mafeking successfully relieved today.'

BALMORAL, May 24th, 1900

AGAIN MY OLD BIRTHDAY RETURNS, my eighty-first! God has been very merciful and supported me, but my trials and anxieties have been manifold, and I feel tired and upset by all I have gone through this winter and spring. Beatrice came in early with a nosegay to congratulate me. Had my present table in my sitting-room, and received so many pretty things.

WINDSOR CASTLE, June 26th, 1900

AT 9 WE ALL WENT TO THE WATERLOO GALLERY, which was arranged as usual, with lovely flowers, in front of the stage, and a performance of the first act of 'Carmen,' followed by 'Cavalleria Rusticana' was given. Calvé was more charming and wonderful than ever, her voice even more beautiful and powerful than before. Susanne Adams was delightful as Micaela. Saléza as Don Jose did very well and the whole mis en scène, chorus and orchestra were very good. Needless to say Calvé was perfection in my favourite 'Cavalleria,' but was not well supported by de Lucia, who bawled in all the most pathetic parts, in a distressing manner.—After receiving the guests who had been invited, in the Green Drawingroom, saw all the 'artistes', Mme. Calvé coming first, wrapped in a long black cloak. Ld. de Grey presented them all, as well as Mr. Gran and the 2 Conductors Mr. Flean, and Signor Mancinelli. I thanked Calvé for her kindness in coming over, as she has done, on purpose to sing before me and she repeated that it was 'un très-grand honneur que la Reine ait voulue, m'entendre encore une fais.' I gave her a sapphire and diamond pendant, and Lenchen and Beatrice gave the other presents.—Heard from China that Tientsin had been relieved and it was believed the Admiral had reached Pekin and was on his way back with the Foreign Ministers after having had hard fighting. [*The Queen was referring to the Boxer Rising—the last effort made by the Chinese to throw off Western influence. The Rising was suppressed by European troops.*]

WINDSOR CASTLE, July 11th, 1900

At three o'clock left for london, and drove to Buckingham Palace through crowds of most enthusiastic people. I rested a little upstairs, and at five got into the victoria with Alix, as three years ago, for the garden party, going first up to the tent where were all the Royal Family and then drove twice round among the guests in the most broiling heat. After having tea we left, just as we came, at twenty minutes to seven. The crowds were still greater than when we arrived. I was dreadfully hot and rather tired.

OSBORNE, July 31st, 1900

A terrible day! When I had hardly finished dressing Lenchen and Beatrice knocked at the door and came in. I at once asked whether there were any news, and Lenchen replied, 'Yes, bad news, very bad news; he has slept away!' Oh, God! my poor darling Affie gone too! My third grown-up child, besides three very dear sons-in-law. It is hard at eighty-one! It is so merciful that dearest Affie died in his sleep without any struggle, but it is heartrending. Poor darling Marie, who knew of no real danger when she left, such a short time ago, without a fear. It is too terrible also for the poor daughters, who adored their father!

WINDSOR CASTLE, November 9th, 1900

Had felt better through the day and free from pain, but I still have a disgust for all food.

WINDSOR CASTLE, November 10th, 1900

Had an excellent night, but my appetite is still very bad.

Windsor Castle
St George's Hall.
(Gallery).

Luncheon Sitting List. Saturday, 7th July 1900.

The Master of
the Household.

WINDOWS

Household and Officers receiving C.Bs

Household and Officers receiving C.Bs

ENTRANCE FROM GRAND RECEPTION ROOM.

Lieut Colonel V.J.Dawson.	Major Smith-Cunninghame.
Lieut: General Hopton.	Major General McCalmont.
Lt Col:Rt Hon:Sir F.Edwards	Lieut:General Geary.
Sir Thomas Gordon.	The Lord Chamberlain.
Miss Bulteel.	Lady Sophia Macnamara.
Lieut:General Sir Baker Russell	The Earl of Jersey.
Hon: Harriet Phipps.	The Dowager Lady Southampton.
General Sir Charles Johnson	Lord Sandhurst.
Hon: Frances Drummond.	The Hon: Bertha Lambart.
Major General Sir Francis Wingate	General Sir William Olpherts.
Fraulein Margraf	Lord Harris.
Hon: A.Yorke.	Major General John Hills.
Colonel F.Keen.	General Louis Nation.

WINDOWS.

Household and Officers receiving C.Bs

Household and Officers receiving C.Bs

Major General
Sir John McNeill.

ORGAN.

A luncheon presided over by the Master of the Household, Lord Edward Peham-Clinton, in St George's Hall, Windsor Castle, before an investiture on July 7, 1900. Note the beautiful typing with the large typeface which were, for many years afterwards, a feature of letters from members of the Royal Family.

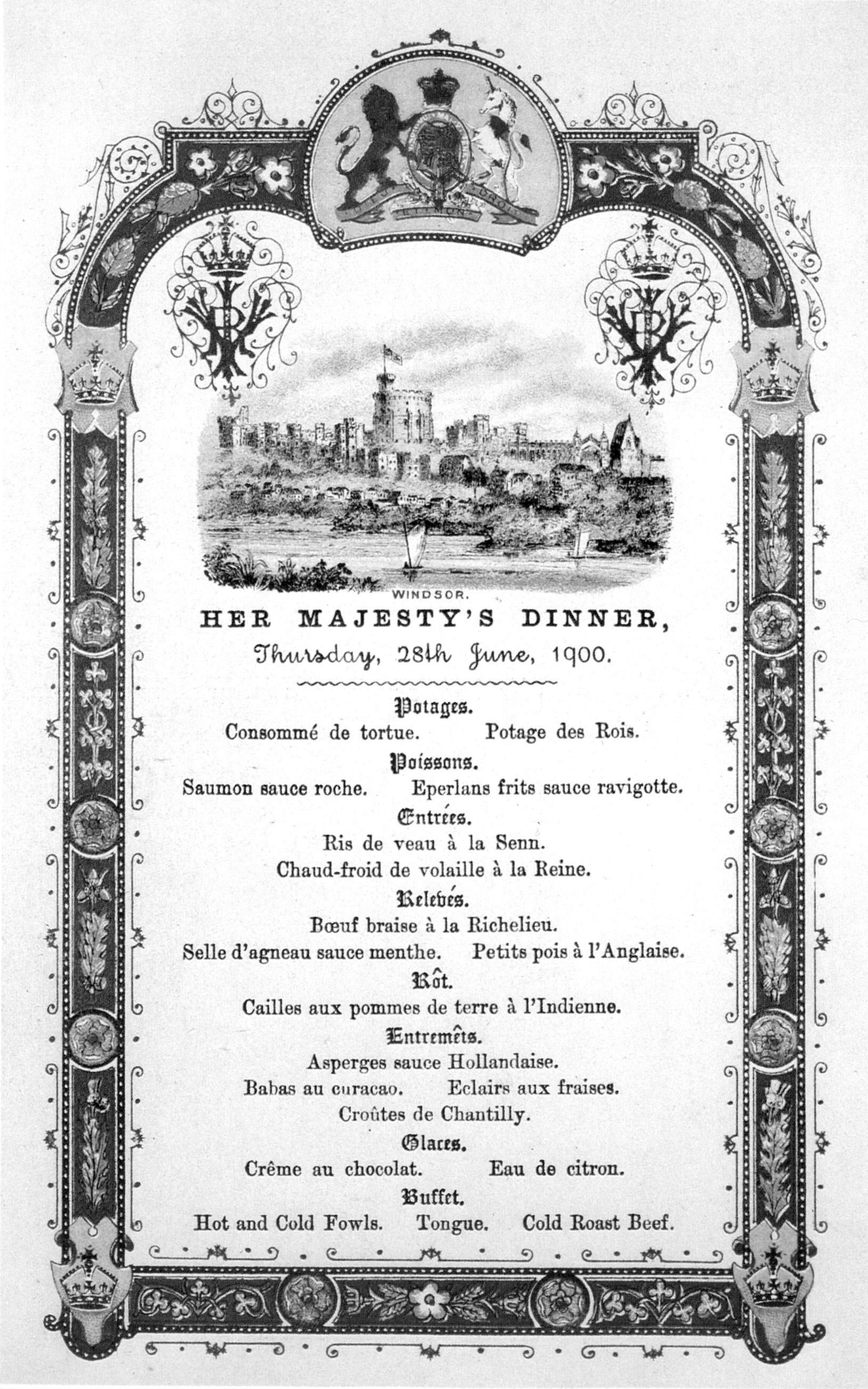

WINDSOR.

HER MAJESTY'S DINNER,

Thursday, 28th June, 1900.

Potages.

Consommé de tortue. Potage des Rois.

Poissons.

Saumon sauce roche. Eperlans frits sauce ravigotte.

Entrées.

Ris de veau à la Senn.

Chaud-froid de volaille à la Reine.

Relevés.

Bœuf braise à la Richelieu.

Selle d'agneau sauce menthe. Petits pois à l'Anglaise.

Rôt.

Cailles aux pommes de terre à l'Indienne.

Entremêts.

Asperges sauce Hollandaise.

Babas au curacao. Eclairs aux fraises.

Croûtes de Chantilly.

Glaces.

Crême au chocolat. Eau de citron.

Buffet.

Hot and Cold Fowls. Tongue. Cold Roast Beef.

RIGHT: *Naturally, only the very best entertainers were good enough for the Queen. She adored opera and members of the Royal Opera Company were welcome and honoured guests at Windsor. The Waterloo chamber or St George's Hall were converted into temporary theatres. After the performance, the Queen always thanked the principal artistes, often giving them valuable presents. Although on this occasion on June 26, 1900, a Signor Mancinelli conducted Mascagni's* Cavalleria Rusticana, *its composer had also conducted it before the Queen.*

WINDSOR CASTLE.

BY COMMAND OF

HER MOST GRACIOUS MAJESTY THE QUEEN

THE

ROYAL OPERA COMPANY

(From the Opera House, Covent Garden)

(UNDER THE DIRECTION OF Mr. MAURICE GRAU)

WILL APPEAR ON

TUESDAY, JUNE 26th, 1900.

HER MAJESTY'S SERVANTS WILL PERFORM

Act I. of BIZET'S Opera

CARMEN

(IN FRENCH.)

Carmen ... ... Mlle. CALVÉ.
Micaela ... ... Mme. SUZANNE ADAMS.
Don José ... ... M. SALÉZA.
Zuniga ... ... M. DECLERY.
Morales ... ... M. DUFRICHE.

Mr. Stedman's Choir.

Conductor ... M. PH. FLON.

FOLLOWED BY

MASCAGNI'S Opera

CAVALLERIA RUSTICANA

(IN ITALIAN.)

Turiddu ... ... Signor DE LUCIA.
Alfio ... ... Signor SCOTTI.
Lola ... ... Miss FANCHON THOMPSON.
Lucia ... ... Mlle. BAUERMEISTER.
Santuzza ... ... Mlle. CALVÉ.

Conductor ... ... Signor MANCINELLI.

Régisseur - M. FERNAND ALMANZ.

Perruquier - M. GUSTAVE.

Special Scenery Painted for this Performance by Mr. BRUCE SMITH & Assistants.

Secretary ... Mr. NEIL FORSYTH.

RIGHT: *Emma Calvé as Carmen, a role for which she was especially acclaimed.*

LEFT: *A mere seven months or so before she died, this was the huge menu set before the Queen on June 28, 1900.*

POST OFFICE TELEGRAPHS.

Government Dispatch No. 3rd — 3 Aug 00

Given in at Coburg
at 11 12 am
Received in Osborne at 12 46 pm
Sent out for delivery at 12 47

This message has passed through the hands of [illegible] Telegraphist [illegible] Writer

TO { Lord Edward Clinton
Osborne England

I am. much touched by
your kind sympathy please accept
and convey my warmest thanks to
all
Marie
Duchess of Coburg

This telegram from Princess Marie, Duchess of Coburg (the widow of Prince Alfred, Duke of Edinburgh and Saxe-Coburg) was received at Osborne at 12.46 pm on August 3, 1900, and sent out one minute later for delivery.

WINDSOR CASTLE, November 11th, 1900

Had a shocking night, and no draught could make me sleep as pain kept me awake. Felt very tired and unwell when I got up, and was not able to go to church to my great disappointment.

WINDSOR CASTLE, November 12th, 1900

Had again not a good night and slept on rather late. My lack of appetite worse than ever. It is very trying.

WINDSOR CASTLE, November 13th, 1900

Had a better night, and was able to take a little breakfast.

WINDSOR CASTLE, November 16th, 1900

After twelve went over to St. George's Hall with Beatrice and the children, where I inspected about one hundred of the Colonial troops, who had been invalided. There

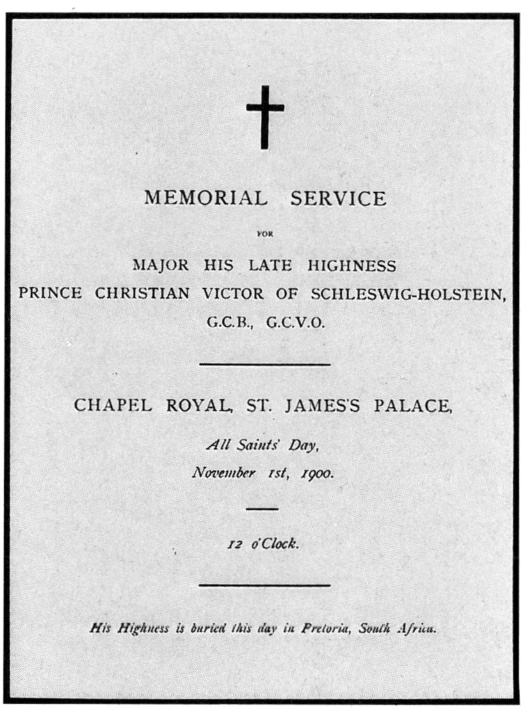

MEMORIAL SERVICE

FOR

MAJOR HIS LATE HIGHNESS

PRINCE CHRISTIAN VICTOR OF SCHLESWIG-HOLSTEIN,

G.C.B., G.C.V.O.

CHAPEL ROYAL, ST. JAMES'S PALACE,

All Saints' Day,

November 1st, 1900.

12 o'Clock.

His Highness is buried this day in Pretoria, South Africa.

The service sheet for the memorial service for the Queen's grandson, Prince Christian ('Christle') of Schleswig-Holstein. He died of enteric fever on October 29, 1900, in Pretoria while serving in South Africa during the Boer War.

were Canadians, Australians, Tasmanians, New Zealanders, and men from the Cape and Ceylon, representing forty-five regiments.

OSBORNE, December 31st, 1900

A TERRIBLY STORMY NIGHT. The same unfortunate alternations of sleep and restlessness, so that I again did not get up when I wished to, which spoilt my morning and day. Got out a little after one with Beatrice. When I came in I had to sign for a new Trustee to my private money, who is Louis Battenburg [*father of the late Earl Mountbatten of Burma*]. Lord Edward Clinton and Sir F. Edwards were witnesses. The afternoon was wet, and I took a short drive in a closed carriage.

OSBORNE, January 1st, 1901

ANOTHER YEAR BEGUN, and I am feeling so weak and unwell that I enter upon it sadly. The same sort of night as I have been having lately, but I did get rather more sleep and was up earlier.

OSBORNE, January 10th, 1901

RATHER A BETTER NIGHT, but I slept on late. Only got out for a short time in the

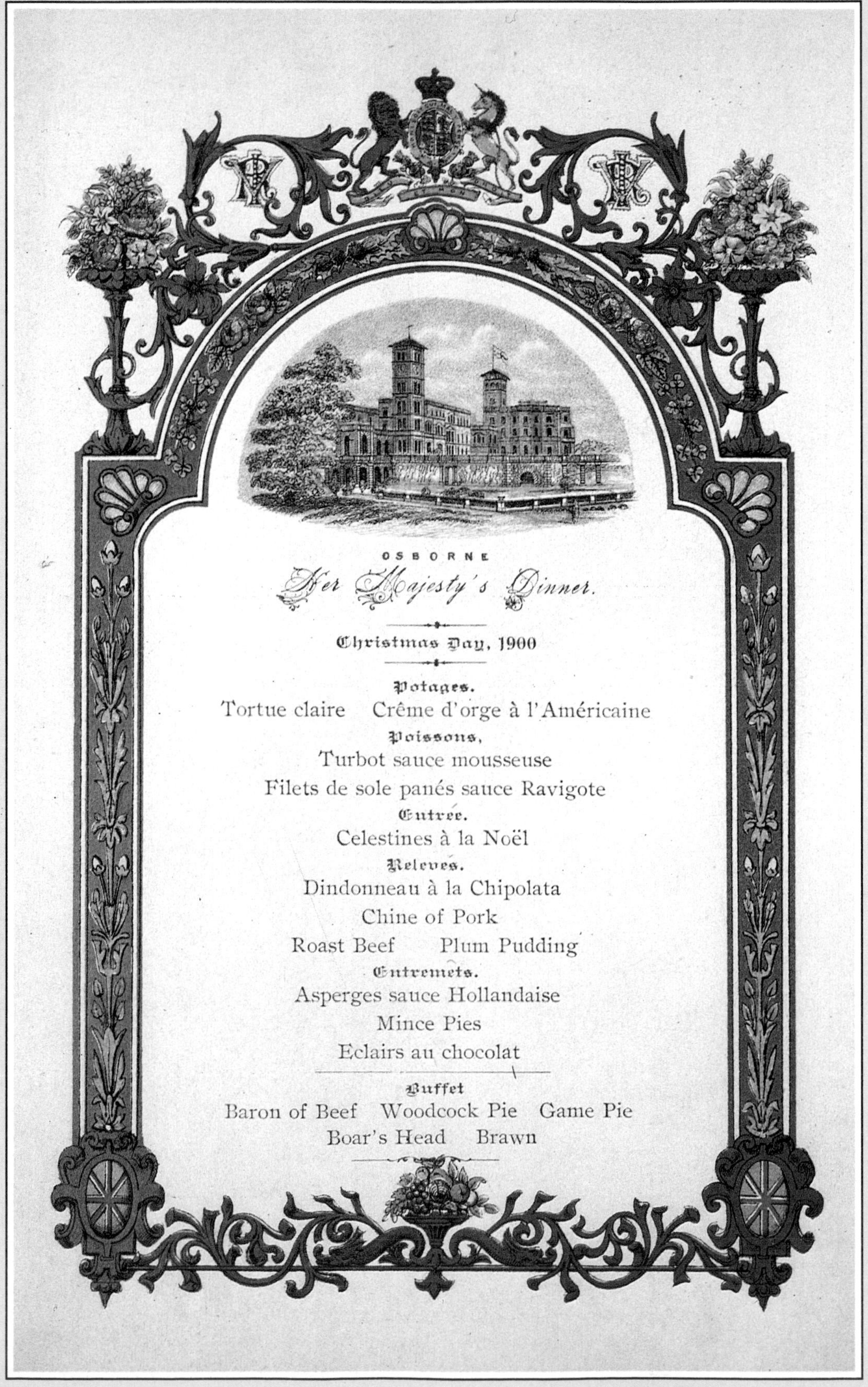

OSBORNE

Her Majesty's Dinner.

Christmas Day, 1900

Potages.

Tortue claire Crême d'orge à l'Américaine

Poissons.

Turbot sauce mousseuse

Filets de sole panés sauce Ravigote

Entrée.

Celestines à la Noël

Releves.

Dindonneau à la Chipolata

Chine of Pork

Roast Beef Plum Pudding

Entremets.

Asperges sauce Hollandaise

Mince Pies

Eclairs au chocolat

Buffet

Baron of Beef Woodcock Pie Game Pie

Boar's Head Brawn

Colonel Lord Edward Pelham Clinton.

. . . SELECTION OF MUSIC . . .

1. Triumphal March "Virtute et Valore." *L. Zavertal*
2. Overture ... "Raymond." ... *Thomas*
3. "Menuet" ... ... *Paderewski*
4. Selection ... "Shamrock." ... *L. Zavertal*
5. "Toreador et Andalouse ... ... *Rubinstein*
   (From the Suite "Bal Costumé.")
6. (a) Anitra's Dance ... ... } *Grieg*
   (b) Dance in the Hall of the King of the Mountains ... }
   (From the Suite "Peer Gynt.")
7. Graceful Dance ("from Henry VIII.") . ... *Sullivan*
8. Overture ... "Ruy Blas." ... *Mendelssohn*

Buckingham Palace,
January 3rd, 1901.

Conductor—Cav. L. Zavertal, R.A.

Lord Edward's place card for the luncheon and the programme of music played during and after the meal.

LEFT: *With less than thirty days to live the Queen was dining privately. This was the menu for her family for Christmas Day, 1900.*

Luncheon at Buckingham Palace:- 3rd January 1901.

2 T.R.H. The Prince and Princess of Wales.
1 H.R.H. Princess Victoria of Wales.
2 The Lady and Gentleman in attendance.
2 T.R.H. The Duke and Duchess of Connaught.
2 T.R.H. Prince Arthur and Princess Margaret of Connaught.
2 The Lady and Gentleman in attendance.
2 H.R.H. Princess Louise(Duchess of Argyll)and the Duke of Argyll.
2 T.R.H. The Duke and Duchess of York.
2 The Lady and Gentleman in attendance.
1 H.R.H. The Duke of Cambridge.
1 The Equerry in attendance.
2 T.S.H. The Duke and Duchess of Teck.
1 H.S.H. Prince Alexander of Teck.
2 Field Marshal the Rt Hon Lord Roberts and Lady Roberts.
2 The Misses Roberts.
2 The Marquis of Salisbury and Lady Gwendolen Cecil.
2 The Marquis and Marchioness of Lansdowne.
2 The Earl and Countess of Selborne.
2 Lord and Lady Walter Kerr.
2 Field Marshal the Rt Hon Viscount Wolseley and Viscountess Wolseley.
1 The Right Hon'ble A.J.Balfour,M.P.
2 The Right Hon'ble J.Chamberlain,M.P,and Mrs Chamberlain.
2 The Rt Hon St John Brodrick,M.P,and Lady Hilda Brodrick.
1 General Sir Evelyn Wood.
2 General Sir Mansfield and Lady Clarke.
2 General Sir Henry and Lady Brackenbury.
4 Lord Roberts' Staff.
1 The Lord Steward.
1 The Master of the Household.

52.

The list of those invited to the luncheon in honour of Lord Roberts is headed by the Prince and Princess of Wales. They represented the Queen who remained at Osborne House.

The Lord Steward is commanded
by Her Majesty to invite
Colonel
The Lord Edward Pelham Clinton
to Luncheon at Buckingham Palace, on Thursday, the
3rd January, 1901, at 1.30 o'clock, on the occasion of the Return
from South Africa of Field Marshal Lord Roberts.

Naval & Military Officers: Blue undress uniform & Cocked Hats.
Other Gentlemen & Ladies: Morning Dress.

See other side.

Lord Edward Pelham-Clinton's invitation to the special luncheon at Buckingham Palace for Field-Marshal Lord Roberts on his return from South Africa.

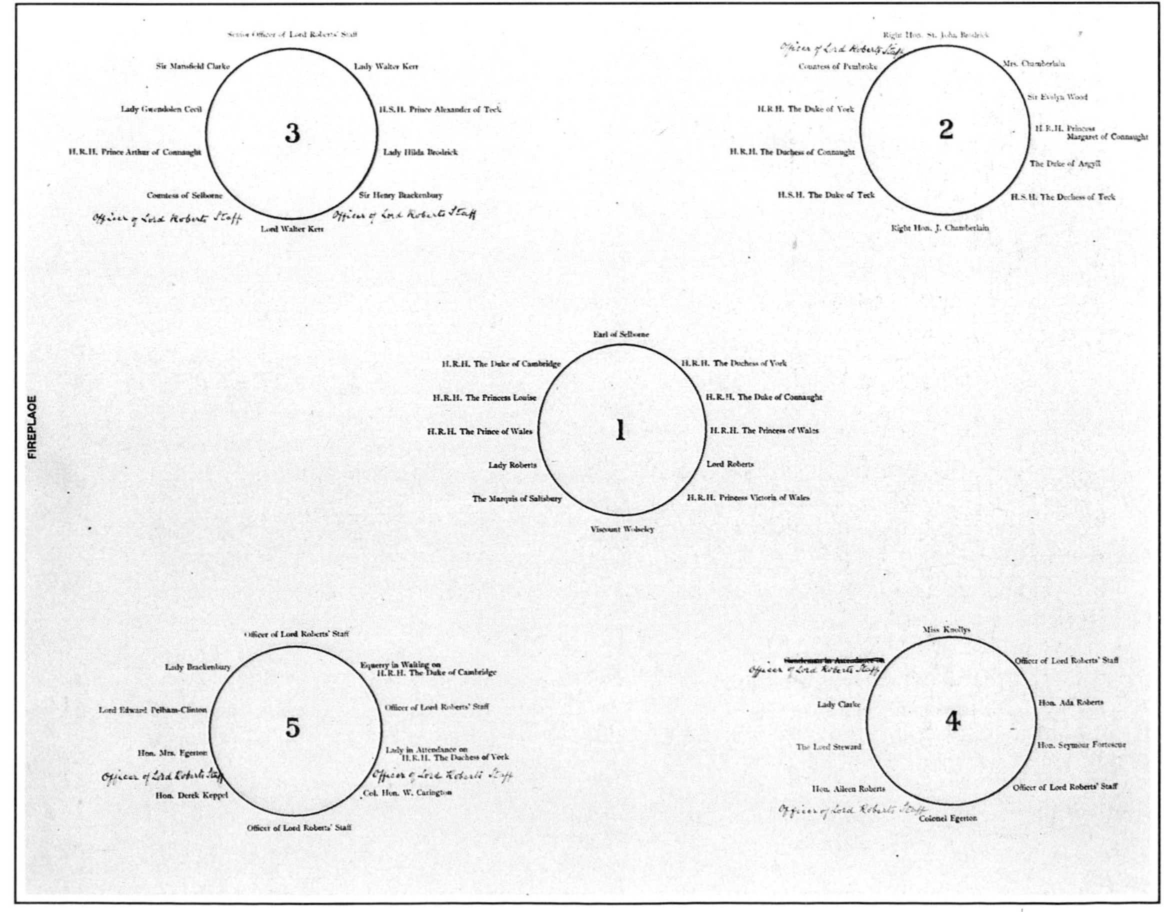

The seating plan for the luncheon in honour of Lord Roberts.

morning, and in the afternoon drove with Lenchen and Beatrice to Newport and back. [*It was during one of these drives towards the end of her life that she sensed that death was very near and said so to Beatrice and the lady-in-waiting. The Queen spoke of 'being united with my beloved Albert very soon'. The lady-in-waiting agreed, and purred: 'Ah yes, ma'am. You'll soon meet Albert in Abraham's bosom.' Perking up a bit, Queen Victoria retorted: 'I refuse to receive Abraham!'*

OSBORNE, January 12th, 1901

HAD A GOOD NIGHT and could take some breakfast better. Took an hour's drive at half-past two with Lenchen.

OSBORNE, January 13th, 1901

HAD A FAIR NIGHT, but was a little wakeful. Got up earlier and had some milk. Lenchen came and read some papers. Out before one, in the garden chair, Lenchen and Beatrice going with me. Rested a little, had some food, and took a short drive with Lenchen and Beatrice. Rested when I came in, and at five-thirty went down to the drawing-room, where a short service was held by Mr. Clement [*the Rev. Canon Clement Smith, Rector of Whippingham, East Cowes*], who performed it so well, and it was a great comfort to me. Rested again afterwards, then did some signing, and dictated to Lenchen.

On Sunday, January 13, 1901, Her Majesty's Journal, which she had kept for almost seventy years, ended.

A few days later, on January 19, a bulletin stated:

'The Queen has not lately been in her usual health, and is unable at present to take her customary drives. The Queen during the past year has had a great strain upon her powers, which has told rather upon her Majesty's nervous system. It has, therefore, been thought advisable by her Majesty's physicians that the Queen should be kept perfectly quiet in the house, and should abstain for the present from transacting business.'

Then, at 6.30 pm, on Tuesday, January 22, 1901 the great Queen-Empress died. The bulletin stated: 'The Queen ... breathed her last, surrounded by her children and grandchildren.' One of those grandchildren was His Imperial Majesty the Kaiser who is said to have been at her side almost motionless for several hours before her death: she virtually died in his arms.

Lord Pelham-Clinton was in Osborne House at this time and was later in Windsor Castle arranging accommodation for the crowned heads and others who attended the Queen's funeral.

New-York Tribune.

Vol. LX....No. 19,793. NEW-YORK, WEDNESDAY, JANUARY 23, 1901.—SIXTEEN PAGES. PRICE THREE CENTS.

A NATION'S SORROW.

THE LOSS OF QUEEN VICTORIA DEEPLY FELT.

HER HEALTH UNDERMINED BY FAMILY ANXIETIES—HER WEALTH EXAGGERATED.

AMERICA'S SYMPATHY.

PRESIDENT'S MESSAGE OF CONDOLENCE TO THE NEW KING.

ALL EUROPE DOES HONOR.

FEELING TRIBUTES FROM CAPITALS ON THE CONTINENT.

TRIBUTES FROM OFFICIALS.

PROFOUND FEELING AMONG FOREIGN REPRESENTATIVES AT WASHINGTON—SYMPATHY VOICED BY CABINET MEMBERS.

SHOCK TO EMPRESS FREDERICK.

DEATH OF QUEEN VICTORIA.

THE AGED SOVEREIGN OF GREAT BRITAIN PASSES PEACEFULLY AWAY AT OSBORNE AT 6:30 P. M.

PREPARING TO PROCLAIM THE NEW KING.

PROCLAIMING NEW KING

DIED AS NIGHT FELL.

PARLIAMENT SUMMONED.

TO ASSEMBLE TO-DAY AND SWEAR ALLEGIANCE TO THE NEW SOVEREIGN.

DEATH CAME PAINLESSLY.

11

DEATH OF THE QUEEN.

It is with the most profound sorrow that we record the death of our much loved Queen.

Throughout yesterday the blow that has overwhelmed in grief the peoples of the British Empire was awaited with universal and almost breathless fear, which grew more tense and poignant as successive bulletins revealed its imminence. At 7 o'clock suspense was ended by the following message from the Prince of Wales to the Lord Mayor, which was instantly made public :—

" Osborne, Tuesday, 6 45 p.m.

" The Prince of Wales to Lord Mayor.

" My beloved mother, the Queen, has just passed away, surrounded by her children and grandchildren.

" ALBERT EDWARD."

Immediately afterwards arrived the final medical bulletin, couched in much the same words :—

" Osborne House, Jan. 22, 6 45 p.m.

" Her Majesty the Queen breathed her last at 6 30 p.m., surrounded by her children and grandchildren.

" JAMES REID, M.D.
" R. DOUGLAS POWELL, M.D.
" THOMAS BARLOW, M.D."

The following are the official bulletins which were issued earlier in the day :—

" Osborne House, Jan. 22, 1901, 8 a.m.

" The Queen this morning shows signs of diminishing strength, and her Majesty's condition again assumes a more serious aspect.

" JAMES REID, M.D.
" R. DOUGLAS POWELL, M.D.
" THOMAS BARLOW, M.D."

" Osborne, 12 o'clock.

" There is no change for the worse in the Queen's condition since this morning's bulletin.

" Her Majesty has recognized the several members of the Royal Family who are here.

" The Queen is now asleep.

" JAMES REID, M.D.
" R. DOUGLAS POWELL, M.D.
" THOMAS BARLOW, M.D."

" Osborne, 4 p.m.

" The Queen is slowly sinking.

" JAMES REID, M.D.
" R. DOUGLAS POWELL, M.D.
" THOMAS BARLOW, M.D."

A *London Gazette* Extraordinary, issued last night, contained the Official Bulletin announcing the death of the Queen which had been received by the Home Secretary.

The Lord Steward of the Household, the Earl of Pembroke, received the following telegram from Osborne from Mr. Balfour, First Lord of the Treasury :—

" The Queen died peacefully at 6 30.

" ARTHUR BALFOUR."

THE LAST HOURS AT OSBORNE.

(FROM OUR SPECIAL CORRESPONDENT.)

COWES, JAN. 22.

All day long the Angel of Death has been hovering over Osborne House. One could almost hear the beating of his wings, but at half-past 6 those wings were folded, and the Queen was at rest. To those who knew her Majesty best and most closely, as some of them have told me, the whole event seems incredible and unreal. To all of them the life of the Queen has seemed a part of the natural order of things, a thing as certain as the rising or the setting of the sun ; and they are simply incapable of realizing what it means,

Newspaper reaction to the announcement of the Queen's death on both sides of the Atlantic. The Times (right) and the New York Tribune for January 23, 1901.

LORD EDWARD'S DIARY

Then, on February 4, 1901, Lord Edward was with the members of the Royal Family at the strictly private interment of the Queen in the royal mausoleum at Frogmore: he was the only commoner present and King Edward VII asked him to scatter earth on Her late Majesty's coffin. 'The last, the very last ceremony that can be performed,' he subsequently wrote in his diary.

On the death of the sovereign, the Master of the Household and other similar officials in the Lord Steward's department cease to exist. Lord Edward stayed on as Master of the Household for six months and then, for the second time in his lifetime, became a Groom-in-Waiting until his death in 1907.

These are extracts from Lord Edward's diary from January 19, 1901 to February 7, 1901.

Saturday, January 19, 1901

Rain nearly all day—and a S.E. gale. At home all day. Busy. Lady Monson, Fraulein Gazerl and Miss Moore leave to make room in the house for Royal Family coming. Prince of Wales and Pss Louise with Knollys [*Francis (later Baron) Knollys, Private Secretary to the Prince of Wales from 1870, and subsequently to him when he became Edward VII*] and Holford [*later, Sir George Holford: his Equerry*] arrive at 5.30. Princess of Wales and Miss Knollys and Sidney Greville [*the Hon. Sidney Greville, Equerry to the Prince of Wales*] arrive at 10.15. Royal dinner of six. Household dinner (14). Queen rather better at six o'clock bulletin.

Sunday, January 20, 1901

Fine and bright rather high wind. The Anniversary of Prince Henry of Battenberg's death; a Service held at Whippingham at 1 p.m. I do not attend it. The Prince of Wales, with Knollys and Holford, leaves at 12.30 for London to receive the German Emperor who is to arrive about 5 o'clock. I walk by the sea between 4 and 5. The Queen about the same at 5 o'clock—all very anxious. Royal dinner of 6 Household dinner of 11.

Monday, January 21, 1901

The Queen was very bad last night and hope almost given up, but there is a slight rally this morning. The German Emperor, Prince of Wales, Duke and Duchess of Connaught and Duke of York with Sir Francis Knollys and Holford arrive about 11.15 a.m. from London. I am at home all morning, feeling very seedy; walk to Osborne Cottage in afternoon. At 5 p.m. Bulletin says—'The slight improvement is maintained'. Sir Robert Barlow M.D. arrives. Royal dinner of (11). Household dinner of (15).

Tuesday, January 22, 1901

THE QUEEN'S DEATH. About 9 a.m. the Royal Family are summoned to the Queen's bedside, she is smiling, however the death does not take place until 6.30 it is quite peaceful. Prince Christian, Duke of Argyll, the Duke of Connaught, family arrive in time. Prince and Pss Louis of Battenberg just too late. Clarendon (Ld Chamberlain) and Mr Balfour arrive. At home all day. [*The Rt Hon. Arthur James Balfour was first Lord of the Treasury and Leader of the House of Commons from 1895 to 1906.*]

Wednesday, January 23, 1901

Prince of Wales, Duke of Connaught, Duke of York, Prince Christian and Duke of Argyll leave for London to attend Privy Council, at 9.30. Between 1 and 4 o'clock, the Household Servants and Tenants are allowed to see the Queen in her bed-room where she died. I go at 1 o'clock—she looks so peaceful, very little changed. Prince of Wales is proclaimed King Edward VII. I see the Queen again later with Mrs. Calthorpe and her daughter.

Lt. Col.
Lord E. Pelham Clinton
K.C.B.

22 JAN 1901
LORD CHAMBERLAIN'S OFFICE

There will be a Privy Council
tomorrow, the 23rd January,
at St James's Palace, at 2 o'clock.
The attendance of the Master of
the Household is required.

Levée Dress. S. Ponsonby Fane

Lord Edward Pelham-Clinton's notification that his presence was 'required' at St James's Palace on January 23, 1901, the day after the Queen's death. The new monarch, Edward VII, was proclaimed King after a formal meeting of the Privy Council, Great Officers of State and high ranking officers of the Royal Household.

Thursday, January 24, 1901

The King, Duke of York, Duke of Connaught, Duchess of Albany, Duke of Albany [*Coburg*] and Princess Alice, and Prince Christian and Duke of Argyll arrive at 2.30 from London. The dining room is being prepared as a Chapel, and the late Queen will be brought down there and have a guard placed from the Rifle Reserve. After dinner in the evening, the King held a sort of levée in the Council room and we were all presented and kissed hands. H.M. most kind and gracious.

Friday, January 25, 1901

This morning, the body of the Queen was brought down from her room and placed in the Chapelle Ardente, which is *so* pretty. All the ladies and gentlemen of Household were at the foot of the stairs to witness it. The Emperor and the King and Royal gentlemen followed into the room and a short service was held in presence of all the Royal Family. A company of Grenadier Guards has arrived to guard the body in the chapel. Ld. Lansdowne arrives and has an audience—he stays at E. Cowes Castle. Large Royal and Household dinner.

Saturday, January 26, 1901

I am at home the whole day, busy answering telegrams and writing. Have a business interview with the King. Princess Victoria and Prince and Princess Charles of Denmark arrive 3.15. Duke of Cambridge, Duke of Teck, Duke of Norfolk [*Henry FitzAlan-Howard, 15th Duke*], Earl Roberts and Mr Brodrick [*Secretary of State for War*] arrive late. Household dinner 23. Royal dinner of 22.

Sunday, January 27, 1901

Blowing a gale. The German Emperor's birthday. At 8.45 all the Queen's Household, the King's Household, the Germany Embassy, the Officers of H.I.M's yacht—assemble in Council room to offer congratulations. The whole Royal Family go to Church at Whippingham, the Bishop of Winchester [*the Rt. Rev. Dr. Randall Davidson*] preaches. I am unable to go being very busy. At home all day. The King goes on board the Emperor's yacht to offer congratulations. Royal dinner 25. Household dinner of 22.

Monday, January 28, 1901

Cold and very heavy rain at times. Duke and Duchess of Connaught go to London for the night. At 10 a.m. an Investiture of the Garter of Crown Prince of Germany—all in Levée dress, the whole Royal Family and their Suites present, with Duke of Norfolk, Earl Roberts, Bishop of Winchester as Prelate of the Order of the Garter. Royal dinner of 22. Household—20.

Tuesday, January 28, 1901

Fine but cold. The King goes to London at 11.30 to receive addresses from the Lords and Commons. The Mistress of the Robes and several Queen's Ladies come at luncheon time to see the Chapelle Ardente. A very short walk at 4.30 the first for a week! The Duke of York has German Measles in the house. Royal Dinner of 22. Household dinner of 20.

Wednesday, January 30, 1901

Very cold, but bright sunshine. Twelve of the Royal Family; the younger members, leave at 1 o'clock. A large number of people visit the Chapelle Ardente. Walk for a short time with Breadallon who comes down to see the Chapelle. The King returns from London about 4.45. Prince Ed. of Saxe Weimar, Pss Frederica of Hanover and Baron Rammingen, Prince Frederick of Mecklenburg Strelitz, Princess Francis and Alexander of Teck and Lady Lytton arrive. Royal dinner—27. Household dinner of 20.

Thursday, January 31, 1901

I leave Osborne by the 9.20 boat, with Fritz Ponsonby—and go to 81 [*Lord Edward's home: 81, Eccleston Square, SW1*] to lunch, then to Pulford and Truefitt (hair cut) and take the 5.5 train to Windsor. Very busy arranging rooms and answering telegrams etc. Dine in my room—Sir R. Collins sits with me. [*Sir Richard Hawthorne Collins, Comptroller of the Household to HRH the Duchess of Albany.*]

Friday, February 1, 1901

Very busy all day, constant telegrams altering arrangements for rooms by sending more Royalties—I begin almost to despair of succeeding, but think all is settled. I get out for a few minutes to go to St George's and to ask Lady Bigge [*a lady-in-waiting and wife of Sir Arthur Bigge, Queen Victoria's Private Secretary*] if she can take in any of the suite—to my great relief she takes in three. Have all meals by myself in my room.

Saturday, February 2, 1901

Dull, and showery in afternoon. The Queen's funeral in St George's Chapel. The trains conveying the late Queen and all the Royalties arrive Windsor at 2 o'clock, after the procession through London—they, the King too, walk through the town with procession, enter at the Long-walk gate, through the quadrangle and so to St George's Chapel. The Royalties (70) lunch in dining-room. Guests about 600 or 700 in St George's Hall. A Royal dinner of 25. Household do—24.

Sunday, February 3, 1901

All the Royal Family attend Service in St George's Chapel at 11—the suites in attendance go there also. The Bishop of Oxford preaches. I am not able to get out all day except to go to St George's. Ld Salisbury [*the Prime Minister*] arrives at 6.15. Royal dinner 27. Household do—35.

Monday, February 4, 1901

Dull and cold wind. Busy all the morning. At 3 p.m. a procession leaves the Memorial Chapel for the final funeral of the Queen at Frogmore in the Mausoleum. A most beautiful and impressive ceremony altogether. The King most kindly allows me to

WINDSOR CASTLE.

VISITORS' LIST.

Saturday, February 2nd, 1901.

THEIR MAJESTIES THE KING AND QUEEN	Edward III. Tower
MISS KNOLLYS	352, Chintz Room
GENERAL SIR DIGHTON PROBYN	335, York Tower
SIR FRANCIS KNOLLYS	331, Sir William Jenner's Room
CAPTAIN HOLFORD	429, North Front
HIS IMPERIAL MAJESTY THE GERMAN EMPEROR...	State Rooms
HIS EXCELLENCY GENERAL VON PLESSEN	The Lord Chamberlain's Room
HIS EXCELLENCY COUNT METTERNICH	The Lord Steward's Room
LIEUT.-COLONEL THE HON. W. CARINGTON	The Lord in Waiting's Room
HIS MAJESTY THE KING OF THE HELLENES	The Tapestry Rooms
THE GENTLEMAN IN ATTENDANCE	433, North Front
HIS ROYAL HIGHNESS THE CROWN PRINCE OF GERMANY..	State Room
COLONEL VON PRITZELWITZ	449, West Front
LIEUT..COLONEL THE HON. H. C. LEGGE	Winchester Tower
HIS IMPERIAL HIGHNESS THE GRAND DUKE MICHAEL OF RUSSIA...	343, Sitting Room, Minister's Rooms
GENTLEMEN IN ATTENDANCE.....................	431, North Front
HIS ROYAL HIGHNESS THE CROWN PRINCE OF DENMARK	Tapestry Rooms
THE GENTLEMEN IN ATTENDANCE........................	432, North Front
H.R.H. THE DUKE OF SPARTA................................	344, Minister's Rooms
H.R.H. PRINCE HENRY OF PRUSSIA........................	State Rooms
ADMIRAL BARON VON SECKENDORFF	446, West Front
ADMIRAL OF THE FLEET SIR EDMUND COMMERELL	Winchester Tower
THEIR ROYAL HIGHNESSES THE DUKE AND DUCHESS OF CONNAUGHT................................	235, York Tower
H R.H. PRINCE ARTHUR OF CONNAUGHT...............	172, Edward III. Tower
T.R.H. THE PRINCESSES MARGARET AND VICTORIA PATRICIA OF CONNAUGHT	176, Edward III. Tower
COLONEL AND THE HON. MRS. EGERTON..............	646 and 647, Round Tower
MISS MILNE	649, Round Tower

Some of the royal visitors (and their suites) who were present at Windsor for the Queen's funeral.

The scene as the gun carriage, on top of which the Queen's coffin rested, waited at the foot of the Great West Stairs of St George's Chapel, Windsor Castle, before it was carried in for the funeral service.

throw the earth on the coffin, during the well known passage in the burial Service: the last, the very last ceremony that can be performed. The Royal dinner is 23. Household dinner—30.

Tuesday, February 5, 1901

I wake to find the ground covered with snow and my voice quite gone. The Emperor leaves at 1 o'clock and lunches with the King who accompanies him, at Marlboro' House. He leaves for Germany in afternoon. I am feeling unwell, send for Reid [*Royal physician Sir James Reid*], he finds my heart out of order from over fatigue and orders complete rest. I lie down and do not go out of my room all the afternoon.

Wednesday, February 6, 1901

Reid finds me better, but advises me to remain in bed till 4 o'clock and then remain on the sofa in sitting room.

Thursday, February 7, 1901

Feeling better, but breakfast in bed and lunch in my sitting room. The King and Queen and other Royalties leave for London at 3.15 and go to Marlborough House. I leave by the 3.25 train and go home to 81—and dine alone—it seems so restful after all I have had to go through.

The Victoria Monument stands at the end of the Mall. Both the monument and the Mall were built as memorials to the Queen during the reign of Edward VII.

ACKNOWLEDGEMENTS

I would like to thank the owner of the 'Lord Edward Pelham-Clinton Collection', Mr Ronald Godfrey Farnham of Quorn, without whose generosity in allowing me unrestricted use of the collection, this book would never have been written. Ronnie Farnham's grandmother, Mrs William (Catherine) Farnham of Quorn was Lord Edward's favourite niece and she became his hostess at Eccleston Square and at The Heights, Witley, after the death of Lady Edward Pelham-Clinton in 1892.

The linking narrative is largely based on extracts from Queen Victoria's Journals. Most of these are taken from *Letters of Queen Victoria*, second and third series, edited by G. E. Buckle (John Murray, 1926–1932). A small number of further extracts has been drawn, by gracious permission of Her Majesty The Queen, from unpublished material in Queen Victoria's Journals. I acknowledge this permission with much gratitude.

I would, in addition, like to thank the owner of the 'Lord Edward Pelham-Clinton Collection', Mr Ronald Godfrey Farnham of Quorn, without whose generosity in allowing me unrestricted use of the collection, this book would never have been written. Ronnie Farnham's grandmother, Mrs William (Catherine) Farnham of Quorn was Lord Edward's favourite niece and she became his hostess at Eccleston Square and at The Heights, Witley, after the death of Lady Edward Pelham-Clinton in 1892.

My sincere thanks go to the following for their practical help or encouragement: First, my nephew, Gerard Ashley Fox who coped splendidly with my (occasional) bad tempers and who gave me excellent practical help. Also to Miss Rosemary Harris the novelist and writer of children's books and her brother, Sir Anthony Harris, Bart. To His Grace the 9th Duke of Newcastle, OBE, to the author Paul James and to my Agent, Miss Pamela Todd and also to my typists, Mrs Sylvia Kloegman and Bryan Bradford and to the following good friends: Robert F. Eddison; Stuart M. F. Greenman; the Reverend Fr. Robin (R. J.) Mark; Hugh Macpherson; and finally to R. E. (Bob) Spence-Grover.

PICTURE CREDITS

The editor and publishers would like to thank the following for supplying illustrations:

COLOUR

Copyright reserved. Reproduced by Gracious Permission of Her Majesty Queen Elizabeth II **2, 3, 14, 36, 40–41, 66–67, 78–79, 169** (above), **196** (below); Bridgeman Art Gallery/Guildhall, London **178–179**/Private Collection **201**; Debrett's Peerage Limited **17**; Eileen Tweedy/Garrick Club **169** (below),/Victoria and Albert Museum, London **191** (below); ET Archive **105, 122**,/Covent Garden Archives **205** (below),/The Gordon Boys' School, Woking **115**,/National Army Museum, London **100–101**,/National Maritime Museum **182** (above); The National Army Museum, London **11, 200**; The National Portrait Gallery, London **89**; Peter Roberts Collection **58–59**; Andy Williams **54, 84, 164–165, 220**; ZEFA **137**.

BLACK AND WHITE

Copyright reserved. Reproduced by Gracious Permission of Her Majesty Queen Elizabeth II **32–33, 50** (above); BBC Hulton Picture Library **15, 20, 21, 22, 23, 25** (above right), **27, 31, 34, 43, 61** (left), **64, 68, 72, 83, 91** (above & below), **94** (right), **97** (above), **107, 119** (right & left), **134, 139, 142, 145, 146, 147** (right & left), **153, 155, 175, 181** (above left); Coutts & Co. **103**; Dickens House Museum **62**; ET Archive **82**; Institution of Electrical Engineers **97** (below); The Mansell Collection **46, 53, 87, 88, 111, 170**; The National Portrait Gallery, London **9, 10, 25** (above left & below), **26, 28, 61** (right), **183** (below right).

INDEX

Page numbers in italic type refer to illustrations.

Aberdeen, Lady 194, 195
Aberdeen, Lord 60, 96
Aix-les-Bains 120
Albani, Madame 119, 138
Albany, Helen Duchess of *142*, 157
Alberta 138, 166
Albert Edward, Prince of Wales (later King Edward VII) 7, *10*, 10, 16, 17, 18, *21*, 29, 31, 37–8, *40–41*, 42, *43*, 45, 56, 68, 69, 74–7, 81–2, 98, 152–3, *155*, 166, 173, 174, 195, 214–17, 219
Albert Edward Victor of Wales (Eddy) 77, 108, 144, 152–3, *153*
Albert Memorial 83–5, *84*
Albert, Prince Consort 9–10, *9*, *10*, 17, 29, 37–8, 42, 47, 48, 49, 51–6, 62, 81, 83, 86, 109, 114, 119, 149, 192, 199
Albert, Prince of Schleswig-Holstein 19
Alexandra of Denmark, Princess of Wales (later Queen Alexandra) 10, *10*, 12, 18, *21*, 31, 38, 39, *40–41*, 42, *43*, 45, 52, 54, 74–6, 80, 90, 152, 160, 166, 173, 174, 189
Alexis of Russia, Grand Duke 90
Alfonso XIII, King of Spain 19
Alfred, Prince, Duke of Edinburgh 18, *21*, 90, *91*, 127, 148, 202
Alice, Princess, Countess of Athlone 13, 18, 142, *142*, 166
Alice, Princess, Duchess of Hesse-Darmstadt 13, 18, *21*, *32*, 37, 42, *43*, 96, 98, 127
Alix of Hesse, Princess, Czarina of Russia 170, *170*
Aosta, Duke of 142
Ashanti Expedition 157
Atholl, Duchess of 102, 120, 138
Argyll, Duke of 19, 83, 215–16
Arnold, Matthew 108
Arthur, Prince, Duke of Connaught 19, *23*, 37, 54, 88, 122, 148, 180, 199
Augusta, Princess of Schleswig-Holstein 127

Baden-Powell, Lord 200–201, *200*
Bagehot, Walter 12–13
Balmoral 58–9, *58*, 72, 122
Barnardo, Dr Thomas *34*
Bath, Order of the 17
Battenberg, Prince Francis Joseph of 160
Battenberg, Prince Henry of 19, 90, 114, 116, 132, 135–6, 138, 144, 146, 148, 153, 157, 171, 214
Battenberg, Prince Louis of 114, 144, 160
Battenberg, Princess Louis of *119*
Battenberg, Ludwig and Victoria 134
Beatrice, Princess (Princess Henry of Battenberg) 9, 19, *20*, 37, *43*, 45, 54, 65, 70, 73–4, 75–7, 86, 90, 96, 109, 111, 114, 116–17, 119, *119*, 132, *134*, 135–6, 138, 143, 148, 152–7, 160, 170, 180, 183, 199, 202, 206–7, 212
Bell, Alexander Graham 96, *97*
Beresford, Lord Charles 95
Bernhardt, Sarah 31, 167, 169–70, *169*
Biarritz 138
Biddulph, Col Sir Thomas 42, 80, 96, 156
Bigge, Col Sir A 138, 143, 156, 160
Bigge, Lady 217
Bismarck, Prince Otto von 11, 46–7, *46*, 65
Blackfriars Bridge 61
Blandford, Lady 120
Boer War 111, 195, 199
Bolitho, Hector 12
Bond, Miss Jessie 148
Booth, General William (Salvation Army) 69
Boxer Rising 202
Brabant, Duchess of 39–51
Bridport, Lord 109, 132
Brown, John 78–82, *78*, 113
Browning, Robert 60, *61*
Bruce, Hon. Katherine 43
Bruce, Lady Augusta (later Lady Augusta Stanley) 37, 51, 60
Bruce, Major-General 38
Buccleuch, Louisa, Duchess of 117, 135, 137, 166
Buckingham Palace 164–5, *164*, 180
Burdett-Coutts, Angela, Baroness 103, *103*
Burdett, William L. A. B. 103

Cadogan, Lord and Lady 199
Calvé, Emma 201–2, 205, *205*
Cambridge, Duchess of 45
Cambridge, George, 2nd Duke of 173, 175, *175*, 216
Cambridge, Lady Mary (later Duchess of Teck) 45
Camden Place 65
Canada 34
Carlyle, Thomas 60, *61*
Carmen 201, 205
Casals, Pablo 7
Cavelleria Rusticana 151, 201
Cetewayo, Zulu King, 98, 111, *111*
Chapel Royal, St James's Palace 17, 42
Charles of Denmark, Prince 166, *167*
Charles, Prince of Wales 142
Charlotte, Princess of Saxe-Meiningen 102
Charlottenburg Castle, Berlin 137, *137*
Charterhouse School 132
Chelmsford, Lord 98
Chelsea Pensioners 176
Children, Queen Victoria's 18–23
Christian, Prince of Schleswig-Holstein 8, 19, 34, *50*, 51, 54, 148, 160, 215
Christian Victor of Schleswig-Holstein, Prince 19, 55
Christy Minstrels 60
Churchill, Lady Jane 43, 80, 86
Churchill, Lord Randolph 127, 146
Cimiez 167
Clarence, Duke of 18, 145; *see also* Albert Edward Victor of Wales
Clarendon, Lord 47, 51, 63
Clarke, Sir James 37, 63
Clayton, Dr Oscar 30
Clementine, Princess of the Belgians 146
Coburg, Prince Ernest of 45
Coburg, Marie 173
Cole, Mrs Henry 52
Colonial and Indian Exhibition 119
Concerts, State 106
Connaught, Duke and Duchess of 215; *see also* Arthur, Prince, Duke of Connaught
Connaught, Princess Margaret of 166, 170, *170*
Connaught, Princess Patricia of 166, 170, *170*
'Court Kalendar' *162*
Coutts & Co. 103
Cranbrook, Lord 122
Crystal Palace 64
Csarewitch (later Czar Nicholas II) 154, 169

Dagmar, Princess of Denmark (later Empress of Russia) 39
Daimler, Gottlieb 107
Darmstadt 144
Darwin, Charles 107
Davidson, the Rt Revd Dr Randall 216
Dawson-Damer 16
Death duties 7, 146
Delhi 17
Denmark, King and Queen of 39, 52, 134, 166, 189
Derby, Earl of 24, *25*, 34, 94
Devonshire, Duke and Duchess of 192, 195
Diamond Jubilee 146, 149, 171, 178–9
Dickens, Charles 9, 34, 62–3, *62*
Dinizulu, Zulu King 111
Disraeli, Benjamin (later Lord Beaconsfield) 24, *26*, 34, 56–7, *57*, 60, 68–9, 81, 94–8, *97*, 107, 109
Ditton Park 135
Divorcees 120
Dodgson, Charles Lutwidge (Lewis Carroll) 147
Dona, Empress of Germany 144–5, 149, 195
D'Oyly Carte Opera Co. 13, 148
D'Oyly Carte, Richard 148
Drawing Rooms 104–5, *105*, 120, 137
Dublin 199
Dufferin, Lord 199
Duleep Singh, Prince 45, 102
Dunlop, John Boyd 108

Eames, Madame 187
Edison, Thomas Alva 68
Education, Board of 147
Edward of York, Prince (later Edward VIII) 146, *155*
Edwards, Sir Fleetwood 156, 207
Eleveden Hall 102
Elgar, Sir Edward 147, *147*
Elgin, 7th Earl of 37
Elizabeth of Russia (Grand Duchess Serge) 127

Ely, Jane, Dowager Marchioness of 47, 63, 65, 86, 96, 102, 117, 132, 144
Ena, Queen of Spain (Princess Victoria Eugénie of Battenberg) 19, 151, 160
Eton College 13, 109, 180
Eugénie, Empress of France 56, 63, *64*, 65, 77, 86, 102
Eurydice 15

Fenians 56, 80
Feodore, Princess Henry of Reuss 102
Feodore, Princess of Hohenloe-Langenburg 37
Fife, Duke and Duchess of 18, 153
Fitzroy, Lord Charles 65, 80
Foley, Admiral 15
Franco-Prussian War 70
Franz-Ferdinand, Archduke of Austria 173
Franz Joseph, Emperor 136
Frederick, Empress of Germany (The Princess Royal of England) 13, 18, *20*, 29, 42, *43*, 145–6, 174, 177, 180
Frederick William, Prince of Prussia (later Emperor Frederick II of Germany) 18, *20*, 45
Freud, Sigmund 146, *146*
Frogmore 42, 51, 55–6, 63, 94–5, 122, 127, 132, 135, 173, 214, 217

Garibaldi, Giuseppe 31
Garter, Order of the 17, 43, 45, 51, 88, 216
George of York, Prince (later George V) 9, 16, 18, 145, *145*, 152–4, *155*, 166, 184, 217
Gilbert, W. S. 13, 148
Gilbert and Sullivan 108
Gladstone, the Rt Hon. W. E. 7, 24, 27, 38, 46, 69–70, 75–6, 81, 108, 145–7, 184, 185
Golden Jubilee 120, 122, 127–36
Gondoliers, The 148–9, *150*
Gordon, General Charles *115*, 116
Gounod, Charles 187
Granby, Violet, Dowager Duchess of Rutland 138
Grande Chatreuse 120
Granville, Lord 51, 145
Greece, William of (George I of Greece) 134
Greville, Sidney 214
Grey, General 37, 42, 52, 56, 156

Haakon VII, King of Norway 18; *see also* Charles of Denmark, Prince
Hamilton, 10th Duke of 17, 29
Hardinge, General 80
Hardy, Thomas 69, 108, 145
Hartington, Lord 127
Hartopp, Matilda (Lady Edward Pelham-Clinton) 17; *see also* Pelham-Clinton, Lady
Hartopp, Sir William Craddock 17
Hedda Gabler 108
Helena, Princess (Princess Christian of Schleswig-Holstein) 8, 19, *21*, 34, 37, *43*, 49, *50*, 51, 120, 160
Helena Victoria of Schleswig-Holstein, Princess 19, 120, *134*, 148, 156, 162
Helena of Waldeck-Pyrmont, Princess 19; *see also* Albany, Helena, Duchess of
Helps, Mr 51, 63
Henry of Prussia, Prince 127
Hesse-Darmstadt, Grand Duke of 18, *21*, *32*, *43*
Holford, Sir George 214
Houseman, A. E. 146
Hughenden 96

Ibsen, Henrik 69, 108
Independent Labour Party 145
India 69, 94, 95
Indian servants *134*, 141, 143
Ireland 109, 147, 199
Isle of Man 82
Italy 98
Italy, Crown Princess of 174
Italy, King of 149

Jane Eyre 103
Jenner, Sir William 37, 72–5, 113

'Kaiser Bill' *see* Wilhelm II, Emperor of Germany
Kensal Green Cemetery 144
Kent, Duke and Duchess of 17
Khartoum 116
Kimberley, Lord 111
Kitchener, Lord 7, 147
Klondike Gold Rush 146
Knollys, Sir William 74
Kodak, George Eastman 108

Ladysmith 147, 195
Landsdowne, Lord and Lady 195
Landseer, Sir Edwin 89, *89*
Lathom, Lord 138
Lausanne Gazette 81
Lear, Edward 108
Legge, Major 143
Lehzen, Baroness 63–4, *64*
Leiningen, Marie (Princess Ernest) 37, 51, 160
Lennox, Lady Caroline 49
Leopold, King of the Belgians 10, 37, 39, 146
Leopold, Prince, Duke of Albany 19, *20*, 54, 107, *107*, 113, 142
Leopold, Prince, Duke of Brabant (later King of the Belgians) 51
Levées 105–6
Lichfield, Lord 52
Lincoln, Abraham 31, *31*
Lincoln, Earl of 29
Lister, Lord 34, 72–3, *72*
Lohlein, Herr 42
London Volunteer Rifle Brigade 17, 102
London, Lord Mayor of 88, 120, 149, 176
Londonderry, Lord and Lady 29
Lord Chancellor, the 11, 12, 51, 70, 77
Lorne, Marquis of (later Duke of Argyll) 34, 54, *67–8*, 68, 98, 143, 148
Louis Napoleon *see* Napoleon III, Emperor of France
Louise of Wales, Princess, Duchess of Fife 18, 170, *170*
Louise, Princess, Marchioness of Lorne (later Duchess of Argyll) 19, *23*, 34, 54, *66–7*, 68, 98, 143, 148, 153
Louise, Princess of Prussia, Duchess of Connaught 19, 170, *170*
Louise of Schleswig-Holstein, Princess 132, 138
Luncheon lists 189, 210

Maclean, Roderick 107
McNeill, Ina 156
McNeill, Sir J. 138, 142–3, 156, 166
Mafeking 147, 201, *201*
Maget, Herr 42
Magnus, Sir Philip 9
Mahdi, the 116
Manchester Ship Canal 146
Marconi, Guglielmo 146
Marie, Grand Duchess of Russia (Duchess of Edinburgh) 18, 90, 127, 148, 202
Marie-Louise of Schlewig-Holstein, Princess (Princess Aribert of Anhalt) 19, 148, 151
Marlborough House 52
Martin, Theodore 51
Mary (May) of Teck, Princess, Duchess of York (later Queen Mary) 9, *14*, 16, 18, 134, 145, *145*, 152–4, 184
Mascagni, Pietro 151
Maud of Wales, Princess (later Queen of Norway) 18, 166–7, *167*
Meath, Lord 199
Mecklenburg-Strelitz, Prince and Princess of 134, 217
Melbourne, Viscount 24
Mensdorff, Albert 156
Menus *112*, *118*, *133*, *161*, *168*, *190*, *193*, *204*, *208*
Methuen, Lord 43, 184
Mikado, The 108, 149
Minter, Dr 38
Mordaunt, Miss Violet 120
Morris, William 31
Muller, Professor Max 119

Naples, the Prince of 145, 149, 173
Napoleon III, Emperor of France *64*, 65, 68, 70, 77, 86, 102
National Trust, the 146
Netherlands, Queen-Regent of 157
New York Times *213*
Newcastle, 5th Duke of 17, 28, *28*, 29, 37
Nicholas II, Czar of Russia *169*, *170*; *see also* Czarewitch
Nobel, Alfred 146
Norfolk, Duke of 216
Northcote, Sir S. 94

O'Connor, Arthur 68, 81, 110
Omdurman 147
Osborne House 17, 36, *36*, *78–9*

Paderewski, I. 148
Paget, Lord Arthur 52, 90
Palmerston, Lord 24, *25*, 34, 37–8, 46–7
Parliament, State Opening of 10, 48–9, 70, 145
Parratt, Sir Walter 183, *183*
Pasteur, Louis 31, *31*
Patti, Adelina 82, *82*
Peel, Sir Robert 24, 60
Pelham-Clinton family 28–30
Pelham-Clinton, Col the Lord Edward 7, *8*, 16–17, 28–30, 102, 155–6, 176–7, 212, 214ff
Pelham-Clinton, Lady 17, 102
Pelham-Clinton, Lady Susan (Lady Adolphus Vane Tempest) 29
Persia, Shah of 88–9, *88*
Pevsne, Professor Sir Willi Nikolas 53
Phipps, Sir C. 37–8, 42
Phipps, Harriet 138, 142, 166
Phoenix Park, Dublin 201
Ponsonby, Arthur 143
Ponsonby, Betty 143
Ponsonby, Fritz 166
Ponsonby, General Sir Henry 74, 96, 109, 143, 148, 156
Ponsonby, 'Johnnee' 142
Portugal, King and Queen of 127
Presentations at Court 104–6, *105*
Prime Ministers 24–7
Prince Imperial of France 65, 69, 86, 102
Princess Royal of England, the, *see* Frederick, Empress of Germany
Programmes *140–41*, *150–51*, *183*, *186*, *188*, *209*
Promenade Concerts 189
Prussia, Crown Prince Frederick *see* Frederick William, Prince of Prussia
Prussia, Princess Henry of 184
Prussia, Queen of 56

Queen's Hall Orchestra 189

Railway timetables *85*, *110*, *114*, *122*, *123–5*
Reske, Edouard and Jean de 138, 187
Ripon, Bishop of (Boyd-Carpenter) 142
Roberts, Field-Marshal Lord 7, *11*, 183, 195, 199, 216
Romeo et Juliet 187
Röntgen, Professor 146
Rosebery, Lord 24, *27*, 146, 157
Rosenau Castle, Coburg 17
Rossetti, Dante Gabriel 107
Rorke's Drift 98, *99*, 100–101
Roxburghe, Duchess of 56, 74, 109, 132
Royal Albert Hall 34, 52–5, 68, 119
Royal College of Music 107, 195
Royal Opera House, Covent Garden 13
Rubens Room, Windsor Castle 90
Rubenstein, Anton 149
Ruland, Mr 37
Rumania, King and Queen of 18
Russell, Earl 12, 24, *25*, 34, 39, 46, 51, 69, 96
Russia, Emperor and Empress of 90

Saint George's Hall, Windsor Castle 54, 90, 134, 148, 195, 206

Saint Paul's Cathedral 176–9
Salisbury, Marquis of 24, 27, 94, 108, 127, 134, 146, 157, 217
Salvation Army 69
San Sebastian 138
Sandringham 74–6
Sarajevo 173
Sarasate, Pablo de 151
Sardinia, King of 90
Saxe-Coburg & Gotha, Duke of 54
Saxe-Weimar, Prince Edward of 45, 160, 217
Saxony, King of 8, 127, 132
Schleswig-Holstein 46, 52
Scots Guards 196, *196*
Scott, Sir George Gilbert 83, *83*
Seating plans/lists *117*, *128–31*, *173*, *189*, *198*, *203*, *211*
Serge of Russia, Grand Duke 127, 132, 134
Sherwood Rangers Yeoman Cavalry 17
Smith, Revd Clement 212
Smuts, General 195
South African War 147, 195; *see also* Boer War
Spain, King of 102
Spain, Queen Regent of 138
Spithead 182, *182*
Stanley, Constance 63
Stanley, the Very Revd Dr Arthur Penrhyn, Dean of Westminster 38, 42, 60
Stanley, Colonel 98
State Balls 106
Stockmar, Baron 199
Suez Canal 4, 34, 94
Sullivan, Sir Arthur 13, *68*, 119, 147–9
Sussex, Duke of 116
Sutherland, Duchess of 43

Tate Gallery 147
Tchaikovsky, P. I. 69
Teck, Duchess of 70, 134, 217; *see also* Cambridge, Lady Mary
Teck, Duke of 134, 147, 160, 217
Tennyson, Alfred, Lord 113, 119
Thackeray, W. M. 31
Thompson, Alexander 'Greek' 83
Times, The 81, 154, *213*
Titles Bill 95
Torrington, Lord 102
Toulouse-Lautrec, Henri 145
Toward, Mr 37
Twain, Mark 108

USA 38, 47–8

Vane-Tempest, Lord Adolphus 29
Verdi, Giuseppe 31
Vice-Regal Lodge, Dublin 199
Victoria, Queen 2, *6*, 7–16, *9*, *10*, *15*, 17, 29, 37–65, *41*, *43*, *53*, 70–106, *78–9*, *87*, 97, *105*, 109–22, *119*, 127, 132–8, *134*, 142–4, *145*, 148–57, *155*, 160, 163, 166–7, *169*, *170*, 170–73, 176–7, *178*, 180, 184, 187, 189, 192, 195, *196*, 199, 201–2, 206–7, 212, 214–19; and assassination attempts 80, 109–10; and children 13; and funerals 7, 157, 160; and John Brown 78–82, 113; and marriage 143; and smoking 7, 8; and the Kaiser 15, 138, 144, 149, 192, 195, 212, *see also* Wilhelm II, Emperor of Germany; and the Prince Consort 8, 9–10, 37–8, 39, 40, 47, 51, 52, 56, 63, 70, 74, 81, 83, 86, 192, *see also* Albert, Prince Consort; her children's weddings 31, 34, 38, 39, 45, 49–50, 114, 116–17, 154, *see also* entries for individual children; death 212, 215; Empress of India 7, 12, 69, 95; illnesses 72–3, 113, 154, 202, 206–7, 212, 214; length of reign 7, *see also* entries for Golden and Diamond jubilees; sense of humour 13, 15–16; widowhood 8, 9–10, 12, 13, 40, 51, 52, 53, 55, 61, 63, 75–6, 95, 96, 109, 143
Victoria & Albert 160
Victoria and Albert Museum 191–2, *191*
Victoria and Albert, Order of 88
Victoria of Hesse, Princess (Princess Louis of Battenberg) 108
Victoria Park, Hackney 87–8, *87*
Visitors, list of *197*
Volunteer Fire Brigades 127

Wagner, Richard 34, 94, *95*, 107, 189
Waldegrave, Lord 180
Walpole, Robert 56
Waterloo Chamber, Windsor Castle 90, 134, 148, 151, 187, *187*, 201
Waterpark, Lady 52, 95, 98, 142
Wellesley, Very Revd George 42
Wells, H. G. 147
Westminster Abbey 17
Whippingham Church 160
Wilde, Oscar 147, *147*
Wilhelm II, Emperor of Germany ('Kaiser Bill') 13, 15, *15*, 18, 45, 108–9, 127, 136, 138–9, *139*, 144–5, 147, 149, 192, 195, 214–16, 219
Wilhelmina, Queen of the Netherlands 157
William IV
Willis, Henry 54
Wilton, Lord and Lady 95
Winchester, Bishop of 216
Windsor Castle *92–3*
Windsor Park 13
Winterhalter, Franz 89, 91
Wolseley, Lord 69, 116, 180, *181*, 195
Wolverhampton 51–2
Wood, Sir C. 47
Wood, Sir Henry 188

Yorke, the Hon. Sir Alick 13

Zanzibar, Sultan of 108
Zulu War 65, 98